MW00379874

Theism and Humanism

The Book that Influenced C. S. Lewis

by

Arthur James Balfour

British Prime Minister, 1902–1905
President of the British Association
for the Advancement of Science, 1904
Author of the Balfour Declaration
that created the State of Israel

with

Three Additional Letters by
C. S. Lewis

Edited by

Michael W. Perry

Being the Gifford Lectures
Delivered at the University of Glasgow, 1914

Inkling Books   Seattle   2000

Theism and Humanism was written by Arthur J. Balfour. This new edition contains all the original text along with additional material.

The main text of this book comes from the definitive 1915 edition of *Theism and Humanism: Being the Gifford Lecture Series*. That edition was authored by Arthur J. Balfour and published by George H. Doran Company on September 23, 1915. For a list of the minor differences between that text and this, see Appendix D. Graphic illustrations are derived (with some changes) from political cartoons in *Punch* magazine published during Balfour's political career. Newspaper accounts describing the original lectures are from *The Times* of London on the dates noted. Other material has been taken from writings and speeches by Arthur Balfour as noted. The glossary, index and some other material in this book are new and have never been published before. This second Inkling edition corrects typographical errors in the first edition, makes minor rearrangements, and adds the articles from *The Times* and the letters by C. S. Lewis.

The 1915 original was based on a lecture series that the author gave at the University of Glasgow in early 1914. This newly typeset and enhanced edition has been retitled *Theism and Humanism: The Book that Influenced C. S. Lewis* to reflect the influence the book had on the well-known Oxford University scholar and popular writer, C. S. Lewis. As an illustration of that literary connection, three letters that Lewis wrote to Sheldon Vanauken have been included as Appendix E.

The 1915 edition had the following dedication:

"To the professors and students of the University of Glasgow, who gave so kind a reception to these lectures on their delivery in the Bute Hall, I dedicate this volume."

Library Cataloging Data

Balfour, Arthur James, Earl of (1848–1930)

Theism and Humanism: The Book that Influenced C. S. Lewis

Editor: Perry, Michael W. [Wiley] (1948–)

Other author: C. S. Lewis (1898–1963)

203 pages, 23 cm.

Second Edition.

Includes 5 appendices, endnotes, glossary, index and 9 illustrations.

ISBN 1-58742-005-8 (paper)

LC 00-108654

1. Humanism. 2. Theism. 3. Balfour, Arthur James (author). 4. Perry, Michael W. (editor) 5. Lewis, C. S. (other author).

Keywords: Humanism Theism Naturalism Science Religion Evolution

BL200 .B2 2000

211 .B2 2000

Inkling Books, Seattle, WA Internet: http://www.InklingBooks.com/

Published in the United States of America on acid-free paper

First Printing: October 2000

Contents

Second Edition Foreword

Even today, many call him "Darwin's Bulldog" for the zeal he displayed defending Charles Darwin's then-new theory of evolution. Certainly no one in the English-speaking world ever did more than Thomas H. Huxley (1825–95) to persuade Englishmen that the ideas of a much shyer Darwin should be treated as accepted fact.

But Huxley's cultural agenda included much more than evolution. In the last years of his life, he was inordinately proud of the fact that he had coined the term "agnostic" in an 1859 *Spectator* article. He invented the word to describe his belief that we cannot know for certain whether God exists or not. It was a clever move by a man who excelled at clever moves. In the rough and tumble of debate it is much easier to defend agnosticism than atheism. But Huxley never solved his real problem: a claim to *know* that we can never prove God's existence is no more skeptical (in Huxley's eyes, the best of all attitudes) than a claim to *know* God exists. In the end all live by faith. No one can be certain that some time in the future will bring definitive proof of God's existence or not.

Huxley's defensiveness about his belief in unbelief shows through most clearly in two articles he wrote in 1895. The first was published as "Mr. Balfour's Attack on Agnosticism" in the March issue of *The Nineteenth Century*. The second did not become public until after his death in June of that year. In both the target of Huxley's wrath was Arthur J. Balfour and his popular book of that same year, *The Foundations of Belief*. Huxley recognized that he had found in Balfour a worthy foe. The author, he notes, has a "charm of a style which flows like a smooth stream, sparkling with wit and rippling with sarcasms enough to take away any reproach of monotony." He notes that Balfour, an up-and-coming young politician, was "sure to go higher, not merely in official rank, but, if I may have an opinion on such a matter, in the estimation of his countrymen."

In his assessment of Balfour's future, Huxley proved quite accurate. Seven years later Balfour became Britain's Prime Minister and throughout his life he would be respected by friend and foe alike for his talent and integrity. During World War I, he would replace Winston Churchill as First Lord of the Admiralty, and in 1916 he became Foreign Secretary. Modern Israel owes its existence to the November 1917 Balfour Declaration promising that the British government would "view with favour the establishment in Palestine of a national home for the Jewish people."

Clearly, for Britain's aged champion of unbelief, the talented young Balfour was a man to be feared. Huxley's difficulties were increased by the fact that, though not a scientist himself, Balfour had many friends in the scientific community. His brother, Francis M. Balfour (1851–82) is considered the founder of modern embryology for his *A Treatise on Comparative Embryology* (1880–81). Only an early death in a climbing accident in the Alps prevented Francis from having a career in science as distinguished as his brother's was in politics.

Much like this present book, Balfour's chosen target in *Foundations* was Naturalism. Here the contrast between Balfour and Huxley gets interesting. It is Balfour, the champion of tradition and a Conservative politician, who was flexible with language, while Huxley, the champion of skepticism and a freethinker, was irritable, pedantic and insistent that what he considers the proper terms be used for everything.

Huxley was upset to find Balfour "curiously shy of naming" what set of beliefs he places in opposition to Naturalism and claimed that Balfour offered nothing more than "the sadly vague appellation of 'current teaching.'" The fault lies with the critic rather than with Balfour. Huxley had failed to understand one of his opponent's most basic points. The beliefs that Balfour called "current teachings" in *Foundations* are those he calls "inevitable" and the "creed of common sense" in this book. If asked, Balfour would have no doubt told his famous critic that they were beliefs that Huxley—whose Victorian morality was as stern as anyone's—taught his own children. Balfour would readily admit that many genuine followers of Naturalism also subscribed to his "current teachings." The question was not what they believe, but whether they had a solid foundation for those beliefs.

The contrast between the two comes through most clearly in the draft Huxley wrote for the second of his two articles on Balfour's book. In *Foundations,* Balfour offered "A Catechism for Naturalism" (reprinted here as Appendix A). There Balfour offered five pairs of beliefs. The first of each pair was the current belief of almost everyone in that era; the second was a belief that Balfour suggested should be part of a naturalistic creed. Take, for instance, the first pair:

A: The universe is the creation of Reason, and all things work together towards a reasonable end.

B: So far as we can tell, reason is to be found neither in the beginning of things nor in their end; and though everything is predetermined, nothing is foreordained.

"I am really curious to know," Huxley asks, "where Mr. Balfour found his authority, either among agnostics or following natural science, for B. To me the former of the two propositions which it contains is absurd. If, according to natural science, reason is absent from the universe, how is it that men of science talk about, 'laws of nature' which are expressions in terms of reason of the order of nature?"

How indeed? But Huxley was the one in the wrong. Even Darwin questioned how his 'monkey mind' could understand the universe when it was merely a chance-created tool evolved to aid in our struggle against larger and fiercer foes. To think that mind can *reason* its way to the truth about life's deeper questions makes as little sense in the naturalistic world view as assuming that a leg, because it does well at propelling us along the ground, should work equally well at flying through the air. Yet that is what every naturalist, almost without exception, does each and every day.

In his reply, Huxley demonstrated the very point Balfour made. The contrast between the two creeds lies in concepts such as foresight and planning. In a universe that is "the creation of Reason [God]" all things *can* "work together towards a reasonable end." But, looking through the eyes of Naturalism, Huxley can see only, "the energy of the cosmos" working "according to fixed principles towards a definite result." He takes as an example, "the whole solar system [which] was once represented by an ocean of similar molecules, unless the energy which set these molecules in motion followed fixed rules of action—unless in that it operated rationally—the solar system could never come out of it."

But—and this is the point Huxley missed completely—that "ocean of similar molecules" did not *set out* to create a solar system. It lacked the capacity to even imagine such a thing, much less accomplish it. True, everything in Huxley's universe was "pre-determined" (Balfour) by "fixed principles" (Huxley). But nothing in it will ever be "fore-ordained" (Balfour) because that requires a reasoning and planning mind. In short, fixed law is not reason and mechanism, however complex, is not mind. Huxley had claimed that no agnostic believed Balfour's naturalistic creed and then went on to express exactly those beliefs. (In Chapter 8 of this book, Balfour takes up Huxley's argument, pointing out that natural laws create no more than an "irrational mimic of reason.")

Huxley never had a chance to comment on *Theism and Humanism*. The series of speeches on which it is based came almost twenty years after his death. But in a sense this book is a continuation of their 1895 debate. Huxley faulted Balfour for not having a word to describe his own beliefs. In this book Balfour has just such a word. That word is Theism—

a far better choice than two clumsy words Huxley coined for his use: "Theologism" and "Demômism." So, in a very real sense, this book—*Theism and Humanism*—is a continuation of that earlier debate. That is why so many of the quotes that I have added to this text come from *Foundations*. The two books complement one another.

For all their disagreements, there was one point on which Huxley expressed "entire agreement" with Balfour. That was Balfour's remark that: "Naturalism is in reality the only system which ultimately profits by any defeats which Theology may sustain, or which may be counted on to flood the spaces from which the tide of Religion has receded." On that point, both men were right. Beneath all our superficial debates about this issue or that, lie the great issues which determine what we believe about almost everything. The greatest of those is the one that engaged Balfour and Huxley—the irreconcilable conflict between Naturalism and Theism. It was Balfour's contention that the only humanly appealing answer lay in Theism or, as he put it in the last chapter of the original edition of this book: "My desire has been to show that all we think best in human culture, whether associated with beauty, goodness, or knowledge, requires God for its support, that Humanism without Theism loses more than half its value."

Like a torch passed to a new generation, *Theism and Humanism* would continue to influence lives long after the author's death in 1930. In a 1962 letter to *Christian Century,* the popular writer, C. S. Lewis, numbered it among the ten books that had most shaped his philosophy of life. As *The C. S. Lewis Readers Encyclopedia* explained: "the thesis and even the language of Balfour's first Gifford lectures permeates the first five chapters of *Miracles.* It was from Balfour that Lewis derived the self-refutability of naturalism. And Balfour's 'plain man's point of view, the creed of common sense' greatly appealed to Lewis."

In his 1944 paper, "Is Theology Poetry," Lewis noted that *Theism and Humanism* was "a book too little read." It is my wish that by publishing it again, I can transform it into a book that is very much read and appreciated. I hope that its readers find it as stimulating to read as it has been for me to edit.

MICHAEL W. PERRY
SEATTLE, WASHINGTON
OCTOBER 4, 2000

1915 Preface

This volume contains the substance of the Gifford Lectures delivered at the University of Glasgow in January and February, 1914. I say the *substance* of the lectures, lest any of those who formed part of my most kindly audience should expect a verbal reproduction of what they then heard. No such reproduction would have been either expedient or possible. The lectures were not read: they were spoken (with the aid of brief notes) in such terms as suggested themselves at the moment; and their duration was rigidly fixed, to suit my academic audience, so as just to occupy the customary hour. Although, therefore, they were largely (though not wholly) based upon written drafts, none of the language, and not all the ideas and illustrations contained in the original could be reproduced in the spoken lectures, nor did everything in the spoken lectures represent passages in the written originals.

It is not, in these circumstances, surprising that the work has had, in large measure, to be rewritten, though the argument itself, and the order in which its various parts are presented for consideration, remains substantially unchanged.

I should not have troubled the reader with this very unimportant narrative except for the purpose of explaining the long interval that has elapsed between the delivery of the lectures and their publication. Literary composition I have always found laborious and slow, even in favourable conditions. But the conditions have not been favourable. My anxiety to make the argument easy to read for persons who take little interest in, and have small knowledge of, philosophical controversies did not make it easy to write; while external circumstances were singularly unfavourable to rapid composition. No one who took any part in public affairs between March 1914 and the outbreak of the war, or between the outbreak of the war and the present moment, is likely to regard these months as providing convenient occasion for quiet thought and careful writing. I say this, however, not as an excuse for poor workmanship, but only as an explanation of long delay.

It may be desirable to warn the intending reader before he embarks on these lectures, that though the basis of the argument is wide, its conclusion is narrow: and though that conclusion is religious, the discussions leading up to it are secular. I make no dialectical use of the religious sentiment; nor do I attempt any analysis of its essential character. Still less do I deal with any doctrines outside what is called "natural" religion; for to "natural" religion the Gifford Lecturer is expressly confined. But even themes which might well be deemed to fall within these limits are scarcely referred to. For example, God, freedom, and immortality have been treated by at least one eminent writer as the great realities beyond the world of sense. I believe in them all. But I only discuss the first—and that only from a limited point of view.

One other caution I must give, though it is hardly necessary. No one, I suppose, is likely to consult this small volume in the hope of finding an historic survey, properly "documented," of the great theistic controversy. But, if so misguided an individual exists, he is doomed to the severest disappointment. There have been, and will be, Gifford Lecturers well equipped for so great an undertaking; but most assuredly I am not among them.

My warm thanks are due to my brother, Mr. Gerald Balfour; my sister, Mrs. Sidgwick, and my brother-in-law, Lord Rayleigh, for the trouble they have taken in reading the proofs, and for the aid they have given me in correcting them. In connection with a passage in the ninth lecture, Sir Oliver Lodge has been good enough to give me an interesting note on "energy," which appears in its proper place.

ARTHUR J. BALFOUR
4 CARLTON GARDENS
MAY 24, 1915

------------ Editor's Note ------------

As editor for this new edition of Balfour's classic work, I have enhanced the 1915 original (created under wartime conditions) with additional quotes from Balfour's other writings, appendices, a glossary, an index and explanatory endnotes. Readers are encouraged to take full advantage of each.

Readers may notice mention of a second Gifford lecture series by Balfour and planned for 1915. It was not delivered until after the war and was published in 1923 as *Theism and Thought*.

With this second Inkling edition I have added the coverage that *The Times* of London gave to each of the original Gifford Lectures. I hope they will convey some of the excitement that the original lectures generated. In addition, given the influence that Balfour had on C. S. Lewis, I have included (as Appendix E) three letters that Lewis wrote to Sheldon Vanauken. As I note in that appendix, those letters touch on great issues that are similar to those Balfour discussed in this book.

CHAPTER

1

Introductory

There are for all men moments when the need for some general point of view becomes insistent; when neither labour, nor care, nor pleasure, nor idleness, nor habit will stop a man from asking how he is to regard the universe of reality, how he is to think of it as a whole, how he is to think of his own relation to it.

MR. BALFOUR ON THEISM
The Plain Man's Picture of Philosophy
Opening Gifford Lecture
(From Our Special Correspondent)
GLASGOW, JAN. 12

The list of Glasgow lecturers on Lord Gifford's foundation includes some famous names. Max Müller delivered the first series in 1888, and Edward Caird as Master of Balliol returned to Glasgow in 1900 to speak once more *ex cathedra* in the University in which he had taught for nearly 30 years. No course of lectures, however, has aroused more interest than that which was begun to-day by Mr. Balfour, who, like the only other living ex-Prime Minister, is also an ex-Lord Rector of the University of Glasgow. The Bute Hall was filled half an hour before the arrival of the lecturer, and the audience included a large number of citizens and many students as well as almost the whole of the teaching staff. The Principal, though now convalescent, was not allowed by his doctors to undertake the duty of presiding.

Mr. Balfour had a reception so wildly enthusiastic that in acknowledging it he remarked that it was more gratifying to himself than consonant with the great theme to which he proposed to draw the attention of his audience. The precise nature of his subject had not been revealed and he did not at once announce it, but from the first moment he riveted the sympathetic attention which a Glasgow audience so generously bestows, and the undergraduates did not fail to respond to the few opportunities of expressing their approbation as, for example, when the lecturer incidentally remarked that if Bacon took all knowledge for his province he was a young man when he did so.

The Inadequacy of Philosophy

The lecture was introductory and expository and Mr. Balfour attempted to do no more than to indicate the topics to which he would devote the 20 lectures,

10 in two successive years, which are required by the Gifford Trust. He spoke of the great problems which every man has to face, and he admitted the failure of philosophy to solve these problems to the general satisfaction. Hardly any man of science treats philosophy seriously, and the plain man feels that philosophy does not meet his difficulties or even look at them from the same point of view. The plain man's picture of philosophy was of men generally quarrelling in an unknown tongue. He himself had never been able to accept any of these great systems. He had none to offer, and he did not intend to devote much time to showing where he differed from those of others. At this point, Mr. Balfour told his audience that his subject is to be Theism, and he felt it necessary to say at once that he could not be satisfied with the conclusion that from the very notion of experience the idea of God could be extracted by a logical process. **"When I speak of God," he said, "it is not the Absolute of which I am speaking. It is the God Whom a man may easily love and adore, not merely the end or conclusion of a logical process."** Some critics might describe his statement as anthropomorphism, but he hoped to commit worse crimes than that in their eyes. If the modern man's idea of God was descended from ancient and corrupt myths, the very permanence of that idea was proof that it could not be ignored; and it was inadequate, but not untrue, to say that God takes sides and works for great ends and asks us to work with Him. The plain man's conception of God and the philosophical conception must ultimately be brought into harmony and connexion.

Method of the Lectures

After this description of his subject, Mr. Balfour proceeded to unfold the outlines of his method. He intended to deal with what he described as the inevitable beliefs of mankind on all subjects except theology, for theology was the end of his argument, and so would not be among his premises. Many things which we believe cannot be described as axiomatic, and yet are held without reference to logical proof. The existence of an external world and other individuals, for example, are inevitable beliefs in spite of philosophical disputes, and are held by philosophers as well as by savages. There is a difference in the way of holding these beliefs, and, using what he described as a dangerous phase, Mr. Balfour said that, while their form was identical, their substance was constantly changing, and never more rapidly than to-day. The views of physicists about matter were widely different from what they were 15 years ago. He had chosen these inevitable beliefs, scientific, ethical, aesthetic, as his materials because each of them possessed an essential peculiarity, having its place as a natural phenomena, both in a causal series and in a rational series. This body of inevitable belief is the interaction of reason and cause. Only in a theistic setting could those beliefs be treated as reasonable. Mr. Balfour's closing sentence was necessarily a hurried indication of a line of thought to be expanded in his next lecture on Wednesday, and they left his audience a little mystified, but with their curiosity thoroughly aroused.

—*The Times,* Tue. Jan. 13, 1914, 8d.

THEISM AND HUMANISM

❖ Metaphysics and the 'Plain Man'

Those responsible for the selection of Gifford Lecturers have made it clear that, in their interpretation of Lord Gifford's Trust, studies in a very wide range of subjects are relevant to the theme of Natural Religion. Gifford lectures have been devoted to such diverse themes as Comparative Religion, Primitive Mythologies, Vitalism, Psychology of Religious Experiences, the History of Religious Development at particular Epochs. And, in addition to these, we have had expounded to us systems of Metaphysics of more than one type, and drawing their inspiration from more than one school.

When I was honoured by an invitation to take a share in the perennial debate which centres round what Lord Gifford described as Natural Religion, I had to consider what kind of contribution I was least unfitted to make. Perhaps if this consideration had preceded my reply to the invitation, instead of following it, I might have declined the perilous honour. Neither in my own opinion nor in that of anybody else, am I qualified to contribute a special study of any of the scientific, psychological, anthropological, or historical problems which may throw light upon the central issue. This must of necessity be the work of specialists. No metaphysical system, again, am I in a position to provide—for reasons which will appear in the sequel. A merely critical commentary upon the systems of other people might hardly meet either the expectations of my audience, or the wishes of those who appointed me to the post. Indeed, the enormous range of modern philosophic literature, and the divergent tendencies of modem philosophic thought would make the task, in any case, one of extreme difficulty. Few, indeed, are those who, by the width of their reading and the quickness of their intellectual sympathy, are qualified to survey the whole field of contemporary speculation; and, assuredly, I am not among them.

——————— **Natural Theology** ———————

Natural theology expounds the theological beliefs which may be arrived at by a consideration of the general course of Nature as this is explained to us by Science. It dwells principally upon the numberless examples of adaptation in the organic world, which apparently display the most marvellous indications of ingenious contrivance, and the nicest adjustments of means to ends. From facts like these it is inferred that Nature has an intelligent and powerful Creator.[1]

The vast amplitude of relevant material daily growing with the growth of knowledge, cannot but hamper the sincerest efforts of those who desire to take a comprehensive view of the great problems which

Lord Gifford desired to solve. Most men are amateurs in all departments of activity but the one, be it scientific or practical, or artistic, to which they have devoted their lives. Bacon, indeed, with the magnificent audacity of youth took all knowledge for his province. But he did so in the sixteenth century, not in the twentieth; and even Bacon did not escape the charge of being an amateur. No one, while human faculty remains unchanged, is likely to imitate his ambitions. More and more does the division and subdivision of labour become necessary for knowledge, as for industry. More and more have men to choose whether they shall be dabblers in many subjects or specialists in one. More and more does it become clear that, while each class has its characteristic defects, both are required in the republic of knowledge.

So far as specialists are concerned, this last proposition is self-evident. Specialists are a necessity. And it may well be that those who have successfully pressed forward the conquering forces of discovery along some narrow front, careless how the struggle towards enlightenment fared elsewhere, may be deemed by the historian to have been not only the happiest, but the most useful thinkers of their generation. Their achievements are definite. Their contributions to knowledge can be named and catalogued. The memory of them will remain when contemporary efforts to reach some general point of view will seem to posterity strangely ill-directed, worthless to all but the antiquarian explorers of half-forgotten speculation.

Yet such efforts can never be abandoned, nor can they be confined to philosophers. There are for all men moments when the need for some general point of view becomes insistent; when neither labour, nor care, nor pleasure, nor idleness, nor habit will stop a man from asking how he is to regard the universe of reality, how he is to think of it as a whole, how he is to think of his own relation to it.

Now I have no wish to overpraise these moments of reflection. They are not among the greatest. They do not of necessity involve strenuous action, or deep emotion, or concentrated thought. Often they are periods of relaxation rather than of tension, moods that pass and leave no trace. Yet it is not always so; and when the pressure of these ancient problems becomes oppressive, then those who, from taste or necessity, have lived only from hour to hour, seek aid from those who have had leisure and inclination to give them a more prolonged consideration.

Of these there is no lack; some speaking in the name of science, some in the name of religion, some in the name of philosophy. The founder of these lectures regarded philosophy, and (if I mistake not) philosophy in its most metaphysical aspect, the surest guide to the truths of which he was in search. And certainly I am the last to criticise such a view. It is clearly the business of metaphysicians, if they have any business at all, to provide us with a universal system. They cannot lose themselves in concrete details, as may happen to men of science. They are neither aided nor trammelled, as all working organisations, whether in Church or State, are necessarily aided and trammelled, by institutional traditions and practical necessities. They exist to supply answers to the very questions of which I have been speaking. Yet metaphysics does not appeal, and has never appealed, to the world at large. For one man who climbs to his chosen point of view by a metaphysical pathway, a thousand use some other road; and if we ask ourselves how many persons there are at this moment in existence whose views of the universe have been consciously modified by the great metaphysical systems (except in so far as these have been turned to account by theologians), we must admit that the number is insignificant.

──────── **Philosophy, Science and Religion** ────────

Philosophy has never touched the mass of men except through religion. And, though the parallel is not complete, it is safe to say that science will never touch them unaided by its practical applications.[2]

Now, I do not think this is due to the fact, so often commented upon, both by the friends of metaphysics and its foes, that in this branch of inquiry there is little agreement among experts; that the labours of centuries have produced no accepted body of knowledge; that, while the separate sciences progress, metaphysics, which should justify them all, seems alone to change without advancing. Mankind is not so easily discouraged. New remedies are not less eagerly adopted because old remedies have so often failed Few persons are prevented from thinking themselves right by the reflection that, if they be right, the rest of the world is wrong. And were metaphysical systems what men wanted, the disagreements among metaphysicians would no more destroy interest in metaphysics than the disagreements among theologians destroy interest in theology. The evil, if evil it be, lies deeper. It is not so much that mankind reject metaphysical systems, as that they omit the preliminary stage of considering them. Philosophy is now, perhaps has always been, an academic discipline which touches not our ordinary life. A general knowledge of the historic schools of thought may indeed be acquired by the young as part of their education; but it is commonly forgotten by the middle-aged; and, whether forgotten or remembered, is rarely treated as in any vital relation to the beliefs and disbeliefs which represent their working theories of life and death.

If you desire confirmation of this statement, consider how few men of science have shown the smallest interest in metaphysical speculation. Philosophers, with one or two notorious exceptions, have commonly had a fair amateur acquaintance with the science of their day. Kant, though I believe that his mechanics were not always beyond reproach, anticipated Laplace in one famous hypothesis. Descartes and Leibnitz would be immortalised as mathematicians if they had never touched philosophy, and as philosophers if they had never touched mathematics. In our own day Huxley not only contributed to biology, but wrote on philosophy. Yet, speaking generally, metaphysics has in modem times been treated by men of science with an indifference which is sometimes respectful, more commonly contemptuous, almost always complete.

Nor can we attribute this attitude of mind, whether on the part of scientific specialists or the general public, to absorption in merely material interests. There are some observers who would have us believe that the energies of Western civilisation are now[3] entirely occupied in the double task of creating wealth and disputing over its distribution. I cannot think so; I doubt whether there has been for generations a deeper interest than at this moment in things spiritual—however different be its manifestations from those with which we are familiar in history. We must look elsewhere for an explanation of our problem. There must be other reasons why, to the world at large, those who study metaphysics seem to sit (as it were) far apart from their fellow-men, seeking wisdom by methods hard of comprehension, and gently quarrelling with each other in an unknown tongue.

Among these reasons must no doubt be reckoned the very technical character of much metaphysical exposition. Some of this could be avoided, much of it could not; and, in any case, philosophers might well ask why people should expect metaphysics—to say nothing of logic and psychology—to be easier of comprehension than the differential calculus or the electromagnetic theory of light. Plainly, there is no reason: and, in so far as the thoughts to be expressed are difficult, and the language required to express them is unfamiliar, the evil admits of no remedy.

But there is something more to be said. It must, I think, be admitted that most men approach the difficulties of a scientific exposition far more hopefully than the difficulties of a metaphysical argument. They will take more trouble because they expect more result. But why? In part, I think, because so much metaphysical debate is not, or does not appear to be, addressed to the problems of which they feel the pinch. On the contrary, it confuses what to them seems plain; if raises doubts about what to them seems obvious; and, of the doubts which they *do* entertain, it provides no simple or convincing solution.

The fact is, of course, that the metaphysician wants to re-think the universe; the plain man does not. The metaphysician seeks for an inclusive system where all reality can be rationally housed. The plain man is less ambitious. He is content with the kind of knowledge he possesses about men and things—so far as it goes. Science has already told him much; each day it tells him more. And, within the clearing thus made for him in the tangled wilderness of the unknown, he feels at home. Here he can manage his own affairs; here he needs no philosophy to help him. If philosophy can speak to him about questions on which science has little to say, he will listen; provided always that the problems dealt with are interesting, and the treatment of them easily understood. He would like, for example, to hear about God, if there be a God, and his Soul, if he has a Soul. But he turns silently away from discussions on the One and the Many, on Subject and Object, on degrees of Reality, on the possibility of Error, on Space and Time, on Reason and Intuition, on the nature of Experience, on theological characteristics of the Absolute. These may be very proper topics for metaphysicians, but clearly they are no topics for him.

Now I am far from saying that in these opinions the plain man is right. His speculative ambitions are small, and his tacit assumptions are many. What is familiar seems to him easy; what is unfamiliar seems to him useless. And he is provokingly unaware of the difficulties with which his common-sense doctrines are beset. Yet in spite of all this, he has my sympathy; and I propose, with due qualifications and explanations, to approach the great subject, described by the Trust as Natural Religion, from his—the plain man's—point of view.

The Failures of Philosophy

Philosophers have mined for truth in many directions, and the whole field of speculation seems cumbered with the dross and lumber of their abandoned workings. But though they have not found the ore they sought for, it does not therefore follow that their labours have been wholly vain. It is something to have realised what not to do. It is something to discover the causes of failure, even though we do not attain any positive knowledge of the conditions of success.[4]

❖ Inevitable Beliefs and 'Common Sense'

But what *is* the plain man's point of view? What *is* the creed of common sense?

It has never been summed up in articles, nor fenced round with definitions. But in our ordinary moments we all hold it; and there should be no insuperable difficulty in coming to an agreement about certain of its characteristics which are relevant to the purposes of my immediate argument. One such characteristic is that its most important formulas represent beliefs which, whether true or false, whether proved or unproved, are at least inevitable. All men accept them in fact. Even those who criticise them in theory live by them in practice.

Now this category of "inevitableness" is not often met with in metaphysics; indeed, so far as I know, it is not met with at all. We hear of innate beliefs, *a priori* judgments, axioms, laws of thought, truths of reason, truths the opposite of which is "inconceivable" and so forth. These various descriptions are all devised in the interests of epistemology, i.e., the theory of knowledge. They are intended to mark off classes of judgments or beliefs which possess peculiar validity. But none of these classes are identical with the class "inevitable." There are inevitable beliefs which nobody would think of describing either as *a priori* or axiomatic. There are others of which the contradictory is perfectly conceivable; though no one who had other things to do would take the trouble to conceive it. An inevitable belief need not be self-evident, nor even, in the last analysis, self-consistent. It is enough that those who deem it in need of proof yet cannot prove it, and those who think it lacks coherence yet cannot harmonise it, believe it all the same.

But, are there such inevitable beliefs? There certainly are. We cannot, in obedience to any dialectical pressure, suppose the world to be emptied of persons who think, who feel, who will; or of things which are material, independent, extended, and enduring. We cannot doubt that such entities exist, nor that they act on one another, nor that they are in space or time. Neither can we doubt that, in the world thus pictured, there reigns an amount of stability and repetition, which suggests anticipations and retrospects—and sometimes justifies them.

These beliefs are beliefs about what are sometimes called "facts" and sometimes "phenomena"—neither term being either very convenient or very accurate. They are assumed in all sciences of nature, in all histories of the past, in all forecasts of the future, in all practice, in all theory, outside philosophy itself. But there are two other kinds of beliefs which must, I think, be also regarded as inevitable, of which I shall have to speak in the course of these lectures. They have unfortunately no generic names, and I must defer any description of them till future lectures. It is sufficient for the moment to say that one of them relates to the ends of action, and includes morals; while the other relates to objects of contemplative interest, among which is beauty. In some shape or other—perhaps in shapes which seem to us utterly immoral or disgusting—beliefs of both kinds are, so far as I can judge, entertained by all men. And though they have not the coercive force possessed by such beliefs as those in the independent existence of things and persons, they may be counted, for my purposes, among the inevitable.

Here, then, are three classes of belief which in some shape or other common sense holds, has always held, and cannot help holding. But evidently the shapes in which they may be held are many. They vary from age to age and from person to person. They are modified by education, by temperament, by the general condition of learning, by individual opportunities, and by social pressure. The common sense of the twentieth century A.D. is very different from the common sense of the twentieth century B.C. Yet, different though it be, it possesses unalterable similarities, and up to a certain point submits to the same classification.

If you desire an illustration, consider the case of matter, or of material things. All men believe in what is commonly called the "external world"—they believe in it with evidence, or without evidence, sometimes (like David Hume) in the teeth of evidence, in any case independently of evidence. But as to what this "external world" really is they differ profoundly. The expert of to-day differs from the expert of yesterday, both differ from the average man, the average man of the twentieth century differs from his predecessors, and they differ from each other according to the stage of general and scientific culture at which they have severally arrived.

──────── **Believing in a Material World** ────────

Compare, for example, the central truth of theology—"There is a God"—with one of the fundamental presuppositions of science (itself a generalised statement of what is given in ordinary judgments of perception)—"There is an independent material world." I am myself disposed to doubt whether so good a case can be made out for accepting the second of these propositions as can be made out for accepting the first.[5]

❖ The Character of the Theism To Be Established

But, though all this be granted, to what, you may be disposed to ask, does it lead? What has it got to do with Theism? It is not alleged that in any shape these inevitable beliefs are necessarily true; it is admitted that in most of the shapes in which men have held them they are actually false; it is not even suggested that a belief in God is to be counted among them. How, then, is Natural Theology advanced?

To answer this question would be to anticipate the nine lectures which are still to come. In the meanwhile, it may be enough to say that these beliefs of common sense supply the material on which I propose to work; that I shall treat them as a developing and improving system, of which the present phase is the most developed and the best. It is with this phase that I am chiefly concerned. If, for example, I make use of beliefs about the "external world" they will be (mainly) the beliefs of contemporary or recent science so far as I know them. If I make use of ethics or aesthetics, it will be the ethics and aesthetics of Western civilisation, not of Melanesia. I shall not add to them nor subtract from them. I shall not criticise nor question them. I shall accept them at their face values. But I shall ask what this acceptance implies. I shall ask how these values are to be maintained. And in particular I shall inquire whether the course of development, whose last known stages these beliefs represent, can be regarded as a merely naturalistic process without doing fatal damage to their credit.

The answer I shall give to this last question will be in the negative. **And, if the only alternative to Naturalism be Theism, as from the common-sense standpoint it certainly is, then the effect of my argument, for those who accept it, will be to link up a belief in God with all that is, or seems, most assured in knowledge, all that is, or seems, most beautiful in art or nature, and all that is, or seems, most noble in morality.**

———— Naturalism and Rationalism ————

Naturalism, then, the naturalism whose practical consequences have already occupied us so long, is nothing more than the result of rationalising methods applied with pitiless consistency to the whole circuit of belief. It is the completed product of rationalism, the final outcome of using the "current methods of interpreting sense-perception," as the universal instrument for determining the nature and fixing the limits of human knowledge.[6]

Now what is Rationalism? Some may be disposed to reply that it is the free and unfettered application of human intelligence to the problems of life and of the world: the unprejudiced examination of every question in the dry light of emancipated reason. This may be a very good account of a particular intellectual ideal: an ideal which has been sought after at many periods of the world's history, although assuredly it has been attained in none. Usage, however permits and even encourages us to employ the word in a much more restricted sense: as indicating a special form of that reaction against dogmatic theology which became prominent at the end of the seventeenth century;

THEISM AND HUMANISM

which dominated so much of the best thought in the eighteenth century, and which has reached its most complete expression in the Naturalism which occupied our attention through the first portion of these Notes.[7]

At this point you will inevitably ask me to explain what sort of Deity He is whose existence I wish to establish. Men have thought of God in many ways. In what way is He thought of in these lectures?

The question is legitimate, though I am in some doubt how far you will regard my answer as satisfactory. I, of course, admit that the conception of God has taken many shapes in the long-drawn course of human development, some of them degraded, all of them inadequate. But this, or something like this, was inevitable on any theory of development; and the subject-matter of theology does not seem to have fared differently in this respect from the subject-matter (say) of physics or psychology. It is in all cases the later stages of the process which mainly concern us.

There is, however, something more to be said. The highest conceptions of God seem to approximate to one of two types, which, without prejudice, and merely for convenience, I may respectively call the religious and the metaphysical. The metaphysical conception emphasises His all-inclusive unity. The religious type emphasises His ethical personality. The metaphysical type tends to regard Him as the logical glue which holds multiplicity together and makes it intelligible. The religious type willingly turns away from such speculations about the Absolute, to love and worship a Spirit among spirits. Which of these types is contemplated in the argument that follows?

To this question I would reply by another. Are the two conceptions incompatible? Must we abandon the second if we accept the first? If so, it is the second of which I propose to speak. It is the God according to religion, and not the God according to metaphysics, whose being I wish to prove. But there are theologians and philosophers of repute who think the two conceptions can be harmonised. They hold that belief in a personal and transcendent God is consistent with the acceptance even of those forms of Absolute Idealism which their friends call logical and their critics call intellectual—in both cases, perhaps, without sufficient justification.

For myself, I must admit that I have never succeeded to my own satisfaction in fusing the two conceptions. Yet I do not profess to be content with their separation. The attribution of personality to God, though much truer, I think, than the denial of it, is manifestly inadequate to the full reality we are struggling to express. Some of the greatest religious teachers, Christian and non-Christian, that the world has seen have more or less explicitly held both, or at least have leaned towards neither exclusively. This is surely true, for example, of Plato the Greek philosopher, of Philo the platonising Jew, of St. Paul the Christian Apostle, of St. Augustine the patristic theologian. Nor (so far as I know), has religious mysticism ever felt the least difficulty in bridging the chasm by which, in the eyes of discursive reason, the two conceptions seem to be divided. This may well represent the highest wisdom. **But, the argument of these lectures has a narrower scope: and when, in the course of them, I speak of God, I mean something other than an Identity wherein all differences vanish, or a Unity which includes but does not transcend the differences which It somehow holds in solution. I mean a God whom men can love, a God to whom men can pray, who takes sides, who has purposes and preferences, whose attributes, howsoever conceived, leave unimpaired the possibility of a personal relation between Himself and those whom He has created.**

But is not this (it may be objected) the degradation of religion? What is a deity so conceived but the old tribal god, with his character improved and his local limitations swept away? If God be not the Absolute, can He be more than a magnified man? Can you hope to cleanse these religious conceptions from the mud in which they once so rankly flourished?

Now there are plenty of unsolved, and perhaps insoluble, difficulties involved in the religious, or indeed in any other, conception of God. But I hardly count among them the lowly origin and crime-stained history of religious development. On this point you will be able to form a better opinion as these lectures proceed. But, in the meanwhile, it may be observed that though no tragic accompaniments attach to the growth of a purely Absolutist philosophy, this by no means implies that metaphysics is better than religion. It is true that, for the sake of a purely logical Absolute, no man has been moved to do what a later and higher morality condemns—to placate it, for example, with bloody rites or obscene revels. But this is because, for the sake of such an Absolute, no man has ever yet been moved to do anything at all. A belief in it may be the conclusion of our intellectual labours; but hardly (as it seems to me) their motive or their reward.

❖ What the Argument Is Not
Let me now bring this introductory lecture to a close by adding to what, so far, must seem a bare and obscure suggestion of what my argument *is,* a warning hint as to what, at first sight, it might seem to be, but is *not.*

It is not an argument from common sense, as that phrase ought properly to be interpreted. It does not say to the opponents of Theism: "You accept current beliefs in science, in morality, in ethics. In some shape or other common sense has always accepted them, in some shape or other you cannot help accepting them. You do, in fact, probably accept them in the shape which finds favour with the 'best thought of the age' or what you conceive to be such. This is common sense. Why not do in the sphere of religion what you are admittedly doing in these other spheres of theory and practice? Would not this be common sense also? True, there is one important difference between the two cases. Theological beliefs are not inevitable—at least not at our present stage of culture. It is possible to be an atheist; and easy to be an agnostic. But inevitableness, in itself, is no ground of philosophic certitude. So this point may be ignored; and in all other respects the parallel seems to be complete. Some form of Theism has been prevalent from an immemorial past. It has strongly appealed to the needs and feelings of mankind. You do not pause before accepting beliefs about things and persons till philosophy has solved all the speculative doubts about them which philosophy itself has raised. Why, then, should you apply a standard of rationality to religion which, with general approval, you reject in the case of science?"

Now I do not suggest that this is bad advice. Quite the contrary. Neither is it necessarily bad argument. But it is not the argument of these lectures. Whatever be its intrinsic merits, it has, from my point of view, the defect of implying a theory of knowledge—a very modest and unassuming theory indeed; but still a theory. And it therefore comes into competition with all other theories of knowledge—Absolutist, Empirical, Pragmatic, Neo-Kantian, Neo-Hegelian, Realist, New Realist, to say nothing of Professor Mach's philosophy of science, or M. Bergson's world-famous speculations.

Now I preach no theory of knowledge; partly because I have none to preach, partly because, in these lectures, I desire to dogmatise as little as I can about fundamentals, and to be constructive rather than critical. If you ask me how it is possible to be constructive without first settling fundamentals, and how it is possible to settle fundamentals without first being critical, I reply that it is only possible if you start from premises which are practically accepted by both parties to the controversy, however little agreement there may be as to their speculative proof; and this is what I am trying to do.

Nor ought this procedure to be deemed unworthy of the attention of serious thinkers. It is provisional, no doubt; but I do not think it shallow. It can never give us a metaphysic of the universe; but the creators of such a metaphysics when they come, will not find it stand in their way. Moreover, it takes account of facts as they are. A creed of some kind, religious or irreligious, is a vital necessity for all, not a speculative luxury for the few: and the practical creed of the few who speculate has a singular, and even suspicious, resemblance to that of the many who do not. While those rare individuals who have thought deeply about the theory of knowledge are profoundly divided as to why we should believe, they largely agree as to what we should believe with that vast multitude who, on the theory of knowledge, have never thought at all. Is not this a circumstance in itself most worthy of closer consideration? May it not guide us to some approximate solution of our present perplexities? The present lectures are an attempt to answer this question.

Is my argument, then, nothing better than an appeal from the competent to the incompetent, from the few to the many? By no means. Progress, though of small account unless it touch the many, gets its vital impetus always from the few. It is to the patient labours of those rare intelligences who possess originality, courage, subtlety, and sympathy that we must look for the gradual working out of a theory of the universe which shall as fully satisfy our reason and our conscience as the limitations of our faculties permit. But that consummation is not yet. And since, whether we be philosophers or not, we all act on a working body of root-beliefs about men and things: since we are also in general agreement as to the form in which those beliefs can best express the present state of knowledge, is it not legitimate to ask whether, on the basis thus provided, a still larger measure of practical harmony cannot in the meantime be reasonably established? It is true that Theism could never by such methods acquire a certitude either greater than, or independent of, the beliefs of science and common sense. But, could it acquire as much, theologians might well be content, though philosophers most rightly strove for more.

THEISM AND HUMANISM

2

An Argument to Design

The choice, therefore, is not between two accounts of the universe, each of which may conceivably be sufficient. The mechanical account is not sufficient. It doubly fails to provide a satisfactory substitute for design.

MR. BALFOUR ON DESIGN
Our Logical Series of Beliefs
Second Gifford Lecture
(From Our Special Correspondent)
GLASGOW, JAN. 14

Some 2,000 people again assembled in the Bute Hall this afternoon to hear Mr. Balfour's second Gifford lecture. He had another enthusiastic welcome, and even as he approached the deeper aspects of his high theme some of the younger members of his audience remained conscious of the interests attaching to the personality of the lecturer. When he happened to take a drink of water just after introducing a subject with the remark, "I will now fulfil the pledge I gave," the sound of unexpected cheers surprised the lecturer and most of those who were following his argument.[8] No other Gifford lecturer has ever attracted so large and so varied an audience.

The Arguments from and to Design

Mr. Balfour began by remarking that his view that beliefs can best be treated as reasonable in a theistic setting might seem to carry us no further than the argument from design, the dregs of old-fashioned apologetics, and a discussion of that argument would form the preface to his lecture. If the argument from design was sound, what, he asked, could it prove? It could answer the question "Is matter due ultimately to mind or is the mind of finite creatures due solely to matter?" But its reply to this question did not carry us very far, for the mere belief that mind lies behind matter is compatible with the wildest heresies in the development of thought. Yet the idea of mind as existing behind matter is a big step towards natural theology, and there is force in design when we do not consider matter by itself and when the design we find is a design which has value for sentient beings. At this point Mr. Balfour illustrated his view by a criticism of Herbert Spencer, who had never told how the transition is effected between the evolving universe of matter and the biological and social stages which are a later form of the same process. Why should atoms diffused in nebulae be inferior to atoms arranged in suns? Evolution is, he said, meaningless without consciousness, and the old argument from design in the material world is open to the same criticism. **For himself he believed that the heavens do declare the glory of God, but only if there are men and if there is a God, and he held with Bacon that if the universe is the result of blind chance, the glory vanishes.**

But this is an argument, not from design, but to design. The "argument to design" became the keynote of the lecture. The two arguments are, Mr. Balfour insisted, vitally different, and he would have frequent occasion to refer to the latter, but he had still something to say about the former. The argument from design is from an adaptation to a contriver, and it has force in dealing with organic life. Recent advance in biology has increased the force a thousand times. Why, then, do we not agree that we cannot be dealing with mere chance? The answer is that Darwin had shown that, given certain conditions, you could build up an infinite wealth of varied organic life. Natural selection shows a method by which design can be mimicked, given the premises of life and variation, and yet he thought that Kelvin's view stills stands that, if we trace back the present distribution of energy into the past, we come to a time when our arguments fail us. There was a beginning of the physical universe as we know it, and we are approaching a time, not to be absolutely reached till after an infinite duration, in which there will be no more transformation of energy out of which work may be obtained. We have a regular process before us, after which we can infer nothing. In the middle we have life, feeling, thought, the equations of which settle the relations of energy, and matter remained the same, but there were added the feelings of feeling beings and the thought of thinking beings. This fact, important from the point of view of the argument from design, was, he said, still more important from the point of view of the argument to design, for it is reasonable to conclude that because matter cannot make will and reason, then will and reason must have made matter.

The Rational Values of our Beliefs

The discussion of the argument from design occupied the greater part of the lecture, and Mr. Balfour, in concluding, reverted to his position that all our beliefs belong to a logical series, passing from premises to conclusions and to a series of causes and effects rooted in the general procession of events in the natural world.

The causal series must have a reaction upon the value of the rational series, and Mr. Balfour illustrated this point by a remark made to him by a famous agnostic, "It is only necessary to explain, not to refute, Christianity." It was a natural view for an opponent of Christianity, but he himself thought that all beliefs could be explained if we knew enough to follow the whole train of antecedents, and if the epigram were to be accepted, it followed that all beliefs could be refuted. The moral of the anecdote followed. The relation between the two series is of great philosophic import, though it has not greatly interested philosophers. The causal series may seriously affect the rational value of the logical process and to preserve the rational values of the great body of our beliefs we must find a causal pedigree which will not prove destructive of the values in which the whole trust and confidence in life naturally rests. **Unless behind our reasoning there is ultimately a rational cause, behind our ethics a moral cause, and behind our belief in beauty, a belief in a God who cares for beauty, then our scientific, our ethical, and our aesthetic beliefs all lose value to a degree which nobody can seriously contemplate.** It might be asked, "Cannot natural selection which can mimic design mimic also creative reason?" This, said Mr. Balfour, is an important objection which he proposed to keep in view, but for some reason or another all things which have the greatest value for thought, for morality, and for beauty seemed to him to have no survival virtue at all, and they cannot be mimicked because they do not affect the survival of the fittest or the multiplication of the race.

With this answer to an attempt to turn his position, Mr. Balfour indicated that in succeeding lectures he would show how our aesthetic values, our moral values, and the great body of intellectual, and especially of scientific, beliefs are dependent on the theistic principle.

—*The Times*, Thur. Jan. 15, 1914, 4c.

❖ Design and Selection

The argument, then, which I propose to lay before you, though its material is provided by our common-sense beliefs, is not an argument from common sense. It does not extend to theology those uncritical methods which we accept (most of us without protest) in the sphere of our everyday activities. Is it, then, you may be tempted to ask, some form of the yet more familiar argument from design? Is it more than Paley[9] and the Bridgwater treatises[10] brought up to date? And, if so, has not the vanity of all such endeavours been demonstrated in advance: from the side of sceptical philosophy by Hume; from the side of idealist philosophy by Kant and his successors; from the side of empirical philosophy by the nineteenth-century agnostics; from the side of science by the theory of Natural Selection? Do not the very catch-words of the argument—"contrivance," "design," "adaptation," exercised by the "Architect of the Universe" fill us with a certain weariness? Do they not represent the very dregs of stale apologetics; the outworn residue of half-forgotten controversies?

———— The Old Argument from Design ————

Consider the old argument from Design. But that argument from Design was based mainly on the fact that material nature was orderly, was uniform, showed the marks (as Maxwell said of the atom) of having been manufactured, of having come out of one mould, or of having been designed by one mind. But the real strength of that argument from Design rested upon adaptation between the living animals, whether man or the lower animals, and the mechanical world which they inhabited. The religious philosopher said: "Can you supposed that animals would be created so happily adapted to their surroundings unless created by an intelligent Creator? Could that be the result of chance, due to a fortuitous concurrence of atoms?" And the argument seemed extremely strong. But then came natural selection, then came the Darwinian doctrine, which indicated that all these wonderful adaptations were explained, or were explainable, by an action between the living organism and its environment, and that what was supposed to be due to design really had nothing in it of final causes, but was due to action and interaction of the living organism with its dead environment.[11]

For my own part, I do not think the argument from contrivance bad, but I do think it very limited; limited in respect of its premises; limited also in respect of its conclusions. It may, perhaps, be worth dwelling on some of these limitations, if only to make my own position clearer by contrast.

In the first place, it must be noted that, from a consideration of inanimate nature alone it is difficult, perhaps impossible, to infer design. The mere existence of natural laws is not, as it seems to me, a sufficient basis for the argument; we require also that these laws should combine to subserve an end. Were the universe, for example, like a huge impervious reservoir of some simple gas, where nothing rested but nothing changed, where amid all the hurry and bustle of colliding atoms no new thing was ever born, nor any old thing ever perished, we might find in it admirable illustrations of natural law, but no hints, so far as I can see, of purpose or design. Nor is the case really mended if, instead of thus artificially simplifying inanimate nature, we consider it in all its concrete complexity. Even cosmic evolution of the Spencerian type will scarcely help us. Herbert Spencer, as we know, regarded the world-story as a continuous progress from the simple to the complex, in which the emergence of the living out of the not-living is treated as a harmonious episode in one vast evolutionary drama. The plot opens in the first chapter with diffused nebulae; it culminates in the last with the social organisation of man. Unfortunately its central episode, the transition from the not-living to the living, was never explained by the author of the *Synthetic Philosophy*; and the lamentable gap must be filled in by each disciple according to his personal predilections. For the moment, however, we are concerned only with one part of the story, that which deals with the evolution of inanimate nature. Can this be regarded as displaying design? I hardly think so. Granting, for the sake of argument, the validity of the Spencerian physics, granting that the material Universe exhibits this general trend from the simple to the complex, from a loose diffusion of nebulous matter to the balanced movements of suns and satellites, does this of itself give any hint of purpose? Only, I believe, if we confound evolution with elaboration and elaboration with improvement, and read into it some suggestion of progress borrowed from biology or ethics, sociology or religion.

────────────── **Inferring God from the World** ──────────────

An induction which may be perfectly valid within the circle of phenomena, may be quite meaningless which it is employed to account for the circle itself. You cannot infer a God from the existence of the world as you infer an architect from the existence of a house, or a mechanic from the existence of a watch.[12]

────────────────────────────────

But we have not the slightest right to do this. Apart from life and thought, there is no reason to regard one form of material distribution as in any respect superior to another. A solar system may be more interesting than its parent nebula; it may be more beautiful. But if there be none to unravel its intricacies or admire its splendours, in what respect is it better? Its constituent atoms are more definitely grouped, the groups move in assignable orbits; but why should the process by which these results have been achieved be regarded as other than one of purposeless change superinduced upon meaningless uniformity? Why should this type of "evolution" have about it any suggestion of progress? And, if it has not, how can it indicate design?

Spencer himself was, of course, no advocate of "design" after the manner of Paley; and I only mention his cosmic speculations because their unavowed optimism—the optimism that is always apt to lurk in the word "evolution"—makes of them material peculiarly suitable for those who seek for marks of design in lifeless nature. But let us add two touches to Spencer's picture, and see how the argument then stands.

I have already commented on the great omission which mars the continuity of his world-story—the omission, I mean, of any account of the transition from the not-living to the living. I shall have again to refer to it. But there are, besides this, two other omissions, one at the beginning of his narrative, and the other at the end, whose significance in relation to "design" should receive a passing comment.

As I understand the matter, an intelligence sufficiently endowed—let us call him Laplace's calculator—might infer the past state of the material universe from the present by a process of rigorous deduction, on accepted physical principles.[13] But, if he carried back his investigations into a period sufficiently remote, be would find a point at which certain fundamental processes reach a theoretical limit; and, though we must believe that this condition of things had antecedents, yet infinite powers of calculation, based upon infinite knowledge of the present, could not, it seems, tell us what they were.

So much for the past. Now for the future. Here our calculator would be more successful. His prophecy, unlike his history, would not break helplessly against any impassable barrier. He could range at will over the illimitable future. But the prospect, though unbounded, would not be exhilarating. No faintest tinge of optimism would colour his anticipations. Everything that happened, good or bad, would subtract something from the lessening store of useful energy, till a time arrived when nothing could happen any more, and the universe, frozen into eternal repose, would for ever be as if it were not.

Do our ideas of material evolution, thus corrected and supplemented, lend themselves easily to the argument from design? I hardly think so. It is true that in retrospect we can ideally reach a limit which no calculations, based upon physical laws, will permit us to overpass, and that where (what in old-fashioned language were called) "secondary causes" fail us, a First Cause may plausibly be invoked; but, if we gaze forward instead of backward, the physical course of nature does not merely fail to indicate design, it seems loudly to proclaim its absence. A world where all energy suffers inevitable degradation, considered by itself, appears atheistic on the face of it: nor can even life consciousness or thought redeem it, if they, too, are doomed to perish when further transformations of energy become impossible.

It is not, therefore, on any general survey of material nature that, in the present state of our knowledge, we can base the argument from "design." Nor is this the foundation on which those who use the argument have chiefly built. They have always sought for proofs of contrivance rather among the living than among the dead. In the intricate adjustment of different parts of an organism to the interests of the whole; in the adaptation of that whole to its environment, they found the evidence they required. Arrangements which so irresistibly suggested purpose could not (they thought) be reasonably attributed to chance.

This argument possessed immense force in what was, comparatively speaking, the infancy of biology. Has that force been lessened by the growth of knowledge? Yes and No. **If we consider organic adaptations and adjustments in themselves, scientific discovery has increased a thousand-fold our sense of their exquisite nicety and their amazing complexity. I take it as certain that, had no such theory as Natural Selection been devised, nothing would have persuaded mankind that the organic world came into being unguided by intelligence. Chance, whatever chance may mean, would never have been accepted as a solution. Agnosticism would have been scouted as stupidity.**

————————— **Balfour Knew Darwin** —————————

Some of us—I am proud to think that I am one among many in this room—knew Charles Darwin personally.[14]

All this has been changed, as every one knows, by Darwin. But what exactly was it that, in this connection, Darwin did? He is justly regarded as the greatest among the founders of the doctrine of organic evolution; but there is nothing in the mere idea of organic evolution which is incongruous with design. On the contrary, it almost suggests guidance, it has all the appearance of a plan. Why, then, has Natural Selection been supposed to shake teleology to its foundation?

The reason, of course, is that though the fact of Selection does not make it harder to believe in design, it makes it easier to believe in accident; and, as design and accident are the two mutually exclusive alternatives between which the argument from design requires us to choose, this comes to the same thing. Before Darwin's great discovery those who denied the existence of a Contriver were hard put to it to explain the

THEISM AND HUMANISM

appearance of contrivance. Darwin, within certain limits and on certain suppositions, provided an explanation. He showed how the most complicated and purposeful organs, if only they were useful to the species, might gradually arise out of random variations, continuously weeded by an unthinking process of elimination. Assume the existence of living organisms, however simple, let them multiply enough and vary enough, let their variations be heritable, then, if sufficient time be granted, all the rest will follow. In these conditions, and out of this material, blind causation will adapt means to ends with a wealth of ingenuity which we not only cannot equal, but which we are barely beginning to comprehend.[15]

The theory of selection thus destroys much of the foundation on which, a hundred years ago, the argument from design was based. What does it leave untouched?

It leaves untouched all that can be inferred from the existence of the conditions which make organic evolution possible: matter which lives, multiplies, and varies; an environment which possesses the marvellously complex constitution required to make these processes possible. Selection may modify these conditions, but it cannot start them. It may modify the manner in which multiplication is secured; it may modify the lines which variations follow; it may enable organic species to adapt their powers to their environment, and (within narrow limits) their environment to their powers. But it cannot produce either the original environment or the original living matter. These must be due either to luck or to contrivance; and, if they be due to luck, the luck (we must own) is great. How great we cannot say. We cannot measure the improbability of a fortuitous arrangement of molecules producing not merely living matter, but living matter of the right kind, living matter on which selection can act. Here, indeed, Laplace's calculator might conceivably help us. But suppose him to have, done so, suppose him to have measured the odds against the accidental emergence of the desired brand of protoplasm, how are we to compare this probability with its assumed alternative—intelligent design? Here, I think, even Laplace's calculator would fail us; for he is only at home in a material world governed by mechanical and physical laws. He has no principles which would enable him to make exhaustive inferences about a world in which other elements are included: and such a world is ours.

For a Greek philosopher to assert that the world is material was legitimate enough. He was in search of a universal principle; and if he found it in matter we need neither wonder nor criticise. After all, matter lies round us on every side; we are immersed in it; we are largely dependent on it. It may well seem but a small step further, and a very natural one, to treat it as the essence of all that is.

But, as it seems to me, we now know too much about matter to be materialists. The philosophical difficulties in the way of accepting a materialistic world-system are notorious—at least to philosophers. But I am not speaking of them. I am thinking of the scientific difficulties, those that cannot but suggest themselves when we consider the breach of continuity involved, in the appearance of life, and still more obviously of feeling, at particular points in the long procession of material causes and effects. The very essence of the physical order of things is that it creates nothing new. Change is never more than a redistribution of that which never changes. But sensibility belongs to the world of consciousness, not to the world of matter. It is a new creation, of which physical equations can give no account. Nay, rather, which falsifies such equations; which requires us to say that, before a certain date in the history of the universe, energy in one shape was converted into precisely the same amount of energy in another shape, and into nothing more; that matter in one position was transferred to another position without increase or diminution: but that, after this date, the transformations of energy and the movements of matter were sometimes accompanied by psychical "epiphenomena" which differ from them in kind, which are incommensurable with them in amount, and which no equations can represent.

Babbage, in order to show how occasional "miracles" might "naturally" break the continuity of the longest sequences, devised a machine which produced numbers according to a particular law for an indefinite period, then broke this uniformity by a single exception, and, thereafter, reverted for ever to its original principle of action. But Babbage's results, however startling, depended wholly on known mathematical and mechanical laws. Their irregularity was only apparent. To Laplace's calculator, they would have seemed not merely inevitable but obvious. It is quite otherwise with the appearance and disappearance of feeling, thought, will, consciousness in general, within the strictly determinal series of mechanical causes and effects. Here the anomaly is real: the breach of continuity inexplicable by any physical laws and indeed incompatible with them. I am not at this moment concerned either to deny or to assert that at the critical frontier where mind and matter meet, the even course of nature suffers violence. I am not suggesting, for example, that, if a given physiological state were exactly repeated, the psychical state formerly associated with it would not be repeated also. My point is different. It is that in a strictly determined physical system, depending on the laws of matter and energy alone, no room has been found, and no room can be found, for psychical states at all. They are novelties, whose intrusion into the material world cannot be denied, but whose presence and behaviour cannot be explained by the laws which that world obeys.

────────── **Spiritual Invasion** ──────────

Unexampled invasions of the physical sphere by the spiritual are not indeed to be lightly believed. But they are certainly not to be rejected merely because historians cannot bring themselves to accept the "miraculous."[16]

The difficulty is a very familiar one; and I cannot see that the progress either of science or philosophy has brought us nearer to its solution. But what (you may be disposed to ask) has it to do with the argument from design? At least this much:

Those who refuse to accept design do so because they think the world-story at least as intelligible without it as with it. This opinion is very commonly associated with a conception of the universe according to which the laws of matter and energy are sufficient to explain, not only all that is, but all that has been or that will be. If we thus know the sort of explanation which is sufficient to cover the facts, why (it is asked) should we travel further afield into the misty realms of theology or metaphysics?

But the explanation does not cover the facts, even when all has been conceded to the opponents of design that I, at least, am ready to concede. Grant that the inorganic world, considered in and for itself, does not suggest contrivance; grant that the contrivance which the organic world does undoubtedly suggest may in great part be counterfeit—there still remains a vast residue of fact quite recalcitrant to merely physical explanation. I will not argue whether in this residue we should or should not include life. It is enough that we must undoubtedly include feeling and all other phases of consciousness. We must include them, even if they be no more than the passive accompaniments of material change; still more must we include them if we speculatively accept (what I deem to be) the inevitable belief that they can, within limits, themselves initiate movement and guide energy. **The choice, therefore, is not between two accounts of the universe, each of which may conceivably be sufficient. The mechanical account is not sufficient. It doubly fails to provide a satisfactory substitute for design.** In the first place, it requires us to believe that the extraordinary combination of material conditions required for organic life is due to hazard. In the second place, it has to admit that these material conditions are insufficient, and have somehow to be supplemented. We must assume, that is to say, an infinitely improbable accident, and, when we have assumed it, we are still unprovided with an explanation. Nay, the case is even worse—for the laws by whose blind operation this infinitely improbable accident has been brought about are, by hypothesis, mechanical; and, though mechanical laws can account for rearrangements, they cannot account for creation; since, therefore, consciousness is more than rearrangement, its causes must be more than mechanical.

To me, then, it seems that the common-sense "argument from design" is still of value. But, if it carries us beyond mechanical materialism, it must be owned that it does not carry us very far towards a religious theology. It is inconsistent with Naturalism: it is inconsistent with Agnosticism. But its demands would be satisfied by the barest creed which acknowledged that the universe, or part of it, showed marks of intelligent purpose. And, though most persons willing to accept this impoverished form of Theism will certainly ask for more, this is not because they are swept forward by the inevitable logic of the argument, but because the argument has done something to clear a path which they were already anxious to pursue.

———————————— **Scientific Knowledge** ————————————

Extend the boundaries of knowledge as you may; draw how you will the picture of the universe; reduce its infinite variety to the modes of a single space-filling ether; re-trace its history to the birth of existing atoms; show how under the pressure of gravitation they became concentrated into nebulae, into suns, and all the hosts of heaven; how, at least in one small planet, they combined to form organic compounds; how organic compounds became living things; how living things, developing along many different lines, gave birth at last to one superior race; how from this race arose, after many ages, a learned handful, who looked round on the world which thus blindly brought them into being, and judged it, and knew it for what it was: perform (I say) all this, and though you may indeed have attained to science, in nowise will you have attained to a self-sufficing system of beliefs. One thing at least will remain, of which this long-drawn sequence of causes and effects gives no satisfying explanation; and that is knowledge itself. Natural science must ever regard knowledge as the product of irrational conditions, for in the last resort it knows no others. It must always regard knowledge as rational, or else science itself disappears. In addition, therefore, to the difficulty of extracting from experience beliefs which experience contradicts, we are confronted with the difficulty of harmonising the pedigree our beliefs with their title to authority. The more successful we are in explaining their origin, the more doubt we cast on their validity. The more imposing seems the scheme of what we know, the more difficult it is to discover by what ultimate criteria we claim to know it.[17]

❖ **Argument from Values**

As the conclusions which I desire to establish are richer in contents than any which can be derived merely from marks of contrivance, so the method of arriving at them is essentially different. In the first place, it is based not upon considerations drawn from external nature, but from the mind and soul of man. Stress is laid, not upon contrivances, adjustments, and the happy adaptation of means to ends, but on the character of certain results attained. **It is not an argument from design, but an argument from value. To emphasise the contrast, it might be called an argument** *to* **design. Value (we assert) is lost if design be absent. Value (you will ask) of what? Of our most valuable beliefs, (I answer) and of their associated emotions.**

We are, no doubt, accustomed to connect the notion of value rather with things believed in, than with the beliefs of which they are the subjects. A fine symphony, an heroic deed, a good dinner, an assured livelihood, have admitted values. But what values can we attribute to beliefs and judgments, except in so far as they are aids and instruments for obtaining valuable objects?

This question, however, is based, as I think, upon an insufficient survey of the subject. We are in search of a world outlook. Creeds, therefore, are our concern. The inquiry with which these lectures are concerned is whether, among the beliefs which together constitute our general view of the universe, we should, or should not, include a belief in God. And to this question it is certainly relevant to inquire whether the elimination of such a belief might not involve a loss of value in other elements of our creed—a loss in which we are not prepared to acquiesce.

But how, you will ask, is this loss of value brought about? What is the connection between a belief in God and a belief concerning (say) beauty, or goodness, or natural law? Evidently the connection is not, in the ordinary sense, a logical one. Neither aesthetic, nor ethic, nor scientific judgments can be 'deduced' from Theism; nor can Theism be 'deduced' from them. We are not dealing with premises and conclusions bound together by a formal chain of inference. How, then, is our procedure to be described?

——————————— **Editor's Note** ———————————

From this point on, Balfour's argument hinges on two characteristics shared by all beliefs. First, everything we believe is part of a *cognitive* series. This means that we believe B is true because we believe it can be logically derived from A. In such cases, the truth of B depends on our reasoning powers as well as the truth of A. If we try to base all our beliefs on such a foundation, we would be being very rationalistic. But Balfour points out that we often forget that our beliefs are also part of a *causal* series that is heavily dependent upon how we came to be the person we are. We may believe in D, for instance, because we were born at a particular time and place. In the chapters that follow, Balfour argues that Naturalism has a serious problem defending the *causal* series that lies behind many of its beliefs. Because what it believes about the evolutionary roots of our love of beauty, our moral codes, and our ability to reason, it has no sound reason for attaching any importance to what we believe about them. In the final analysis, each is just an illusion that exists because it gives us advantages in the struggle for existence. Theism, in contrast, doesn't have this problem because in its *causal* series our beliefs about beauty, morality and reason come directly from God who is himself the final source of all beauty, morality and reason. What Balfour is saying is similar to the argument in the first few verses of John's gospel: "In the beginning was the Word . . . [and] through him all things were made; without him nothing was made that has been made." Naturalistic theories may provide a seemingly valid answer to the origin of our physical natures, but they can never provide a sound explanation for our deeper concerns. (For more on this topic, see Appendix B, "The Evolution of Belief.")

In order to make this clear, I must call your attention to a double aspect possessed by all beliefs alike, whatever be the subject-matter with which they deal. All beliefs have a position, actually or potentially, in a *cognitive series*; all beliefs, again, have a position, known or unknown, in a *causal series*. All beliefs, in so far as they belong to the first kind of series, are elements in one or more collections of interdependent propositions. They are conclusions, or premises, or both. All beliefs, in so far as they belong to the second kind of series, are elements in the temporal succession of interdependent events. They are causes, or effects, or both.

It has, further, to be noted that whereas reasons may, and usually do, figure among the proximate causes of belief, and thus play a part in both kinds of series, it is always possible to trace back the causal series to a point where every trace of rationality vanishes; where we are left face to face with conditions of beliefs—social, physiological, and physical— which, considered in themselves, are quite a-logical in their character.

It is on this last point that I particularly desire to insist. We are all very familiar with the equivocal origin of most human creeds. To be sure, we observe it chiefly in the case of other people. In our own case, we dwell by preference on those causes of our beliefs which are also reasons. But in our detached studies of the opinions we do not share, we easily perceive how insufficient are the arguments officially urged on their behalf, and how often even these insufficient arguments have only a nominal connection with the convictions of which they claim the legal paternity. We must, however, go yet one step further. We must realise that, on any merely naturalistic hypothesis, the rational elements in the causal series lie always on the surface. Penetrate but a short way down, and they are found no more. You might as easily detect life in the minerals wherein plants are rooted, as reason in the physiological and physical changes to

THEISM AND HUMANISM

which the source of our most carefully reasoned beliefs must, in the last resort, be traced.

Consider, for example, an extreme case—say a proposition of Euclid. Here we have a belief logically inferred from well-assured premises—so, at least, we were accustomed to suppose before mathematicians became so very fastidious in the matter of proof. Can we not say that in this case the elements of the two series are in a sense identical, that all the causes for our belief are also reasons for it? Certainly we are not moved by prejudice, or affection, or authority. It is neither self-interest nor party passion that induces us to believe, for example, that the three angles of a triangle are equal to two right angles. Has our thought, then, in this case freed itself from the dominion of a-logical conditions? Is our belief the child of uncontaminated reason? I answer—No. Though the argument, *qua* argument, is doubtless independent of time, the argumentative process by which we are in fact convinced occurs in time, and, like all psychological processes, is somehow associated with physiological changes in the brain. These, again, are part of the general stream of physical happenings, which in themselves have nothing rational about them. Follow up this stream but a little further and every trace, not only of mind but of life, is completely lost; and we are left face to face with unthinking matter and its purposeless movements. Logical inference is thus no more than the reasoned termination of an unreasoning process. Scratch an argument, and you find a cause.

If this be admitted, the question at once arises whether we can treat the two kinds of series thus intimately connected as separable when we are estimating the values of the beliefs with which they are both associated. Is it permissible, is it even possible, to ignore the genesis of knowledge when we are considering its validity? Do not origins qualify values?

In many cases they notoriously do. A distinguished agnostic once observed that in these days Christianity was not refuted, it was explained. Doubtless the difference between the two operations was, in his view, a matter rather of form than of substance. That which was once explained needed, he thought, no further refutation. And certainly we are all made happy when a belief, which seems to us obviously absurd, is shown nevertheless to be natural in those who hold it.

But we must be careful. True beliefs are effects no less than false. In this respect magic and mathematics are on a level. Both demand scientific explanation; both are susceptible of it. Manifestly, then, we cannot admit that explanation may be treated as a kind of refutation. For, if so, the more successfully science carried out its explanatory task, the more completely would it shatter its own principles. This way lies universal scepticism. Thus would all intellectual values be utterly destroyed.

But we have not to do with intellectual values alone. There are beliefs (as I have already said) round which crystallise complex emotions, aesthetic and ethic, which play no small part in our highest life. Without the beliefs the emotions would dwindle; without the emotions the beliefs would lose their worth. Though they do not imply each other in the world of logic, they are mutually necessary in the world of values. Here, of course, there is no question of a contrast between the logical and the causal series. Emotions are always effects; they are never inferences. In their case, therefore, the relation of value to origin is not obscured by considerations like those which must occupy us in the case of mere beliefs; and we have to face in a simpler and more direct form the central problem of these lectures: the problem of the relation which origin bears to value. It is with this branch of my subject as it is raised by aesthetic and by ethic emotions that I shall be mainly occupied in the next two lectures. And as in the later part of my course I shall contend that it is destructive of rational values to root them in unreason, so I shall now contend that the emotional values associated with, and required by, our beliefs about beauty and virtue must have some more congruous source than the blind transformation of physical energy. **If I am successful in my endeavour I shall have done something to show that "design" is demanded by all that we deem most valuable in life, by beauty, by morals, by scientific truth: and that it is design far deeper in purpose, far richer in significance, than any which could be inferred from the most ingenious and elaborate adjustments displayed by organic life.**

——————— **Music and Human Ancestry** ———————

The procedures of those who account for music by searching for the primitive association which first in the history of man or of his ancestors conferred aesthetic value upon noise, is as if one should explain the Amazon in its flood by pointing to the rivulet in the far Andes which, as the tributary most distant from its mouth, has the honour of being called its source. This may be allowed to stand as the geographic description, but it is very inadequate as a physical explanation. Dry up the rivulet, and the huge river would still flow on, without abatement or diminution. Only its titular origin has been touched; and if we would know the Amazon in its beginnings, and trace back the history of the vast result through all the complex ramifications of its contributory causes, each great confluent must be explored, each of the countless streams enumerated whose gathered waters sweep into the sea four thousand miles across the plain.[18]

3

Aesthetic and Theism

Are we to treat as unconsidered trifles our powers of enjoying beauty and of creating it? Can we be content with a world-outlook which assigns to these chance products of matter and motion so vast a value measured on the scale of culture, and no value worth counting measured on the scale of race survival

EMOTION AND BELIEF
Mr. Balfour on Aesthetic Values
Third Gifford Lecture
(From Our Special Correspondent)
GLASGOW, JAN. 16

Even a Glasgow fog had no appreciable effect upon the numbers who waited in the cold corridors outside the Bute Hall to-day to listen to Mr. Balfour's third Gifford lecture. They were rewarded by an address which excited an enthusiasm with which philosophical disquisitions rarely received, and the cheers, which on Wednesday emanated from youthful anxiety to find a joke, came to-day in more suppressed volume from eager listeners glad to discover that a Gifford lecturer could defend what they themselves had the wish to believe.

Mr. Balfour began by referring to the classification of beliefs with which he concluded his last lecture. He had, he said, adopted that classification because of the varying degree to which emotions are associated with our beliefs. In aesthetics, with which he proposed to deal to-day, emotion absorbs almost the whole of the belief, for the sense of beauty is an emotion and its value lies, not in the judgment, but in the emotions associated with the judgments. In ethics judgments are of fundamental importance, yet the emotions or moral sentiments must be there also. In science emotion is the vanishing quantity, there is an emotional element, but it is of

little value.

Origin of Aesthetic Emotion

What, he proceeded to ask, are aesthetic emotions? And he described them as always existing in contemplation and never leading to action. He admitted, of course, that beautiful things might be used for practical ends, that the creative effort, which produced the beautiful thing was not included in his definition, and the very act of contemplation itself requires much effort and preparation. But when a great artist had put a great effort of concentrated will into a great work of art, and when the observer had put himself into harmony with it, the result was not action but contemplation. It had been said that the essence of tragedy is that it "purifies by terror and pity." "The pity," said Mr. Balfour, "does not suggest assistance; the terror does not prompt to fight. Nobody rushes to rescue Desdemona." How did these aesthetic beliefs, and the contemplative emotions associated with them, come into existence? Are they due to any process of natural selection? He believed, with regard to ethics and knowledge, up to a certain point the beliefs and the emotions connected with them are due, or may be plausibly attributed, to the general process of organic evolution. But he could find no such pedigree for the aesthetic emotions. They cannot be shown to have in any effective sense their root in the attributes bred into the race by the struggle for existence. Herbert Spencer had tried to contribute to the explanation of how we of the 19th or 20th century feel in the presence of a great work of art by saying that our ape-like ancestors howled in moments of emotion. The audience laughed, and Mr. Balfour told them that to ridicule Mr. Spencer was not his object. If Mr. Spencer could have shown in the anthropoid ape any element of musical appreciation, and traced its development into our elaborate appreciation of a symphony of Beethoven, he would have produced a causal connexion between the two. As it was, he had mistaken an historic account of origins for a theory of genesis, and the two were in this instance unconnected. From the naturalistic standpoint, Mr. Balfour insisted, the whole psychical complex of aesthetic emotions and beliefs is a chance by-product, a happy accident of evolution; and the geniuses themselves who produce works of art are equally accidental products, for poets and artists did not greatly contribute to the destruction of tribal enemies and the survival of the fittest. This view, he held, really destroyed the values of aesthetic beliefs. He did not refer to the minor manifestations of the aesthetic emotions, and he admitted that a cinematograph can be enjoyed without reference to cosmical theories.

The Spiritual Intution

It is the aesthetic emotion in its highest manifestations that has most to lose from a purely naturalistic origin. The poet or the artist is generally supposed to have an insight into reality. The men who are most alive to the higher aesthetic emotions feel that their emotions open up something that contains an intuition greater than knowledge. There is always in a work of art the sense of communication from its creator. Behind the poem, the picture, and the symphony are the poet, the painter, and the composer, and works of art must be communicated from one spirit to another spirit. The most perfect kaleidoscope could never be a work of art or convey aesthetic emotion. Could they, he asked, accept this view for works of art and deny it for the manifestations of natural beauty, before which, he thought, the greatest works of art faded into insignificance? Were there two principles of aesthetic? Beauty moves upon the surface. Only what appears is beautiful. If we could perceive the aether and the scattered electrons which are the real facts, such insight would merely excite curiosity and wonder. **We must regard the beauties of nature as signs, as symbols, as a language, just as we do chords and colours. The entire value of the glories of nature is lost unless we conceive behind nature one who has designed it. Art, he pointed out, clings obstinately to personification, in spite of the teachings of science.** We live and move and have our being in available energy, but we cannot write an ode to it. Poetry clings to personification, not by the staying power of long tradition, nor by a feigned literary conceit, but because the naturalistic explanation is felt to be intolerable in that it destroys aesthetic values. It is, of course, possible for a reader of Wordsworth to accept conventionally the notion of a God of nature, while he is reading Wordsworth, just as a man who does not believe in ghosts may read a ghost story with a conventional belief sufficient for his artistic purposes. But it is not possible to enjoy the best of Wordsworth as it should be enjoyed unless you take the same general view of the universe as Wordsworth did.

Mr. Balfour had now reached the culminating point of his argument, and he drove it home in some eloquent sentences. He argued that what is true of Wordsworth is true also of natural beauty, and he invited his hearers to recall the moments, too rare in any life, when the sight of some magnificent spectacle seems to drive out not merely all the smaller cares and anxieties of life, but all the smaller preoccupations of art itself. At such moments it is true that a man has something better to do than to think of cosmology. But, just as no pain is so severe but that it leaves a man some corner of consciousness in which to ask, how long it will last, so there is no beauty, however overpowering, but allows of the thought that it means something and is not simply a matter of aether and electrons, and brain and visual nerves. To persuade a man to attribute no such significance is to weaken fatally those aesthetic values which can only exist if, behind that great appearance is a reality, and if it contains a message from spirit to spirit. If we desire to produce those values, to argue to design from one can say unless men are willing to sacrifice the aesthetic emotion in its highest development and in the greatest example, we should believe in a Greek spirit whose manifestations these things are.

—*The Times,* Sat. Jan. 17, 1914, 5f.

❖ Aesthetic Described

In this lecture I have undertaken to consider certain beliefs and emotions relating to beauty, and to inquire how far their value is affected by our views as to their origin.

The poverty of language, however, makes it rather difficult to describe with any exactness the scope of such an inquiry. Beauty is an ill-defined attribute of certain members of an ill-defined class; and for the class itself there is no very convenient name. We might describe its members as "objects of aesthetic interest" always bearing in mind that this description (as I use it) applies to objects of the most varying degrees of excellence—to the small as well as the great, the trifling as well as the sublime: to conjuring and dancing; to literature, art, and natural beauty.

It follows from this description that, while all things of beauty possess aesthetic interest, not all things of aesthetic interest would in common parlance be described as beautiful.[19] They might, for example, display wit, or finish, or skill. They might, therefore, properly excite admiration. But beauty is a term whose use may well be confined to the qualities which excite only the highest forms of aesthetic interest, and it is thus I propose to employ it.

Now what are the characteristics which distinguish objects of aesthetic interest from interesting objects generally? I will mention two.

In the first place, the value of aesthetic objects depends on the intrinsic quality of the emotions they arouse, and not upon the importance of any ulterior purpose which they may happen to subserve. In the second place, the emotions themselves, whatever be their value, must be *contemplative*. They must not prompt to action or reach forward to any end. They must be self-sufficient, and self-contained.

Of course, I do not suggest that works of art are useless. A building may be beautiful, although it is also convenient. A sword most delicately damascened may be an admirable engine of destruction. We may even go further and admit that utility unadorned may have about it an aesthetic flavour. Nice adjustment and fitness exquisitely accomplished are without doubt agreeable objects of contemplation. But, in the first two of these cases, beauty is deliberately added to utility, not organically connected with it. An ill-proportioned building might have been equally fitted for its purpose; a plain sword might have been equally lethal. In the third case the connection between utility and aesthetic interest is organic, yet undesigned. From the very nature of the case it forms no part of the purpose for which the mechanism was contrived.

Again—when I say that aesthetic interest does not prompt to action, I am, of course, speaking of those who enjoy, not of those who are laboriously trying to enjoy, still less of those who create what is to be enjoyed. It commonly requires effort, conscious and unconscious, to be a good spectator; it always requires effort to become a good artist. Yet these are no real exceptions to the principle. Aesthetic interests, once aroused, do not prompt to action; and it is, I conceive, of their essence that they should not. The most emotional spectator does not rush to save Desdemona from Othello; and, though tragedy may (or may not) purify by "pity and terror," the pity does not suggest a rescue, nor the terror urge to flight.

❖ Whence Comes It?

Now these characteristics of aesthetic emotions and beliefs raise problems of great interest. How came they to be what they are? To what causal process are they due? In the case of ethics (to anticipate a discussion that will occupy us in the next lecture) the earlier stages at least are seemingly due to selection. They lead to action, and to action which has survival value. But what survival value have aesthetic judgments and feelings at any stage of culture? It is true that actions which are sometimes represented as primitive forms of artistic creation play their part in the drama of animal courtship. Some animals dance, some sing, some croak; some flaunt colours, some exhale smells. Apes (it seems) make inarticulate noises which (according to Spencer) were the humble beginnings, not only of speech, but of music. I own that to me this sort of explanation leaves our aesthetic interests quite unexplained. Grant, for the sake of argument, that, were our knowledge sufficient, we could trace a continuous history of musical emotions from the simple satisfaction excited in the female ape by the howling of the male, down to the delicate delights of the modern musician, should we be nearer an answer to the problem of aesthetic causation? I doubt it. **Certainly we should not have succeeded in coupling the development of our feelings for beauty to the general process of organic evolution. Before this can be satisfactorily accomplished it must be shown, not merely that the tastes of anthropoid apes are useful to anthropoid apes, but that the tastes of men are useful to men, and in particular that the tastes of civilised men are useful to civilised men. Nor would even this be enough unless usefulness be carefully defined in terms of survival value. It must, in other words, be shown that communities rich in the genius which creates beauty and in the sensibility which enjoys it, will therefore breed more freely and struggle more successfully than their less gifted neighbours. And**

I am not aware that any attempt to establish such a doctrine has ever been seriously undertaken.

———————— Our Delight in Music ————————

What is said to be the cause of our delight in Music? It is sometimes hastily said to have originated in the ancestors of man through the action of sexual selection. This is of course impossible. Sexual selection can only work on materials already in existence. Like other forms of selection, it can improve, but it cannot create; and the capacity for enjoying music (or noise) on the part of the female, and the capacity for making it on the part of the male, must both have existed in a rudimentary state before matrimonial preferences can have improved either one gift or the other.[20]

But, if so, our aesthetic sensibilities must be regarded (from the naturalistic standpoint) as the work of chance. They form no part of the quasi design which we attribute to selection; they are unexplained accidents of the evolutionary process. This conclusion harmonises ill with the importance which civilised man assigns to them in his scheme of values. On this point, at least, there reigns a singular unanimity. However people may differ as to what we should admire, all are agreed that we should admire something. However they may differ about the benefits to be derived from aesthetic, all are agreed that the benefits are great. The pessimist finds in art the solitary mitigation of human miseries. A certain type of agnostic treats it as an undogmatic substitute for religion. He worships beauty, but nothing else; and expects from it all the consolations of religious experience without the burdens of religious belief. Even those who would refuse to art and literature this exalted position, are prepared to praise them without stint. They regard the contemplative study of beautiful things as a most potent instrument of civilisation; in countless perorations they preach its virtues; delicacy of aesthetic discrimination they deem the surest proof of culture, and the enjoyment of aesthetic excellence its highest reward.

The case is apparently, but not really, different when we turn from beauty to the minor aesthetic interests—the popular novel, the music-ball song, the cricket-match (as spectacle), the cinematograph, and so forth. Nobody, it is true, greatly praises these things, but multitudes greatly enjoy them. The space they occupy in the life of the community has increased beyond computation. As locomotion becomes easier and leisure greater that space will increase yet more. This may be good or bad; but none will deny that it is important. What a paradox this seems! Theories of selection were devised to explain the complex structures and the marvellous adjustments of the organic world without needlessly postulating design. We should think but poorly of them if they accounted for some organs by methods quite inapplicable to others—if they showed us, for example, how the eye had developed, but appealed to some wholly different principle (say special creation) when they set to work on the ear; or taught that the nose must be regarded as an evolutionary accident not to be explained on any general principle at all. If what required explanation was of small biological importance, this last hypothesis would not seem perhaps startling. The most convinced selectionist is not obliged to suppose that selection eliminates everything which does not make for survival. Useless variations may be spared if they be harmless. Even harmful variations may be spared if they be linked to variations so advantageous that their joint effect proves beneficial on balance. But is this the case with aesthetic? **Are we to treat as unconsidered trifles our powers of enjoying beauty and of creating it? Can we be content with a world-outlook which assigns to these chance products of matter and motion so vast a value measured on the scale of culture, and no value worth counting measured on the scale of race survival? If design may ever be invoked where selection fails and luck seems incredible, surely it may be invoked here.**

—————— No Beauty Under Naturalism ——————

The persistent and almost pathetic endeavours of aesthetic theory to show that the beautiful is a necessary and unchanging element in the general scheme of things, if they prove nothing else, may at least convince us that mankind will not easily reconcile themselves to the view which the naturalistic theory of the world would seemingly compel them to accept. . . . However little, therefore, we may be prepared to accept any particular scheme of metaphysical aesthetics—and most of these appear to me to be very absurd—we must believe that somewhere and for some Being there shines an unchanging splendour of beauty of which in Nature and in Art we see, each of us from our own standpoint, only passing gleams and stray reflections, whose different aspects we cannot now co-ordinate, whose import we cannot fully comprehend, but which at least is something other than the chance play of subjective sensibility or the far-off echo of ancestral lusts. No such mystical creed can, however, be squeezed out of observation and experiment; Science cannot give it us; nor can it be forced into any sort of consistency with the Naturalistic Theory of the Universe.[21]

❖ Values and the Higher Emotions

These observations are applicable, more or less, to the whole body of our aesthetic interests—whether they be roused by objects we deem relatively trivial, or by objects which are admittedly rare and splendid. But while neither fit comfortably into a purely naturalistic framework, it is only the second which, in virtue of their intrinsic quality, demand a source beyond and above the world of sense perception. Here, then, we are face to face with a new question. So far we have been concerned to ask whether that which is admittedly valuable can be plausibly attributed to chance. Now we must ask whether that which is attributed to chance can thereafter retain its value. Of these questions the first is germane to the ordinary argument from design. It is the second which chiefly concerns us in these lectures.

Perhaps an affirmative answer may seem to have been already given by implication. The admission that the second problem only touches the highest values in the aesthetic scale may be thought to render the whole inquiry vain. And the admission cannot be avoided. No one supposes that when we are looking (for example) at an acrobat, it matters in the least what we think of the universe. Our beliefs and disbeliefs about the Cosmic order will not modify either in quantity or quality such satisfaction as we can derive from the contemplation of his grace and agility. Where, then, it will be asked, do we reach the point in the aesthetic scale at which values begin to require metaphysical or theological postulates? Is it the point where beauty begins? If so, who determine where this lies; and by what authority do they speak?

Evidently we are here on difficult and delicate ground. On questions of taste there is notoriously the widest divergence of opinion. Nor, if we regard our aesthetic interests simply as the chance flotsam and jetsam of the evolutionary tides, could it well be otherwise. If there be practically no "limits of deviation" imposed by selection; if, from a survival point of view, one taste be as good as another, it is not the varieties in taste which should cause surprise so much as the uniformities.

——————— 1909 Romanes Lecture at Oxford ———————
Music is the art which perhaps most clearly shows how futile is the search for agreement among men of "trained sensibility."[22]

To be sure, the uniformities have often no deep aesthetic roots. They represent no strong specific likes and dislikes shared by all men at a certain stage of culture, but rather tendencies to agreement (as I have elsewhere called them), which govern our social ritual, and thereby make social life possible. We rail at "fashion," which by an unfelt compulsion drives multitudes simultaneously to approve the same dresses, the same plays, the same pictures, the same architecture, the same music, and the same scenery. We smile at the obsequious zeal with which men strive to admire what the prophets of the moment assure them is admirable. But admitting, as I think we must, that these prophets neither possess any inherent authority, nor can point to any standard of appeal, we must also admit that if in Art there were no orthodoxies, if the heresies themselves were unorganised, if every man based his aesthetic practice on a too respectful consideration of his own moods and fancies, the world we live in would be even more uncomfortable than it is.

However this may be, it is clear that this second portion of my argument, which is not based, like the first, on any objective survey of the part played in human affairs by general aesthetic interests, has special difficulties to surmount. For it rests on experiences of high emotion rare for all, unknown to many, roused in different men by different objects. How can any conclusions be securely based on foundations at once so slender and so shifting?

I agree that the values dealt with in this part of the argument are not values for everybody. Yet everybody, I think, would be prepared to go some way in the direction I desire. They would acknowledge that, in art, origin and value cannot be treated as independent. They would agree that those who enjoy poetry and painting must be at least dimly aware of a poet beyond the poem and a painter beyond the picture. **If by some unimaginable process works of beauty could be produced by machinery, as a symmetrical colour pattern is produced by a kaleidoscope, we might think them beautiful till we knew their origin, after which we should be rather disposed to describe them as ingenious.** And this is not, I think, because we are unable to estimate works of art as they are in themselves, not because we must needs buttress up our opinions by extraneous and irrelevant considerations; but rather because a work of art requires an artist, not merely in the order of natural causation, but as a matter of aesthetic necessity. It conveys a message which is valueless to the recipient, unless it be understood by the sender. It must be expressive.

Such phrases are no doubt easily misunderstood. Let me, therefore, hasten to add that by an "expressive" message I do not mean a message which can be expressed in words. A work of art can never be transferred from one medium into another, as from marble to music. Even when words are the medium employed, perfect translation is impossible. One poet may paraphrase, in a different language, the work of another; and a new work of art may thus be produced. But however closely it follows the original, it will never be the same. On the other hand, if the medium used be (for example) colour, or sound, or stone, the work of art cannot be translated into words at all. It may be described; and the description may better the original. Yet it cannot replace it. For every work of art is unique; and its meaning cannot be alternatively rendered. But are we, therefore, to conclude that it has no meaning? Because its message cannot be translated, has it therefore no message? To put these questions is to answer them.

Many people, however, who would travel with me so far would refuse to go further. They would grant that a work of art must be due to genius, and not, in the first instance, to mechanism or to chance. But whether, in the last resort, mechanism or chance has produced the genius, they would regard as, from the aesthetic point of view, quite immaterial. Music and poetry must have a personal source. But the musician and the poet may come whence they will.

And perhaps, in very many cases, this is so; but not, I think, in all, nor in the highest. If any man will test this for himself, let him recall the too rare moments when beauty gave him a delight which strained to its extremest limit his powers of feeling; when not only the small things of life, but the small things of Art—its technical dexterities, its historical associations—vanished in the splendour of an unforgettable vision; and let him ask whether the attribution of an effect like this to unthinking causes, or to an artist created and wholly controlled by unthinking causes, would not go far to impair its value.

To such an appeal it is not difficult to raise objections. It may be said, for example, that, under the stress of emotions like those I have described, no man troubles his head about problems of cosmology; thought is merged in feeling; speculation is smothered. But though this is true, it is not wholly true. As no pain, I suppose, is so intense as to exclude all reflections on its probable duration, so no rapture is so absorbing as to exclude all reflections on its probable source. I grant that at such moments we do not philosophise; we do not analyse a problem, turning it this way or that, and noting every aspect of it with a cool curiosity. Nevertheless, for those accustomed to reflect, reflection is never wholly choked by feeling. Nor can feeling, in the long run, be wholly unaffected by reflection.

Again, it may be said that such moments too seldom occur in any man's experience to justify even the most modest generalisations—let alone generalisations that embrace the universe. But this objection seems to rest on a misapprehension. We must remember that the argument from aesthetic values is not a scientific induction or a logical inference. There is here no question of truth and falsehood, or even of good taste and bad taste. We are not striving to isolate what is essential to beauty by well-devised experiments; nor are we concerned with psycho-physical determination of the normal relation between feeling and stimulus. If it be urged that some particular example of deep aesthetic emotion quite outruns the merits of its object, so that sound canons of criticism require its value to be lowered, we need not deny it. We are not dealing with sound canons of criticism; though I may observe, in passing, that if they lower emotional values in one direction without raising them in others, good taste becomes a somewhat costly luxury. **My point is different. I am not appealing to all men, but only to some men—to those and to those only who, when they explicitly face the problem, become deeply conscious of the incongruity between our feelings of beauty and a materialistic account of their origin.**

────────── Poets and Artists ──────────

Poets and artists have been wont to consider themselves and to be considered by others, as prophets and seers, the revealers under sensuous forms of hidden mysteries, the symbolic preachers of eternal truths. All this is, of course, on the naturalistic theory, very absurd. They minister, no doubt, with success to some phase, usually a very transitory phase, of public taste; and what they tell us, though it may be very agreeable, is seldom true, and never important. This is a conclusion which, howsoever it may accord with sound philosophy, is not likely to prove very stimulating to the artist, nor does it react with less unfortunate effect upon those to whom the artist appeals. . . . For such a feeling carries with it, at its best, an inevitable reference not less inevitable because it is obscure, to a Reality which is eternal and unchanging; and we cannot accept [that] without suffering the conviction that in making such a reference we were merely the dupes of our emotions, the victims of a temporary hallucination induced, as it were, by some spiritual drug.[23]

The extreme individualism of this point of view may seem repulsive to many. Are the feelings (they will ask) of some transient moment to be treated as authentic guides through the mysteries of the universe, merely because they are strong enough to overwhelm our cooler judgment? And, if so, how far is this method of metaphysical investigation to be pressed? Are we, for example, to attach transcendental value to the feelings of a man in love? There is evidently a close, though doubtless not a perfect, parallel between the two cases. It is true that love is rooted in appetite, and that appetite has a survival value which I, at least, cannot find in the purely contemplative emotions. But romantic love goes far beyond race requirements. From this point of view it is as useless as aesthetic emotion itself. And, like aesthetic emotion of the profounder sort, it is rarely satisfied with the definite, the limited, and the immediate. It ever reaches out towards an unrealised infinity. It cannot rest content with the prose of mere fact. It sees visions and dreams dreams which to an unsympathetic world seem no better than amiable follies. Is it from sources like these— the illusions of love and the enthusiasms of ignorance—that we propose to supplement the world-outlook provided for us by sober sense and scientific observation?

Yet why not? Here we have values which by supposition we are reluctant to lose. Neither scientific observation nor sober sense can preserve them. It is surely permissible to ask what will. And if Naturalism be inimical to their maintenance, the fact should at least be noted.

It is true, no doubt, that these high-wrought feelings have worse enemies even than naturalism. When the impassioned lover has sunk into a good husband, and the worshipper of beauty has cooled into a judicious critic, they may look back on their early raptures with intelligent disdain. In that event there are for them no values to be maintained. They were young, they were foolish, they made a mistake, and there is no more to be said. But there is a higher wisdom. Without ignoring what experience has to teach, they may still believe that through these emotions they have obtained an authentic glimpse of a world more resplendent and not less real than that in which they tramp their daily round. And, if so, they will attribute to them a value independent of their immediate cause—a value which cannot be maintained in a merely naturalistic setting.[24]

This may seem a doctrine too mystical to suit the general tenor of these lectures. Let me, therefore, hasten to add that our ordinary and repeatable experiences of beauty seem to point in the same direction as these rarer and more intense emotions. It is, of course, true that even about these we cannot generalise as we may (for example) about the external world. We cannot, I mean, assume that there is a great body of aesthetic experience which all normal persons possess in common. There is always something about our feeling for beautiful things which can neither be described nor communicated, which is unshared and unsharable. Many normal persons have no such feelings, or none worth talking about. Their aesthetic interests may be great, but they lie at a lower level of intensity. They do not really care for beauty. Again, there are many who do care, and care greatly, who would yet utterly repudiate the doctrine that the highest aesthetic values were in any sense dependent on a spiritual view of the universe. The fact that so much of the greatest art has been produced in the service of religion they would not regard as relevant. They would remind us that one great poet at least has been a passionate materialist; that many have been pessimists; that many have been atheists; that many have been in violent revolt against the religion of their age and country. Of these we cannot say that their art suffered from their opinions, for we cannot imagine what their art would have been like had their opinions been different. Neither can we say that the readers who shared their opinions, became, thereby, less qualified to enjoy their art. Such a paradox would be too violent. How, then (the objectors may ask), are facts like these to be harmonised with the views I am recommending?

Probably they cannot be harmonised. We are confronted with a difference of temperament which must be accepted as final. Yet the contradiction may often be less than at first appears. In the case which I brought forward just now, strong aesthetic emotion was assumed to carry with it, both at the crisis of immediate experience and yet more in periods of reflective retrospect, a demand for some cause emotionally adequate to its effect. In other words, it was assumed that such an experience suggested the question—whence comes it? of matter? or of spirit? and required the answer—if it be not born of spirit it is little, or it is naught. But in many cases this answer is not given because the question is not asked; or, if it be asked, is misunderstood. And there are many reasons why it should not be asked; and many why it should be misunderstood.

For there are two things which must, in this connection, be remembered. The first is that materialism has never been the prevailing creed among lovers of beauty. The second is that though (as I contend) a deeply-lying incongruity infects theories which trace the ultimate genesis of beauty exclusively to causes which neither think, nor feel, nor will, such theories involve no contradiction, nor can those who hold them be taxed with inconsistency. There is, therefore, little in the ordinary routine of artistic criticism which raises the point which we are now discussing. A critic examining some artistic whole—a picture, a poem, a symphony—is much occupied in separating out the elements which contribute to the total effect, and in observing their character, value, and mutual relations. But it is only when we cease to analyses, when we contemplate, directly or in retrospect, the whole as a whole, that the problem of origin arises; and even then it need never become explicit. It may remain in the shape of an unsatisfied longing for a spiritual reality beyond the sensuous impression, or of a vaguely felt assurance that the spiritual reality is there. And in neither case has it developed into a question definitely present—and pressing for a definite reply.

While, then, I am quite ready to believe that there are many persons whose enjoyment of beauty is quite independent of their world-outlook, I am also convinced that there are some who count themselves among the number only because they have never put the matter to the proof. It may be that they have given but little thought to questions of theology or metaphysics. It may be that they are pantheists after the manner of Shelley, or pessimists after the manner of Schopenhauer. Perhaps, again, they hold one or other of the theosophies which pass current in the West as the esoteric wisdom of the East. In any case, they are averse from orthodoxy, or what they regard as such. A lover of the beautiful belonging to any type like these, if asked whether his estimate of aesthetic values depended on his creed, might easily miss the point of the inquiry, and his negative reply would be worthless. Let the question, therefore, be put in different terms. Let him be asked whether beauty would not lose value for him if his world-outlook required him to regard it as a purposeless accident; whether the aesthetic delights which he deems most exquisite would not be somewhat dimmed if reflection showed them to be as vain, as transitory, though not so useful as the least considered pleasures of sense. If he replies in the negative, there is no more to be said. This lecture is not addressed to him. But I believe there are many to whom such an answer would be profoundly unsatisfying; and they, at least, can hardly deny that aesthetic values are in part dependent upon a spiritual conception of the world we live in.

——— **Rationalism Without Naturalism Doomed** ———

Theism, Deism, Design, Soul, Conscience, Morality, Immortality, Freedom, Beauty—these and cognate words associated with the memory of great controversies mark the points at which rationalists who are not also naturalists have sought to come to terms with the rationalising spirit or to make a stand against its onward movement. It has been in vain. At some places the fortunes of battle hung long in the balance; at others the issues may yet seem doubtful. Those who have given up God can still make a fight for conscience; those who have abandoned moral responsibility may still console themselves with artistic beauty. But, to my thinking, at least, the struggle can have but one termination. Habit and education may delay the inevitable conclusion; they cannot in the end avert it. For these ideas are no native growth of a rationalistic epoch, strong in their harmony with contemporary modes of thought. They are the products of a different age, survivals from, as some think, a decaying system. And howsoever stubbornly they may resist the influences of an alien environment, if this undergoes no change, in the end they must surely perish.[25]

❖ Natural Beauty

So far I have been considering art and the beauty expressed by art. But there are two kinds of aesthetic interest, which, though not artistic in the ordinary sense of the word, are so important that something must be said about them before this lecture closes.

The first of these is natural beauty. Hegel, if I rightly understand him, altogether excluded this from the sphere of aesthetic. For him the point of importance was Spirit—the Idea—expressing itself in art; and since nature is not spirit, nor natural beauty art, the exclusion was logical. For me, on the other hand, the main thing is feeling roused by contemplation;

and particularly feeling at its highest level of quality and intensity. Natural beauty, therefore, cannot be ignored; since no feelings of contemplation possess higher quality, or greater intensity, than those which natural beauty can arouse.

Evidently, however, there is, even from my point of view, a great difference between beauty in art and beauty in nature. For, in the case of nature, there is no artist; while, as I observed just now, "a work of art requires an artist, not merely in the order of natural causation, but in the order of aesthetic necessity. It conveys a message which is valueless to the recipient unless it be understood by the sender. It must be significant."

Are we, then, to lay down one rule for artistic beauty and another rule for natural beauty? Must the first be expressive, but not the second? Is creative mind necessary in one case, and superfluous in the other? And if in the case of nature it be necessary, where is it to be found? On the naturalistic hypothesis, it is not to be found at all. The glory of mountain and of plain, storm and sunshine, must be regarded as resembling the kaleidoscopic pattern of which I just now spoke; with this difference only—that the kaleidoscope was designed to give some pattern, though no one pattern more than another; while nature was not designed with any intention at all, and gives us its patterns only by accident.

I know not whether you will think that this train of thought is helped or hindered by bringing it into relation with our scientific knowledge of natural realities. The world which stirs our aesthetic emotions is the world of sense, the world as it appears. It is not the world as science asks us to conceive it. This is very ill-qualified to afford aesthetic delight of the usual type; although the contemplation of complicated relations reduced to law may produce an intellectual pleasure in the nature of aesthetic interest. Yet none, I think, would maintain that mass and motion abstractly considered, nor any concrete arrangement of moving atoms or undulating ether, are beautiful as represented in thought, or would be beautiful could they become objects of perception. We have a bad habit of saying that science deals with nothing but "phenomena." If by phenomena are meant appearances, it is to aesthetics rather than to science that, on the principle of Solomon's judgment, phenomena most properly belong. To get away from appearances, to read the physical fact behind its sensuous effect, is one chief aim of science; while to put the physical fact in place of its sensuous effect would be the total and immediate ruin of beauty both in nature and in the arts which draw on nature for their material. Natural beauty, in other words, would perish if physical reality and physical appearance became one, and we were reduced to the lamentable predicament of perceiving nature as nature is!

Now, to me, it seems that the feeling for natural beauty cannot, any more than scientific curiosity, rest satisfied with the world of sensuous appearance. But the reasons for its discontent are different. Scientific curiosity hungers for a knowledge of causes; causes which are physical, and, if possible, measurable. Our admiration for natural beauty has no such needs. It cares not to understand either the physical theories which explain what it admires, or the psychological theories which explain its admiration. It does not deny the truth of the first, nor (within due limits) the sufficiency of the second. But it requires more. It feels itself belittled unless conscious purpose can be found somewhere in its pedigree. Physics and psycho-physics, by themselves, suffice not. It longs to regard beauty as a revelations—revelation from spirit to spirit, not from one kind of atomic agitation to the "psychic" accompaniment of another. On this condition only can its highest values be maintained.[26]

❖ Aesthetic of History

There is yet one other subject of aesthetic interest on which I desire to say something before the course of these lectures carries me into very different regions of speculation. The subject I refer to is history.

That history has aesthetic value is evident. An age which is both scientific and utilitarian occasionally pretends to see in it no more than the raw material of a science called sociology, and a storehouse of precedents from which statesmen may draw maxims for the guidance of mankind. It may be all this, but it is certainly more. What has in the main caused history to be written, and when written to be eagerly read, is neither its scientific value nor its practical utility, but its aesthetic interest. Men love to contemplate the performances of their fellows, and whatever enables them to do so, whether we belittle it as gossip, or exalt it as history, will find admirers in abundance.

Yet the difference between this subject of contemplative interest and those provided either by beauty in art or beauty in nature is striking.

In the first place, history is not concerned to express beauty. I do not deny that a great historian, in narrating some heroic incident, may rival the epic and the saga. He may tell a tale which would be fascinating even if it were false. But such cases are exceptional, and ought to be exceptional. Directly it appears that the governing preoccupation of an historian is to be picturesque, his narrative becomes intolerable.

This is because the interest—I mean the aesthetic interest—of history largely depends upon its accuracy; or (more strictly) upon its supposed accuracy. Fictitious narrative, whether realistic or romantic, may suggest deeper truths, may tell us more about the heart of man, than all the histories that ever were written; and may tell it more agreeably. But fact has an interest, because it is fact; because it actually happened; because actual people who really lived and really suffered and really rejoiced caused it to happen, or were affected by its happening. And on this interest the charm of history essentially depends.

In this respect there is, I think, a certain analogy between the aesthetic interest aroused by history and that aroused by natural beauty. Our pleasure in a landscape is qualified if we discover ourselves to have been the victims of an optical delusion. If, for example, purple peaks are seen on a far horizon, the traveller may exclaim, "What beautiful mountains!" Something thereupon convinces him that the mountains are but clouds, and his delight suffers an immediate chill. But why? The mountains, it is true, proved unreal; but they had as much reality as mountains in a picture. Where lies the essential difference between a representation accidentally produced by condensed vapour and a representation deliberately embodied in paint and canvas? It is not to be found, as might be at first supposed, in the fact that the one deceives us and the other does not. Were we familiar with this particular landscape, did we know that nothing but a level plain stretched before us to the limits of our vision, we might still feel that, if the clouds on the horizon were what they seemed to be, the view would gain greatly in magnificence. Here there is no deception and no shock of disillusionment. If, therefore, we remain dissatisfied, it is because in this case verisimilitude does not suffice us; we insist on facts.

It has, perhaps, not been sufficiently noticed that brute fact, truth as it is apprehended in courts of law, truth as it is given by an accurate witness speaking on oath, has for some purposes great aesthetic value. That it is all-important in the dealings between man and man would be universally conceded; that it has no importance either in fine art or imaginative literature, and no meaning in music or architecture, most people would be ready to admit. But that it possesses worth where no practical issues are involved, and that this worth is of the contemplative or aesthetic order, is perhaps not so easy of acceptance. Yet so it is. A tale which would be inexpressibly tedious if we thought it was (in the "law court" sense) false may become of absorbing interest if we think it true. And this not because it touches morals or practice, not because it has theoretic interest or controversial importance, but in its own right and on its own merits.

Now this aesthetic quality is, it seems to me, required both from "natural beauty" and historic narrative; but if there is here a resemblance between them, in other respects they are profoundly different. Landscape appeals to us directly. I do not mean that our enjoyment of it, both in quality and quantity, is not largely due to the work of artists. Our tastes have, no doubt, been formed and our sensibilities educated by the interpretation of nature which we owe to painters and poets. But though this is true, it is also true that what we see and what we enjoy is not art but nature, nature at first hand, nature seen immediately, if not as she is, at least as she appears. In the case of history it is otherwise. Except when we happen to have been ourselves spectators of important events, there is always an artist to be reckoned with. It may be Thucydides. It may be Dr. Dryasdust. It may be a mediaeval chronicler. It may be Mrs. Candour at the tea-table. But there is always somebody; and though that somebody might repudiate the notion that his narrative was a work of art, yet he cannot evade responsibility for selection, for emphasis, and for colour. We may think him a bad artist, but, even in his own despite, an artist he is—an artist whose material is not marble or sound, but brute fact.

There is another way in which the aesthetic interest of history characteristically differs from the interest we feel in beauty, whether of art or of nature. It is massive rather than acute. Particular episodes may indeed raise the most poignant emotions. But, broadly speaking, the long-drawn story of man and his fortunes stirs feelings which (to borrow a metaphor from physics) are great in quantity but of low intensity. So it comes about that, whereas in the case of art the emotions stand out prominently above their associated judgments, in the case of history the positions are commonly reversed.

Yet this need not be so; and in particular it need not be so when we are contemplating the historical process as a whole. Details are then merged in a general impression; and the general impression drives us beyond the limits of history proper into questions of origin and purpose, into reflections about man and destiny, into problems of whence and whither. Speculations like these have an emotional as well as an intellectual value, which must be affected by the answers we give them.

Let me illustrate and explain. It is possible, indeed it is easy, to contemplate aspects of history with the coolest intellectual interest. In this mood we might, for instance, study the development of science and religion out of primitive magics and superstitions. In this mood we might observe the characteristics of the city state, or the growth and decay of feudalism, or the history of the Mongols. On the other hand, the interest often becomes tinged with stronger feelings when we sympathetically follow the changing fortunes of particular individuals or communities. We are then, as it were, spectators of a drama, moved by dramatic hopes and fears, dramatic likes and dislikes, dramatic "pity and terror." And our emotions are not merely those appropriate to drama; they have, besides, that special quality (already referred to) which depends on the belief that they are occasioned by real events in a world of real people.

But there is yet a third case to be considered, in which the two previous cases are included and partially submerged. This occurs when the object of our contemplative interest is not episodic but general, not the fate of this man or that nation, this type of polity or that stage of civilisation, but the fate of mankind itself, its past and future, its collective destiny.

Now we may, if we please, treat this as no more than a chapter of natural history. Compared with the chapter devoted, let us say, to the Dinosaurs it no doubt has the disadvantage of being as yet unfinished, for the Dinosaurs are extinct, and man still survives. On the other hand, though the natural history of "Homo Sapiens" is incomplete, we may admit that it possesses a peculiar interest for the biologist; but this interest is scientific, not historical.

For what does historical interest require? Not merely "brute fact," but brute fact about beings who are more than animals, who look before and after, who dream about the past and hope about the future, who plan and strive and suffer for ends of their own invention; for ideals which reach far beyond the appetites and fears which rule the lives of their brother beasts. Such beings have a "natural history," but it is not with this that we are concerned. The history which concerns us is the history of self-conscious personalities, and of communities which are (in a sense) self-conscious also. Can the contemplative values which this possesses, especially in its most comprehensive shape, be regarded as independent of our world-outlook? Surely not.

Observe that history, so conceived, must needs compare faculty with desire, achievement with expectation, fulfilment with design. And no moralist has ever found pleasure in the comparison. The vanity of human wishes and the brevity of human life are immemorial themes of lamentation; nor do they become less lamentable when we extend our view from the individual to the race. Indeed, it is much the other way. Men's wishes are not always vain, nor is every life too brief to satisfy its possessor. Only when we attempt, from the point of view permitted by physics and biology, to sum up the possibilities of collective human endeavour, do we fully realise the "vanity of vanities" proclaimed by the Preacher.

I am not, of course, suggesting that history is uninteresting because men are unhappy: nor yet that naturalism carries pessimism in its train. It may well be that if mankind could draw up a hedonistic balance-sheet, the pleasures of mundane existence would turn out to be greater than its suf-

ferings. But this is not the question. **I am not (for the moment) concerned with the miseries of the race, but with its futility. Its miseries
might be indefinitely diminished, yet leave its futility unchanged. We
might live without care and die without pain; nature, tamed to our
desires, might pour every luxury into our lap; and, with no material
wish unsatisfied, we might contemplate at our ease the inevitable, if
distant, extinction of all the life, feeling, thought, and effort whose
reality is admitted by a naturalistic creed.**

But how should we be advanced? What interest would then be left in
the story of the human race from its sordid beginnings to its ineffectual
end? Poets and thinkers of old dimly pictured a controlling Fate to which
even the Olympian gods were subject. The unknown power, which they
ignorantly worshipped, any text-book on physics will now declare unto
you. But no altars are erected in its honour. Its name is changed. It is no
longer called Fate or Destiny, but is known by a title less august if more
precise, the law of energy-degradation, or (if you please) "the second law
of thermo-dynamics." It has become the subject of scientific experiment;
the physicists have taken it over from the seers, and its attributes are
defined in equations. All terrestrial life is in revolt against it; but to it, in
the end, must all terrestrial life succumb. Eschatology, the doctrine of the
last things, has lapsed from prophecy to calculation, and has become (at
least potentially) a quantitative science.

And, from a scientific point of view, this is quite satisfactory. But it is
not satisfactory when we are weighing the aesthetic values of universal
history. Shakespeare, in the passionate indictment of life which he puts
into the mouth of Macbeth, declares it to be "a tale told by an idiot, full of
sound and fury," and (mark well the climax) "signifying nothing." That is
the point with which in this lecture we are chiefly concerned. It most
clearly emerges when, in moments of reflection, we enlarge the circuit of
our thoughts beyond the needs of action, and, in a mood untouched by
personal hopes or fears, endeavour to survey man's destiny as a whole.
Till a period within the memory of men now living it was possible to
credit terrestrial life with an infinite future, wherein there was room for an
infinite approach towards some, as yet, unpictured perfection. It could
always be hoped that human efforts would leave behind them some
enduring traces, which, however slowly, might accumulate without end.
But hopes like these are possible no more. **The wider is the sweep of our
contemplative vision the more clearly do we see that the rôle of man,
if limited to an earthly stage, is meaningless and futile—that, however it be played, in the end it "signifies nothing."** Will any one assert

that universal history can maintain its interest undimmed if steeped in the atmosphere of a creed like this?

Here, however, we are evidently nearing the frontier which divides aesthetic from ethic. Before I cross it, and begin a new subject, let me very briefly touch on a difficulty which may have occurred to some of my hearers.

The line of thought followed in the last section of this lecture assumes, or seems to assume, that our only choice lies between history framed in a naturalistic, and history framed in a theistic setting. In the first case we have a world-outlook which forbids the attribution of permanent value to human effort; in the second case we have a world-outlook which requires, or, at the least, permits it. But are these the only alternatives? What are we to say, for example, about those metaphysical religions which, whether they be described as theistic, pantheistic, or atheistic, agree in regarding all life as illusion, all desire as wretchedness, and deem the true end of man to be absorption in the timeless identity of the real? Such creeds have no affinity with naturalism. Philosophically they are in sharpest contrast to it. But even less than naturalism do they provide history with a suitable setting. For naturalism does, after all, leave untouched the interest of historical episodes, so long as they are considered out of relation to the whole of which they form a part. As we are content, in the realm of fiction, to bid farewell to the hero and heroine on their marriage, unmoved by anxieties about their children, so, in the realm of "brute fact," we may arbitrarily isolate any period we choose, and treat the story of it without reference to any theories concerning the future destiny of man. But this process of abstraction must surely be useless for those who think of the world in terms of the metaphysical religions to which I have referred. In their eyes all effort is inherently worthless, all desire inherently vain. Nor would they change their opinion even were they persuaded that progress was real and unending; that effort and desire were building up, however slowly, an imperishable polity of super-men. For those who in this spirit face the struggling world of common experience the contemplative interest of universal history must be small indeed.

CHAPTER
4

Ethics and Theism

My main contention rests, not upon the difficulty of harmonising moral ends in a Godless universe, but upon the difficulty of maintaining moral values if moral origins are purely naturalistic. That they never have been so maintained on any large scale is a matter of historic fact. At no time has the mass of mankind treated morals and religion as mutually independent. They have left this to the enlightened; and the enlightened have (as I think) been wrong.

MR. BALFOUR ON ETHICS
Limitations of Natural Selection
Need of a Theistic Setting
(From Our Special Correspondent)
GLASGOW, JAN. 19

Mr. Balfour devoted his fourth Gifford lecture to demonstrating that our ethical ideas can retain their value only in a theistic setting. He began by admitting that natural selection has played a large part in the development of our ideas of right and wrong, for ethical values, unlike aesthetic values, do not hang loosely upon the evolutionary process, but are up to a certain point dependent upon it, while the aesthetic emotions lead only to contemplation. Ethics has essentially to do with action, and if there is any truth in the modern theory of evolution, it would be strange indeed if ethical beliefs and emotions were entirely alien from it.

Altruism in Man and Animals

At this point Mr. Balfour introduced a distinction similar to that on which he based his argument regarding aesthetic values. The whole stress of his reasoning was laid upon the higher values in the ethical scale, and these higher values he defined as being those dependent upon the group of altruistic and unselfish feelings which operate for the interest of other individuals or of the family or of the State, or of mankind. How far, he asked, are our altruistic values the result of the mimicry of design by natural selection? How far can they retain their value if we refuse to put them in a theistic setting? Mr. Balfour began his answer to these questions by pointing out that we find no altruism in the lower organisms; only certain powers of reacting to environment for the benefit of the individual. There is no effort of the individual to serve the species other than instinctive efforts under the impulse of selective forces. Such instinctive efforts were not, indeed, the limits of the power of natural selection. Animals higher in the scale show parental, and especially maternal, love and sacrifice, and give examples of altruism in one of its purest shapes. We cannot, of course, say what goes on in the consciousness of the animal, but we cannot deny it something of true altruism marked by the higher qualities which we admire in the devotion and self-sacrifice of men. This, however, did not amount to social instinct, for it did not outlast the early days or months after birth, and it did not help towards the social organization which is essential for human existence.

It is true that bees and ants give a resemblance to social organization, but each bee has only one desire—that of subserving the good of the whole hive. In the bee, self is lost in the interest of the society, and the very mechanical perfection of those amazing societies impaired their interest. There can never be a conflict of interest in the case of a working bee, never the problem of the self against the whole, or the more difficult problem of the divergent interests of two wholes to each of which the self belongs. Such conflicts we cannot avoid, because we have a choice of ends. Here Mr. Balfour explained that he used the word "whole" to mean such a collection of other individuals as a family, a town, a state, a profession. It is not simply a choice between self-interest and one of those societies to which a man may well, and even a selfish man constantly does, sacrifice his interests, but it is a multiple choice, because the interests of these wholes come into collision. Mankind must have progress, not unchanging perfection. Loyalty to family or tribe is essential to progress, and it was essential to very early and primitive progress, and is therefore a direct product of the individual. The argument that it is folly because it involves a loss to the self-regarding instincts was an appeal from the later stages of evolution to the earlier.

Evolution and Morals

Coming to the central point of his argument, Mr. Balfour said that the essential point is the answer to the question whether, granting that selection has improved the altruistic feelings in their earlier stages, we can attribute the growth of morality and the higher ideals to the continued action of natural selection. The higher emotions, he argued, can have no effect upon the struggle for existence. **Nobody could maintain that in that brute struggle the virtues of mercy, charity, and loving-kindness are to the advantage of the race from the point of view of a biologist, who studies what it is that enables one organism to oust another.** For this view, the lecturer said, he could quote high authority. Nietzsche was perhaps the best known in this country by the reference to superman made by a brilliant dramatic writer [George Bernard Shaw, 1903, *Man and Superman*], but he had many disciples in his own country. Nietzsche held that the higher virtues are what he call denaturalized— that they have no place in the natural development of morals, and that they have only been made possible by religious beliefs. Mr. Balfour summoned him as a witness to his premises, not to his conclusions, because Nietzsche's conclusion was that the higher virtues are not merely express products, but even harmful products, of the biological process, and ought to be stamped out. His own conclusion was diametrically opposite, but he agreed that the higher virtues cannot retain values if they are to be judged simply as helping or hindering the internecine struggle for existence.

As another witness Mr. Balfour

quoted Huxley's Romanes lecture delivered in 1893. It was, he said, an impressive and a pathetic lecture, because, while Huxley accepted no form of religion and was an agnostic, and indeed, the coiner of that convenient word, and while he took a purely naturalistic view of the universe, he felt, as Mr. Balfour himself felt, that the higher values cannot be hitched into the evolutionary process, to which he assigned everything around him and behind which he saw nothing but energy and matter. It was with the utmost diffidence that he differed from so eminent a biologist, but he thought Huxley went too far when he said that all that is ethically best is opposed to success in the cosmic struggle. In opposition to this unhappy conclusion stood maternal love, one of the highest things in the ethical scale, and still unsurpassed. He could not himself pass upon the evolutionary process the same heavy condemnation which was passed on it by that great man, who had done so much to make it intelligible to the world, but he asked how anyone who takes Huxley's view even in a less extreme form could imagine that the higher scale of ethics is going to retain its value as a by-product or a dangerous product of evolution.

In an impressive passage Mr. Balfour then reminded his hearers of the power exercised upon mankind by the phase, "a return to nature." If the simple teaching of nature is that the higher virtues are useless and noxious, is not the teaching of Nietzsche an inevitable conclusion? Men will argue that if development and the course of progress must always be the result of constant internecine warfare, then they must pin their faith on the untrammelled license of that struggle, and the return to nature would mean the abandonment of all the higher and tenderer virtues in which the value of life entirely depends for us.

The Religious Framework

In conclusion, Mr. Balfour referred to the efforts of philosophers and preachers to show that there is no real discrepancy between self-interest and altruism. Such efforts are not founded on past experience; they represent the ideal of a future reconciliation. Such an ideal has no meaning on a naturalistic basis, and we wish to keep and to improve their higher values. If we feel that progress in ethics has been as great as in knowledge and in the arts of life, we cannot rest content with the belief that ethics has now no survival value and no root in some higher moral purpose which, as the world goes on, will ever give it more and more meaning. **"If," says the lecturer, "we are to keep the highest of all values in the scale where religion has placed them and where we instinctively feel they ought to be, we cannot tear away that religious framework and suppose that the ideas remain." A theistic setting, he again insisted, is a necessity for ethics.** The argument from design, he added, might show the ingenuity of the contrivance, but it required such an argument as he had been placing before them to add to the conception of a powerful and, if he might say so, an ingenious Deity, the conception of a God, the author of all that is beautiful and of all that is good.

—*The Times*, Tue. Jan. 20, 1914, 10a.

❖ Ethics Described

I turn now from contemplation to action; from Aesthetics to Ethics. And in so doing I must ask permission to stretch the ordinary meaning of the term which I use to describe the subject-matter of the present lecture, as I have already stretched the meaning of the term which described the subject-matter of the last. "Aesthetics" there included much besides beauty; "Ethics" here will include much besides morality. As, under the first head, were ranged contemplative interests far lower in the scale than (for example) those of art, so I shall extend the use of the word "Ethics" till it embraces the whole range of what used to be called the "springs of action," from the loftiest love down to impulses which in themselves are non-moral, instinctive, even automatic.

The grounds for this procedure are similar in both cases. I am mainly, almost exclusively, concerned with beliefs and emotions touching beauty and goodness. Yet it is important to remember that, considered as natural products, these shade off by insensible gradations into manifestations of life to which the words "belief" and "emotion" are quite inapplicable, where "beauty" and "goodness" have little meaning or none. And as this larger class, when concerned with action, has at present no better name, I may be permitted to describe it as ethical.

I am mainly concerned, however, with that higher part of the ethical scale which all would agree to call Moral, and with the debatable region immediately below it. Of purposive action, or what seems to be such, of a still lower type, I need say little—but we must never forget that it is there.

Morals, as I conceive them, are concerned with ends of action: and principally with ultimate ends of action. An end of action, in so far as it is ultimate, is one which is pursued for itself alone, and not as a means to some other end. Of course an end may be, and constantly is, both ultimate and contributory. It is sought for on its own account, and also as an instrument for procuring something else. It is mainly in the first of these capacities, however, that it concerns morality.

For the purposes of this lecture I shall classify ultimate ends as either egoistic or altruistic—egoistic ends being those that are immediately connected with, or centred in, the agent; altruistic ends being those that are not. But I beg you to remember that this distinction does not correspond to that between right and wrong. Egoism is not necessarily vicious, nor is altruism necessarily virtuous. Indeed, as I shall have occasion to point out later, the blackest vices, such as cruelty and hatred, are often altruistic.

This is an unusual, though not, I think, an unreasonable, use of language. "Egoism" and. "altruism" are terms historically associated with the moral theories which regard happiness as the only end of action, but are under the necessity of distinguishing between actions designed to secure the happiness of the agent and actions designed to secure the happiness of other people. I do not accept these theories, though I borrow their phraseology. Happiness may, or may not, be the highest of all ultimate ends, the one to which all others should give way. But it seems to me quite misleading to call it the only one. To describe the sensual man, the vain man, the merely selfish man, the miser, the ascetic, the man moved by rational self-love, the man absorbed in the task of "self-realisation," the man consumed by the passion for posthumous fame, as all pursuing the same egoistic end by different means, is surely to confuse distinctions of great moral importance without any gain of scientific clarity. In like manner, to suppose that the man who spends himself in the service (say) of his family, his country, or his church, is only striving for the "happiness" of the human race, or of certain selected members of the human race, is (it seems to me) to ignore the plain teaching of daily experience. As there are many egoistic ends besides our own happiness, so there are many altruistic ends besides the happiness of others. The extended sense, therefore, in which I employ these terms seems justified by facts.

❖ Egoism, Altruism and Selection

I shall not attempt to determine the point at which we can first clearly discriminate between the "egoistic" and "altruistic" elements in animal instinct. Evidently, however, it is anterior to and independent of any conceptual recognition either of an *ego* or an *alter*. It might be argued that there is an altruistic element in the most egoistic instincts. Eating, multiplying, fighting, and running away—acts plainly directed towards preserving and satisfying the individual—also conduce to the preservation of the race. But, however this may be, the converse is certainly untrue. There are altruistic instincts into which no element of egoism enters. Of these the most important is parental, especially maternal, love: the most amazing are the impulses which regulate the complex polity of (for example) a hive of bees. In these cases one organism will work or fight or endure for others: it will sacrifice its life for its offspring, or for the commonwealth of which it is a member. Egoism is wholly lost in altruism.

Now, I suppose that, in the order of causation, all these animal instincts, be they egoistic or altruistic, must be treated as contrivances for aiding a species in the struggle for existence. If anything be due to selection, surely these must be. This is plainly true of the egoistic appetites and impulses on which depend the maintenance of life and its propagation. It must also be true of the altruistic instincts. Take, for instance, the case of parental devotion. Its survival value is clearly immense. The higher animals, as at present constituted, could not exist without it; and though, for all we can say to the contrary, development might have followed a different course, and a race not less effectively endowed than man might flourish though parental care played no greater part in the life-history of its members than it does in the life-history of a herring, yet this is not what has actually happened. Altruistic effort, in the world as we know it, is as essential to the higher organisms as the self-regarding instincts and appetites are to organic life in general; and there seems no reason for attributing to it a different origin.

Can this be said with a like confidence about the higher portions of the ethical scale? Are these also due to selection?

Evidently the difference between primitive instincts and developed morality is immense; and it is as great in the egoistic as in the non-egoistic region of ethics. Ideals of conduct, the formulation of ends, judgments of their relative worth, actions based on principles, deliberate choice between alternative policies, the realised distinction between the self and other personalities or other centres of feeling—all these are involved in developed morality, while in animal ethics they exist not at all, or only in the most rudimentary forms.

Compare, for instance, a society of bees and a society of men. In both there is division of labour; in both there is organised effort towards an end which is other and greater than the individual good of any single member of the community. But though there are these deep-lying resemblances between the two cases, how important are the differences which divide them! In the beehive altruism is obeyed, but not chosen. Alternative ends are not contrasted. No member of the community thinks that it could do something different from, and more agreeable than, the inherited task. Nor in truth could it. General interest and individual interest are never opposed, for they are never distinguished. The agent never compares, and therefore never selects.

Far different are the ethical conditions requiring consideration when we turn from bees to men. Here egoism and altruism are not only distinguished in reflection; they may be, and often are, incompatible in practice. Nor does this conflict of ends only show itself between these two great ethical divisions; it is not less apparent within them. Here, then, we find ourselves in a world of moral conflict very faintly foreshadowed in animal ethics. For us, ultimate ends are many. They may reinforce each other, or they may weaken each other. They may harmonise, or they may clash. Personal ends may prove incompatible with group ends: one group end may prove incompatible with another. Loyalty may be ranged against loyalty, altruism against altruism; nor is there any court of appeal which can decide between them.

But there are yet other differences between the ethics of instinct and the ethics of reflection. Instincts are (relatively) definite and stable; they move in narrow channels; they cannot easily be enlarged in scope, or changed in character. The animal mother, for example, cares for its young children, but never for its young grandchildren. The lifelong fidelity of the parent birds in certain species (a fidelity seemingly independent of the pairing season, or the care of particular broods) never becomes the nucleus of a wider association. Altruistic instincts may lead to actions which equal, or surpass, man's highest efforts of abnegation; but the actions are matters of routine, and the instincts never vary. They emerge in the same form at the same stage of individual growth, like any other attribute of the species—its colour, for instance, or its claws. And if they be, like colour and claws, the products of selection, this is exactly what we should expect. But then, if the loyalties of man be also the product of selection, why do they not show a similar fixity?

Plainly they do not. Man inherits the capacity for loyalty, but not the use to which he shall put it. The persons and causes (if any) to which he shall devote himself are suggested to him, often, indeed, imposed upon him, by education and environment. Nevertheless, they are his by choice, not by hereditary compulsion. And his choice may be bad. He may unselfishly devote himself to what is petty or vile, as he may to what is generous and noble. But on the possibility of error depends the possibility of progress; and if (to borrow a phrase from physics) our loyalty possessed as few "degrees of freedom" as that of ants or bees, our social organisation would be as rigid.

The most careless glance at the pages of history, or the world of our own experience, will show how varied are the forms in which this capacity for loyalty is displayed. The Spartans at Thermopylae, the "Blues" and the "Greens" at Byzantium, rival politicians in a hard-fought election, players and spectators at an Eton and Harrow Match, supply familiar illustrations of its variety and vigour. And do not suppose that in thus bringing together the sublime, the familiar, and the trivial, I am paradoxically associating matters essentially disparate. This is not so. I am not putting on a moral level the patriot and the partisan, the martyr to some great cause and the shouting spectator at a school match. What I am insisting on is that they all have loyalty in common; a loyalty which often is, and always may be, pure from egoistic alloy.

Loyalties, then, which are characteristically human differ profoundly from those which are characteristically animal. The latter are due to instincts which include both the end to be sought for and the means by which it is to be attained. The former are rooted in a general capacity for, or inclination to, loyalty, with little inherited guidance either as to ends or means. Yet, if we accept selection as the source of the first, we can hardly reject it as the source of the second. For the survival value of loyalty is manifest. It lies at the root of all effective co-operation. Without it the family and tribe would be impossible; and without the family and the tribe, or some yet higher organisation, men, if they could exist at all, would be more helpless than cattle, weak against the alien forces of nature, at the mercy of human foes more capable of loyalty than themselves. A more powerful aid in the struggle for existence cannot easily be imagined.

We are indeed apt to forget how important are its consequences, even when it supplies no more than a faint qualification of other and more obvious motives. It acts like those alloys which, in doses relatively minute, add strength and elasticity even to steel. The relation (for example) between a commercial company and its officials is essentially a business one. The employer pays the market price for honesty and competence, and has no claim to more. Yet that company is surely either unfortunate or undeserving whose servants are wholly indifferent to its fortunes, feeling no faintest flicker of pride when it succeeds, no tinge of regret when it fails. Honourable is the tie between those who exchange honest wage and honest work; yet loyalty can easily better it. And a like truth is manifest in spheres of action less reputable than those of commerce. Mercenaries, to be worth hiring, must be partly moved by forces higher than punishment or pay, Even pirates could not plunder with profit were their selfishness unredeemed by some slight tincture of reciprocal loyalty.

There are, however, many who would admit the occasional importance of loyalty while strenuously denying that social life was wholly based upon it. For them society is an invention; of all inventions the most useful, but still only an invention. It was (they think) originally devised by individuals in their individual interest; and, though common action was the machinery employed, personal advantage was the end desired. By enlightened egoism social organisation was created; by enlightened egoism it is maintained and improved. Contrivance, therefore, not loyalty, is the master faculty required.

This is a great delusion—quite unsupported by anything we know or can plausibly conjecture about the history of mankind. No one, indeed, doubts that deliberate adaptation of means to ends has helped to create, and is constantly modifying, human societies; nor yet that egoism has constantly perverted political and social institutions to merely private uses. But there is something more fundamental to be borne in mind, namely, that without loyalty there would be no societies to modify, and no institutions to pervert. If these were merely well-designed instruments like steam-engines and telegraphs, they would be worthless. They would perish at the first shock, did they not at once fall into ruin by their own weight. If they are to be useful as means, they must first impose themselves as ends; they must possess a quality beyond the reach of contrivance: the quality of commanding disinterested service and uncalculating devotion.

─────────── **Blotches on a Beetle's Back** ───────────

Kant, as we all know, compared the Moral Law to the starry heavens, and found them both sublime. It would, on the naturalistic hypothesis, be more appropriate to compare it to the protective blotches on the beetle's back, and to find them both ingenious. But how on this view is the "beauty of holiness" to retain its lustre in the minds of those who know so much of its pedigree? In despite of theories, mankind—even instructed mankind—may, indeed, long preserve uninjured sentiments which they have learned in their most impressionable years from those they love best; but if, while they are being taught the supremacy of conscience and the austere majesty of duty, they are also to be taught that these sentiments and beliefs are merely samples of the complicated contrivances, many of them mean and many of them disgusting, wrought into the physical or into the social organism by the shaping forces of selection and elimination, assuredly much of the efficacy of these moral lessons will be destroyed, and the contradiction between ethical sentiment and naturalistic theory will remain intrusive and perplexing, a constant stumbling-block to those who endeavour to combine in one harmonious creed the bare explanations of Biology and the lofty claims of Ethics.[27]

❖ Selection and the Higher Morality

I should therefore be ready to admit, as a plausible conjecture, that the capacity for altruistic emotions and beliefs is a direct product of organic evolution; an attribute preserved and encouraged, because it is useful to the race, and transmitted from parents to offspring by physiological inheritance. On this theory loyalty in some shape or other is as natural to man as maternal affection is natural to mammals. Doubtless it is more variable in strength, more flexible in direction, more easily smothered by competing egoisms; but the capacity for it is not less innate, and not less necessary in the struggle for existence. But when we ask how far selection has been responsible for the development of high altruistic ideals out of primitive forms of loyalty, we touch on problems of much greater complexity. Evidently there has been a profound moral transformation in the course of ages. None suppose that ethical values are appraised in the twentieth century as they were in the first stone age. But what has caused the change is not so clear.

There are obvious, and, I think, insurmountable difficulties in attributing it to organic selection. Selection is of the fittest—of the fittest to survive. But in what consists this particular kind of fitness? The answer from the biological point of view is quite simple: almost a matter of definition. That race is "fit" which maintains its numbers; and that race is fittest which most increases them. The judge of such "fitness" is not the moralist or the statesman. It is the Registrar-General. So little is "fitness" inseparably attached to excellence, that it would be rash to say that there is any quality, however unattractive, which might not in conceivable circumstances assist survival. High authorities, I believe, hold that at this moment in Britain we have so managed matters that congenital idiots increase faster than any other class of the population. If so, they must be deemed the "fittest" of our countrymen. No doubt this fact, if it be a fact, is an accident of our social system. Legislation has produced this happy adaptation of environment to organism, and legislation might destroy it. The fittest to-day might become the unfittest to-morrow. But this is nothing to the purpose. That part of man's environment which is due to man does no doubt usually vary more quickly than the part which is due to nature; none the less is it environment in the strictest sense of the word. The theory of selection draws no essential distinction between (say) the secular congelation of a continent in the ice age, and the workings of the English Poor Law in the twentieth century. It is enough that each, while it lasts, favours or discourages particular heritable variations, and modifies the qualities that make for "survival."

What is more important, however, than the fact that heritable "fitness" may be completely divorced from mental and moral excellence, is the fact that so large a part of man's mental and moral characteristics are not heritable at all, and cannot therefore be directly due to organic selection. Races may accumulate accomplishments, yet remain organically unchanged. They may learn and they may forget, they may rise from barbarism to culture, and sink back from culture to barbarism, while through all these revolutions the raw material of their humanity varies never a bit. In such cases there can be no question of Natural Selection in the sense in which biologists use the term.

And there are other considerations which suggest that, as development proceeds, the forces of organic selection diminish. While man was in the making we may easily believe that those possessing no congenital instinct for loyalty failed, and that failure involved elimination. In such circumstances, the hereditary instinct would become an inbred characteristic of the race. But in a civilised, or even in a semi-civilised, world, the success of one competitor has rarely involved the extinction of the other—at least by mere slaughter. When extinction has followed defeat, it has been due rather to the gradual effects of disease and hardship, or to other causes more obscure, but not less deadly. The endless struggles between tribes, cities, nations, and races, have in the main been struggles for domination, not for existence. Slavery, not death, has been the penalty of failure; and if domination has produced a change in the inherited type, it is not because the conquered has perished before the conqueror, but because, conquest having brought them together, the two have intermarried. **There is thus no close or necessary connection between biological "fitness' and military or political success. The beaten race, whose institutions or culture perish, may be the race which in fact survives; while victors who firmly establish their language, religion, and polity may, after a few centuries, leave scarce a trace behind them of any heritable characteristics which the anthropologist is able to detect.**

This observation, however, suggests a new point. Is there not, you may ask, a "struggle for existence" between non-heritable acquirements which faintly resembles the biological struggle between individuals or species? Religious systems, political organisations, speculative creeds, industrial inventions, national policies, scientific generalisations, and (what specially concerns us now) ethical ideals, are in perpetual competition and conflict. Some maintain themselves or expand. These are, by definition, the "fit." Some wane or perish. These are, by definition, the unfit. Here we find selection, survival, elimination; and, though we see them at work in quite other regions of reality than those explored by the student of organic evolution, the analogy between the two cases is obvious.

But is the analogy more than superficial? Is it relevant to our present argument? Can it explain either the spread of higher moral ideals or their development? Let us consider for a moment some examples of this psychological "struggle for existence." Take, as a simple case, the competition between rival inventions—between the spinning jenny and the hand-loom, the breech-loader and the muzzle-loader, pre-Listerian and post-Listerian methods of surgery. Unless the environment be strongly charged with prejudice, ignorance, or sinister interests, the "fittest" in such cases is that which best serves its purpose. Measurable efficiency is the quality which wins. But this supplies us with no useful analogy when we are dealing with ethics. Morality, as I have already insisted, is not an invention designed to serve an external purpose. The "struggle for existence" between higher and lower ethical ideals has no resemblance to the struggle between the spinning-jenny and the hand-loom. It is a struggle between ends, not between means. Efficiency is not in question.

A like observation applies to that quality of our beliefs which might be described as "argumentative plausibility." This is to abstract theorising what efficiency is to practical invention. It has survival value. Both, of course, are relative terms, whose application varies with circumstances. An invention is only efficient while the commodity it produces is in demand. A theory is only plausible while it hits off the intellectual temper of the day. But if efficiency and plausibility be thus understood, the more efficient invention and the more plausible doctrine will oust their less favoured rivals. They are the "fittest." But as morality is not a means, so neither is it a conclusion. Whatever be its relation to Reason, reasoning can never determine the essential nature of its contents. Plausibility, therefore, is no more in question than efficiency.

I do not, of course, deny that ethics are always under discussion, or that the basis of moral rules and their application are themes of unending controversy. This is plainly true. But it is also true that there is no argumentative method of shaking any man's allegiance to an end which he deems intrinsically worthy, except by showing it to be inconsistent with some other end which he (not you) deems more worthy still. Dialectic can bring into clear consciousness the implicit beliefs which underlie action, but it cannot either prove them or refute them. It is as untrue to say that there is no disputing about morals as to say that there is no disputing about tastes. But also it is as true; and the truth, properly understood, is fundamental.

What pass for opposing arguments are really rival appeals; and it is interesting to observe that the appeal which, to the unreflecting, seems the most rational is the appeal to selfishness. I am told[28] that on any fine Sunday afternoon in some of our big towns you may find an orator asking why any man should love his country. "What," he inquires, "does a man get by it? Will national success bring either to himself or to any of his hearers more food, more drink, more amusements? If not, why make personal sacrifices for what will never confer personal advantage?" To this particular question it might be replied (though not always with truth) that the antithesis is a false one, and that on the whole the selfish ideal and the patriotic ideal are both promoted by the same policy of public service. But there is another question of the same type to which no such answer is possible. We have all heard it, either in jest or in earnest. "Why" (it is asked) "should we do anything for posterity, seeing that posterity will do nothing for us?" The implication is infamous, but the statement is true. We cannot extract from posterity an equivalent for the sacrifices we make on its behalf. These are debts that will never be recovered. The unborn cannot be sued; the dead cannot be repaid. But what then? Altruism is not based on egoism; it is not egoism in disguise. The ends to which it points are ends in themselves; and their value is quite independent of argument, neither capable of proof nor requiring it.

In what, then, consists the psychological (as distinguished from the organic) "fitness" of the higher moral ideals? If it cannot be found in their practical efficiency, nor yet in their argumentative plausibility, where shall we seek it?

Sometimes, no doubt, the explanation is to be found in their association with a culture, other elements of which do possess both these kinds of "fitness." Thus Western morality—or (to be accurate) Western notions of morality—find favour with backward races, because they are associated with Western armaments and Western arts. Again, they may be diffused, perhaps as part of some militant religion, by the power of the sword or by its prestige. They reach new regions in the train of a conqueror, and willingly or unwillingly the conquered accept them.

But these associations are seemingly quite casual. The prestige of Western arts and science may assist the diffusion of Western morals, as it assists the diffusion of Western languages, or Western clothes. Conquests by Mahommedan or Christian States may substitute a higher for a lower ethical creed in this or that region of the world. Such cases, however, leave us still in the realm of accident. The causes thus assigned for the spread of a particular type of ethical ideal have nothing to do with the quality of that type. They would promote bad morals not less effectively than good; as a hose will, with equal ease, scatter dirty water or clean. Moreover, the growth of the higher type in its place of origin is left wholly unexplained. Its "fitness" seems a mere matter of luck due neither to design nor to any natural imitation of design.

The rigour of this conclusion would be little mitigated even if we could connect psychological fitness with some quite non-moral peculiarity habitually associated with the higher morality, but not with the lower. If, for example, the former were found to lead normally to worldly success, its repute would need no further explanation. If, in private life, those endowed with Sir Charles Grandison's merits usually possessed Sir Charles Grandison's estate, if, in political or national life, victory and virtue went ever hand in hand, morality might be none the better, but certainly it would be more the fashion. Heaven would be wearied with prayers for an unselfish spirit, uttered by suppliants from purely selfish motives. Saints would become the darlings of society, and the book of Job would be still unwritten.[29] I can devise no more extravagant hypothesis. But though, if it were true, the "fitness" of the higher morality might seem to have found an explanation, it is not the explanation we require. It is too external. It gives no account of the appeal which the nobler ends of action make to our judgments of intrinsic value. It suggests the way in which a higher ideal might increase the number of its possessors at the expense of a lower, but not the way in which the higher ideal might itself arise. Indeed, we must go further. Few are the moralists who would maintain that indifference to worldly triumphs was not, on the whole, a bar to their attainment. Few are the biologists who would maintain that care and kindness, lavished on the biologically unfit, will never tend to diminish the relative number of the biologically fit. **But, if so, we must agree with Nietzsche in thinking that ethical values have become "denaturalised." In their primitive forms the products of selection, they have, by a kind of internal momentum, overpassed their primitive purpose. Made by nature for a natural object, they have developed along lines which are certainly independent of selection, perhaps in opposition to it.** And though not as remote from their first manifestations as is the aesthetic of men from the aesthetic of monkeys, no evolutionary explanation will bridge the interval. If we treat the Sermon on the Mount as a naturalistic product, it is as much an evolutionary accident as Hamlet or the Ninth Symphony.

——— **Human Sentiments and the Naturalistic Creed** ———

My point is, that in the case of those holding the naturalistic creed the sentiments and the creed are antagonistic; and that the more clearly the creed is grasped, the more thoroughly the intellect is saturated with its essential teaching, the more certain are the sentiments thus violently and unnaturally associated with it to languish or die.[30]

❖ Same Subject Matter Continued

In what setting, then, are we to place morality so that these "denaturalised" values may be retained? Can we be content to regard the highest loyalties, the most devoted love, the most limitless self-abnegation as the useless excesses of a world-system, which in its efforts to adapt organism to environment has overshot its mark?

I deem it impossible. The naturalistic setting must be expanded into one which shall give the higher ethics an origin congruous with their character. Selection must be treated as an instrument of purpose, not simply as its mimic. Theistic teleology must be substituted for Naturalism.

Thus, and thus only, can moral values, as it seems to me, be successfully maintained.

This would not, I suppose, have been denied by Nietzsche and Nietzsche's predecessors in revolt. On the contrary, they would admit the interdependence of morals and religion, as these are commonly understood in Christendom, and they would condemn both. It would, however, have been vehemently denied by agnostics like Huxley; for Huxley accepted, broadly speaking, Christian ethics, while refusing to accept the Christian, or, indeed, any other form of theology.

In my opinion, this position is not permanently tenable. I do not mean that it involves a logical contradiction. I do mean that it involves an emotional and doctrinal incompatibility of a very fundamental kind. And this is a defect which may be even more fatal than logical contradiction to the stability of ethical beliefs.

For what was Huxley's position? His condemnation of evolutionary ethics was far more violent than my own.[31] He states categorically that "What is ethically best involves conduct which in all respects is opposed to that which leads to success in the cosmic struggle for existence." On a biological question I differ from him with misgiving; but, as I have already urged, selection may plausibly be credited with the earlier stages of the noblest virtues. I cannot think that the mother who sacrifices herself for her child, the clansman who dies for his chief, the generation which suffers for the sake of its posterity, are indulging in "conduct which is in all respects opposed to that which leads to success in the cosmic struggle for existence." **But, whether Huxley be right on this point or I, it is surely impossible for the mass of mankind to maintain, at the cost of much personal loss, an ideal of conduct which science tells us is not merely an evolutionary accident, but an evolutionary mistake; something which was, and is, contrary to the whole trend of the cosmic process which brought us into being, and made us what we are.** It requires but a small knowledge of history to show how easily mankind idealises nature; witness such phrases as "the return to nature," the "state of nature," "natural rights," "natural law," and so forth. Appeals founded upon these notions have proved powerful, even when they ran counter to individualistic selfishness. When the two are in alliance, how can they be resisted? Is it possible for the ordinary man to maintain undimmed his altruistic ideals if he thinks Nature is against them?—unless, indeed, he also believes that God is on their side?

To me it appears certain that this clashing between beliefs and feelings must ultimately prove fatal to one or the other. Make what allowances you please for the stupidity of mankind, take the fullest account of their really remarkable power of letting their speculative opinions follow one line of development and their practical ideas another, yet the time must come when reciprocal actions will perforce bring opinions and ideals into some kind of agreement and congruity. If, then, naturalism is to hold the field, the feelings and opinions inconsistent with naturalism must be foredoomed to suffer change; and how, when that change shall come about, it can do otherwise than eat all nobility out of our conception of conduct and all worth out of our conception of life, I am wholly unable to understand.[32]

❖ Theism and the Collision of Ends

Here are questions raised to which there is no parallel in the case of aesthetics. Doubtless differences of aesthetic judgment abound; but they do not produce difficulties quite matching those due to the collision of incompatible ends; nor is their solution so important. On this subject I must say a few words before bringing this lecture to a conclusion. Possible collisions between ends are many, for ends themselves are many. And of these ends some are in their very nature irreconcilable—based on essential differences which reflection only makes more apparent, and moral growth more profound.

Now these collisions are not always between altruism and egoism. Often they are between different forms of altruism—call them, if you please, the positive form and the negative. Enmity, hate, cruelty, tyranny, and all that odious brood whose end and object is the pain and abasement of others are not intrinsically egoistic. Though they be the vilest of all passions, yet they do not necessarily involve any taint of selfish alloy. Often as disinterested as the most devoted love or the most single-minded loyalty, they may demand no smaller sacrifices on the part of those whom they inspire, and the demand may be not less willingly obeyed. It is, perhaps, worth observing that these altruistic ends, the positive and the negative, the benevolent and the malevolent, irreconcilably opposed as they are in moral theory, have often been associated in ethical practice. Family affection has in many half-civilised communities produced the binding custom of family vendetta. Political loyalty, which has blossomed into some of the noblest forms of positive altruism, has also bred cruelty and hatred against those who are outside the pale of the tribe, the state, the party, or the creed. The brightest light has cast the deepest shadows. To torture and enslave, not because it brings profit to the victor, but because it brings pain to the vanquished, has, through long ages, been deemed a fitting sequel to victories born of the most heroic courage and the noblest self-sacrifice; while no small part of moral progress has consisted in expelling this perverted altruism from the accepted ideals of civilised mankind.

Egoism is far more reputable. The agent's own good, considered in itself, is, what negative altruism can never be, a perfectly legitimate object of endeavour. When, therefore, there is a collision between egoism and positive altruism, problems of real difficulty may arise; the competing ends may both have value, and the need for a reconciliation, practical as well as speculative, of necessity impresses both moralists and legislators.

In practice the evils of this conflict arise largely from the fact that the end which has most worth has too often least power. This is not surprising if the account of ethical evolution, which I have provisionally adopted in this lecture, be near the truth. For the extra-regarding instincts are of later birth than the self-regarding. All animals look after themselves. Only the more developed look also after others. The germ of what, in reflection, becomes egoism is of far earlier growth than the germ of what, in reflection, becomes altruism. Being more primitive, it is more deeply rooted in our nature; and, even when recognised as morally lower, it tends, when there is conflict, to prevail over its rival. "The evil that I would not, that I do."[33]

Now this result has, as we all know, serious social consequences. Even the least stable society must be organised on some firm framework of custom, rule, and law; and these, in their turn, must find their main support in the willing loyalty of the general community. But, though loyalty is the great essential, it is not sufficient. Legislators, lawyers, moralists, all agree that in the collision between ends—especially between egoistic and altruistic ends—it is not always the highest end as judged by the agent himself, still less the highest end as measured by the standards of the community, which finally prevails. Therefore must law and custom have the support of sanctions: sanctions being nothing else than devices for bringing a lower motive to the aid of a higher, and so producing better conduct, if not better morals.[34] Public approval and disapproval, the jailer and the hangman, heaven and hell, are familiar examples. Can they in any true sense effect a reconciliation between discordant ends, and, in particular, between altruism and egoism? I hardly think so. When they are effective they doubtless diminish ethical conflict; but it is by ignoring the intrinsic value of one set of ethical ends. In so far as we are honest because honesty is the best policy, in so far as we do not injure lest we

should ourselves be injured, in so far as we benefit that we may be bene-
fited ourselves—just in that proportion we treat altruistic actions merely
as the means of attaining egoistic ends. The two competitors are not rec-
onciled, but a working arrangement is reached under which the conduct
appropriate to the higher ideal is pursued from motives characteristic of
the lower.

**Is any truer reconciliation possible? Scarcely, as I think, without
religion. I do not suggest that any religious theory gets rid of ethical
anomalies, or theoretically lightens by a feather-weight the heavy
problem of evil. But I do suggest that in the love of God by the individual soul, the collision of ends _for that soul_ loses all its harshness,
and harmony is produced by raising, not lowering, the ethical ideal.**

———————— A Moral Code Must Inspire ————————

Practically, human beings being what they are, no moral code can be effective which does not inspire, in those who are asked to obey it, emotions of
reverence; and, practically, the capacity of any code to excite this or any other
elevated emotion cannot be wholly independent of the origin from which
those who accept that code suppose it to emanate.[35]

Kant, by a famous feat of speculative audacity, sought to extract a
proof of God's existence from the moral law. In his view the moral law
requires us to hold that those who are good will also in the end be happy;
and, since without God this expectation cannot be fulfilled, the being of
God becomes a postulate of morality. Is this (you may ask), or any variant
of this, the argument suggested in the last paragraph? It is not. In Kant's
argument, as I understand it, God was external to morality in the sense
that He was not Himself a moral end. It was not our feeling of love and
loyalty to Him that was of moment, but His guidance of the world in the
interests of virtue and the virtuous. My point is different. I find in the love
of God a moral end which reconciles other moral ends, because it
includes them. It is not intolerant of desires for our own good. It demands
their due subordination, not their complete suppression. It implies loyal
service to One who by His essential nature wills the good of all. It
requires, therefore, that the good of all shall be an object of our endeavour; and it promises that, in striving for this inclusive end, we shall, in
Pauline phrase, be fellow-workers with Him.

I will not further pursue this theme. Its development is plainly inappropriate to these lectures, which are not directly concerned with personal
religion. In any case, this portion of my argument, though important, is
subsidiary. **My main contention rests, not upon the difficulty of harmonising moral ends in a Godless universe, but upon the difficulty of**

maintaining moral values if moral origins are purely naturalistic. That they never have been so maintained on any large scale is a matter of historic fact. At no time has the mass of mankind treated morals and religion as mutually independent. They have left this to the enlightened; and the enlightened have (as I think) been wrong.

They have been wrong through their omission to face the full results of their own theories. If the most we can say for morality on the causal side is that it is the product of non-moral, and ultimately of material agents, guided up to a certain point by selection, and thereafter left the sport of chance, a sense of humour, if nothing else, should prevent us wasting fine language on the splendour of the moral law and the reverential obedience owed it by mankind. That debt will not long be paid if morality comes to be generally regarded as the causal effect of petty causes; comparable in its lowest manifestations with the appetites and terrors which rule, for their good, the animal creation; in its highest phases no more than a personal accomplishment, to be acquired or neglected at the bidding of individual caprice. More than this is needful if the noblest ideals are not to lose all power of appeal. Ethics must have its roots in the divine; and in the divine it must find its consummation.

———————————— **The Worth of Creeds** ————————————

Yet, after all, it is in moments of reflection that the worth of creeds may best be tested; it is through moments of reflection that they come into living and effectual contact with our active life. It cannot, therefore, be a matter to us of small moment that, as we learn to survey the material world with a wider vision, as we more clearly measure the true proportions which man and his performances bear to the ordered Whole, our practical ideal gets relatively dwarfed and beggared, till we may well feel inclined to ask whether so transitory and so unimportant an accident in the general scheme of things as the fortunes of the human race can any longer satisfy aspirations and emotions nourished in the Everlasting and the Divine.[36]

Berardus Perdix fecit

Sainct Patrice dryueth ỹ snaykes and baytlefull beestes owt frõ Irelãde

A DREAM OF ST. PATRICK'S DAY.

5

Intellectual Values

I went to Cambridge in the middle sixties with a very small equipment of either philosophy or science, but a very keen desire to discover what I ought to think of the world, and why. For the history of speculation I cared not a jot. Dead systems seemed to me of no more interest than abandoned fashions. My business was with the ground-work of living beliefs; in particular, with the ground-work of that scientific knowledge whose recent developments had so profoundly moved mankind.

MR. BALFOUR ON BELIEF
The Basis of Knowledge Analysed
Need of a Theistic Setting

(From Our Special Correspondent)

GLASGOW, JAN. 21

Before a scarcely diminished audience Mr. Balfour to-day in his fifth Gifford Lecture began the discussion of what he described as a more difficult and complicated topic than the emotions and moral sentiments treated in the last two lectures. He promised to avoid technical metaphysical terminology, but he could not help asking them to look at familiar things from an unusual angle. He proposed to take our body of everyday beliefs and of scientific beliefs, to look at that body both from the causal or genetic point of view and from the logical or rational aspect, and to place the results side by side.

A Personal Allusion

At this point, Mr. Balfour made a personal remark which deeply interested his audience. He had, he said, been charged with having, in writings published many years ago, attempted to promote skepticism in the interests of orthodoxy. It was not only incompetent and unfriendly critics who had accused him of showing how difficult it is to accept ordinary and elementary ideas in order to argue that, as

knowledge is beyond us, we had better accept the beliefs that are most agreeable to us, and that, as everything is illusory, we had better make our illusions as pleasant as possible. "That," he said, "has [never] been my view." His plea had always been in the interests of rationality, and that it should be the object of those who approach knowledge from the widest standpoint to place belief in the most reasonable framework.

Turning to his immediate subject, he said that one of the difficulties lies in the fact that every one is willing to see other people's beliefs in the double light to which he had referred, but no one is willing to apply the same test to his own. We all see that our neighbour's beliefs are the result of their experiences in childhood, their education, their general social surroundings, and the psychological atmosphere in which they live. We all agree that historical causes have influenced the development of belief in historical times, but we shrink from applying these cannons of criticism to ourselves. Our own beliefs, like the beliefs from which we most differ, are part of a causal series and can be genetically explained, and their history goes back through the social history of the community.

How, he asked, does it come about that there is a coincidence between a rational series which is a logical justification of beliefs and a causal series in which reason does not appear till the later stages and then only as one of a set of psychological influences? This question, he said, had never been faced directly and fully. Could it be answered by a reference to natural selection or to selection in some form? It is true that anyone who mistakes the character of the world into which he is born will perish, and that those who make right judgment have the best chance of surviving and leaving offspring. But it is absurd to say that man's powers of discourse and man's insights, limited though it may be, into areas of time and space in which he has no interest whatsoever can have been bred into us by the necessity of obtaining food or of ousting others in the struggle for existence.

Criticism of the Emperics

The rest of the lecture was devoted to a criticism of the empirical philosophy which assigns a privileged position to knowledge derived from experience. He objected to any bisection of knowledge, and he drew attention to the fact that all philosophical controversies rage, and always have raged, over the very question as to what experience means, as to whether we can infer from it, and as to what we can infer from it.

Locke had written that "one unerring mark by which a man may know whether he is a lover of truth in earnest is by not entertaining a belief in a proposition with greater assurance than the proofs that it is built upon will warrant." The words, "with greater assurance than the proofs that it is built upon will warrant," now became Mr. Balfour's text. Leslie Stephen, he said, had called this a platitude. Is it a platitude? Did Locke, did Leslie Stephen, act upon it? Could the world go on if everybody acted upon it? **He appealed for a more courageous view, and he insisted that if the world were suddenly to begin to examine what we believe by the exact amount of assurance which the proofs will warrant, the whole possibility of carrying on the practical or even speculative life would come to an end.**

He asked them to consider the possibility of the education of youth on these terms. The response came in a laugh from the audience, and Mr. Balfour went on to point out that when we come to years of discretion we find ourselves possessed of a body of beliefs and judgments which have been instilled into us, and which we hold without any reason at all.

Reminding them that what he had in mind was not religion or philosophy, but what is called common sense, he asked if they would advise a young man not to enter into practical life until he had made up his mind about these various propositions and the exact degrees of assurance with which he could hold them. It would be ludicrous to start in life without accepting many propositions about which it is easy to argue, and about which philosophers ought to argue, but which even philosophers held with greater assurance than the facts warrant. Let them read Locke's own efforts to get outside the circle of sensations and impressions to the external world in which he firmly believed. Let them turn to psychology for the evidence of each other's existence. He did not want to annoy or to puzzle anyone or to suggest a sceptical view; he only asked them to face the facts about knowledge in a scientific spirit.

Future Lectures

In conclusion, Mr. Balfour indicated the results at which he hoped to arrive in the next five lectures. He hoped to show that there are inevitable processes of thought which are not logical and further that there are probable beliefs of profound importance for practical life. For himself he utterly any scheme of knowledge built simply upon *a priori* doctrines, and he equally rejected the empirical system which held sway in Great Britain when he was young, and which is still largely accepted by ordinary educated men and by men of science. He believed that a confusion between causes and reasons vitiates the whole process of empirical thought, and he would try to show that, when we look at scientific knowledge genetically, we find that there are tendencies running through the whole length of this great and splendid history which it is impossible to attribute to any principle accepted by *a priori* philosophy or by empirical philosophy. He hoped to prove that all their tendencies and inferences which, although they are independent of sound reasoning, are not contrary to it, have moulded our body of knowledge and that without them we should not possess our body of knowledge.

—*The Times,* Thu. Jan. 22, 1914, 10a.

❖ Retrospect

In the preceding lectures I have given reasons for thinking that in two great departments of human interest—Aesthetics and Ethics—the highest beliefs and emotions cannot claim to have any survival value. They must be treated as by-products of the evolutionary process; and are, therefore, on the naturalistic hypothesis, doubly accidental. They are accidental in the larger sense of being the product of the undesigned collocation and interplay of material entities—molecular atoms, sub-atoms, and ether— which preceded, and will presumably outlast, that fraction of time during which organic life will have appeared, developed, and perished. They are also accidental in the narrower sense of being only accidentally associated with that process of selective elimination, which, if Darwinism be true, has so happily imitated contrivance in the adaptation of organisms to their environment. They are the accidents of an accident.

I disagreed with this conclusion, but I did not attempt to refute it. I contented myself with pointing out that it was destructive of values; and that, the greater the values, the more destructive it became. The difficulty, indeed, on which I have so far insisted is not a logical one. We have not been concerned with premises and conclusions. Neither our aesthetic emotions nor our moral sentiments are the product of ratiocination; nor is it by ratiocination that they are likely to suffer essential wrong. If you would damage them beyond repair, yoke them to a theory of the universe which robs them of all general significance. Then, at the very moment when they aspire to transcendent authority, their own history will rise up in judgment against them, impugning their pretensions, and testifying to their imposture.

———————— The Professor of Naturalism ————————

The professor of naturalism rejoicing in the display of his dialectical resources is like a voyager, pacing at his own pleasure up and down the ship's deck, who should suppose that his movements had some important share in determining his position on the illimitable ocean. And the parallel would be complete if we can conceive such a voyager pointing to the alertness of his step and the vigour of his limbs as auguring well for the successful prosecution of his journey, while assuring you in the very same breath that the vessel, within whose narrow bounds he displays all this meaningless activity, is drifting he knows not whence nor whither, without pilot or captain, at the bidding of the shifting winds and undiscovered currents.[37]

❖ Reason and Causation

The inquiry on which I now propose to enter will follow a more or less parallel course, and will reach a more or less similar conclusion. Yet some characteristic differences it must necessarily exhibit. In the higher regions of aesthetics and ethics, emotions and beliefs are inextricably intertwined. They are what naturalists describe as "symbiotic." Though essentially different, they are mutually dependent. If one be destroyed, the other withers away.

But Knowledge—the department of human interest to which I now turn—is differently placed. The values with which we shall be concerned are mainly rational; and intellectual curiosity is the only emotion with which they are associated. Yet here also two questions arise corresponding to those which we have already dealt with in a different connection: (1) what are the causes of our knowledge, or of that part of our knowledge which concerns the world of common sense and of science? (2) does the naturalistic account of these causes affect the rational value—in other words the validity—of their results?

We are, perhaps, more sensitive about the pedigree of our intellectual creed than we are about the pedigree of our tastes or our sentiments. We like to think that beliefs which claim to be rational are the product of a purely rational process; and though, where others are concerned, we complacently admit the intrusion of non-rational links in the causal chain, we have higher ambitions for ourselves.

Yet surely, on the naturalistic theory of the world, all such ambitions are vain. It is abundantly evident that, however important be the part which reason plays among the immediate antecedents of our beliefs, there are no beliefs which do not trace back their origin to causes which are wholly irrational. Proximately, these beliefs may take rank as logical conclusions. Ultimately, they are without exception rooted in matter and motion. The rational order is but a graft upon the causal order; and, if Naturalism be true, the causal order is blind.

──────────── **Reason Under Naturalism** ────────────

Reason, therefore, on the Naturalistic hypothesis, occupies no very exalted or important place in the Cosmos. It supplies it neither with the First cause nor a Final Cause. It is a merely local accident ranking after appetite and instinct among the expedients by which the existence of a small class of mammals on a very insignificant planet is rendered a little less brief, though perhaps not more pleasurable, than it would otherwise be.[38]

❖ Leslie Stephen and Locke's Aphorism

Before I further develop this line of speculation it may help you to understand what I am driving at, if I venture upon an autobiographical parenthesis. The point I have just endeavoured to make I have made before in these lectures, and I have made it elsewhere. It is one of a number of considerations which have led me to question the prevalent account of the theoretical ground-work of our accepted beliefs. Taken by itself, its tendency is sceptical; and, since it has been associated with arguments in favour of a spiritual view of the universe, I have been charged (and not always by unfriendly commentators) with the desire to force doubt into the service of orthodoxy by recommending mankind to believe what they wish, since all beliefs alike are destitute of proof. As we cannot extricate ourselves from the labyrinth of illusion, let us at least see to it that our illusions are agreeable.

This, however, is not what I have ever wanted to say, nor is it what I want to say now. If I have given just occasion for such a travesty of my opinions, it must have been an indirect consequence of my early, and no doubt emphatically expressed, contempt for the complacent dogmatism of the empirical philosophy, which in Great Britain reigned supreme through the third quarter of the nineteenth century. But was this contempt altogether unreasonable?

I went to Cambridge in the middle sixties with a very small equipment of either philosophy or science, but a very keen desire to discover what I ought to think of the world, and why. For the history of speculation I cared not a jot. Dead systems seemed to me of no more interest than abandoned fashions. My business was with the ground-work of living beliefs; in particular, with the ground-work of that scientific knowledge whose recent developments had so profoundly moved mankind. And surely there was nothing perverse in asking modern philosophers to provide us with a theory of modern science!

I was referred to Mill; and the shock of disillusionment remains with me to the present hour. Mill possessed at that time an authority in the English Universities, and, for anything I know to the contrary, in the Scotch Universities also, comparable to that wielded forty years earlier by Hegel in Germany and in the Middle Ages by Aristotle. Precisely the kind of questions which I wished to put, his Logic was deemed qualified to answer. He was supposed to have done for scientific inference what Bacon tried to do, and failed. He had provided science with a philosophy.

I could have forgiven the claims then made for him by his admirers; I could have forgiven, though young and intolerant, what seemed to me the futility of his philosophic system, if he had ever displayed any serious misgiving as to the scope and validity of his empirical methods. If he had admitted, for example, that, when all had been done that could be done to systematise our ordinary modes of experimental inference, the underlying problem of knowledge still remained unsolved. But he seemed to hold, in common with the whole empirical school of which, in English-speaking countries, he was the head, that the fundamental difficulties of knowledge do not begin till the frontier is crossed which divides physics from metaphysics, the natural from the supernatural, the world of "phenomena" from the world of "noumena," "positive" experiences from religious dreams. It may be urged that, if these be errors, they are errors shared by ninety-nine out of every hundred persons educated in the atmosphere of Western civilisation, whatever be their theological views: and I admit that it has sunk deep into our ordinary habits of thought. Apologetics are saturated with it, not less than agnosticism or infidelity. But, for my own part, I feel now, as I felt in the early days of which I am speaking, that the problem of knowledge cannot properly be sundered in this fashion. Its difficulties begin with the convictions of common sense, not with remote, or subtle, or otherworldly speculations; and if we could solve the problem in respect of the beliefs which, roughly speaking, everybody shares, we might see our way more clearly in respect of the beliefs on which many people are profoundly divided.

That Mill's reasoning should have satisfied himself and his immediate disciples is strange. But that the wider public of thinking men, whom he so powerfully influenced, should on the strength of this flimsy philosophy adopt an attitude of dogmatic assurance both as to what can be known and what cannot, is surely stranger still. Thus, at least, I thought nearly half a century ago, and thus I think still.

─────── **Philosophy Supported Theology** ───────

Philosophy, or what passed for such, not only supported Theology in the Middle Ages—it became almost identical with it; it not only supports Science now, but it has almost become a scientific department.[39]

Consider, for example, a typical form of the ordinary agnostic position: that presented by Leslie Stephen. The best work of this excellent writer was biographical and literary; but he was always deeply interested in speculation; and his own creed seems early to have taken its final shape under the philosophical influences of the British empiricists. He regarded the "appeal to experience" as the fundamental dogma of agnosticism, and by the "appeal to experience" he meant what Mill meant by it. He sincerely supposed that this gave you indisputable knowledge of "phenomena," and that if you went beyond "phenomena" you were dreaming, or you were inventing.

This is a possible creed; and it is, in fact, the creed held implicitly, or explicitly, by many thousands of quite sensible people. But why should those who hold it suppose that it must always satisfy impartial inquirers? Why should they assume that those who reject it are sacrificing their reason to their prejudices or their fancies? It may represent the best we can do, but is it, after all, so obviously reasonable? On this subject the empirical agnostic has no doubts. He holds, with unshaken confidence, that nothing deserves to be believed but that which in the last resort is proved by "experience"; that the strength of our beliefs should be exactly proportioned to the evidence which "experience" can supply, and that every one knows or can discover exactly what this evidence amounts to. Leslie Stephen refers to a well-known aphorism of Locke, who declared that "there is one unerring mark by which a man may know whether he is a lover of truth in earnest, viz., the not entertaining any proposition with greater assurance than the proofs it is built on will warrant." Upon which Leslie Stephen observes that the sentiment is a platitude, but, in view of the weakness of human nature, a useful platitude.

Is it a platitude? Did Locke act up to it? Did Hume act up to it, or any other of Leslie Stephen's philosophic progenitors? Does anybody act up to it? Does anybody sincerely try to act up to it?

Read through the relevant chapters in Locke's *Essay*, and observe his ineffectual struggles, self-imprisoned in the circle of his own sensations and ideas, to reach the external world in which he believed with a far "greater assurance" than was warranted by any proofs which he, at all events, was able to supply. Read Hume's criticism of our grounds for believing in a real world without, or a real self within, and compare it with his admission that scepticism on these subjects is a practical impossibility.

But we need not go beyond the first chapter of "An Agnostic's Apology" to find an illustration of my argument. Leslie Stephen there absolves himself from giving heed to the conclusions of philosophers, because there are none on which all philosophers are agreed, none on which there is even a clear preponderance of opinion. On the other hand, he is ready to agree with astronomers, because astronomers, "from Galileo to Adams and Leverrier," substantially agree with each other. Agreement among experts is, in his opinion, a guarantee of truth, and disagreement a proof of error.

But then he forgets that these distressing differences among philosophers do not touch merely such entities as God and the soul, or the other subjects with which agnostics conceive man's faculties are incapable of dealing. They are concerned (among other things) with the presuppositions on which our knowledge of "phenomena"—including, of course,

"astronomy from Galileo to Adams and Leverrier," is entirely con-
structed. What, in these circumstances, is Locke's "sincere lover of truth"
to do? How is he to avoid "entertaining propositions with greater assurance than the proofs they are built on will warrant"? Where will he find a
refuge from the "pure scepticism" which is, in Leslie Stephen's opinion,
the natural result of divided opinions? How is he to get on while he is
making up his mind whether any theory of the world within his reach will
satisfy unbiased reason?

The fact is that the adherents of this philosophic school apply, quite
unconsciously, very different canons of intellectual probity to themselves
and to their opponents. "Why," asks Mr. Stephen, "should a lad who has
just run the gauntlet of examination and escaped to a country parsonage
be dogmatic?" If to be dogmatic is to hold opinions with a conviction in
excess of any reason that can be assigned for them, there seems to be no
escape for the poor fellow. The common lot of man is not going to be
reversed for him. Though he abandon his parsonage and renounce his
Church, though he scrupulously purify his creed from every taint of the
"metempirical," though he rigidly confine himself to themes which his
critics declare to be within the range of his intellectual vision, fate will
pursue him still. He may argue much or argue little; he may believe much
or believe little; but, however much he argues and however little he
believes, his beliefs will always transcend his arguments, and to faith, in
his own despite, he must still appeal.

Those who accept Leslie Stephen's philosophy suppose that for this
young man, as for all others, a way of escape may be found by appealing
to experience. But surely none are so sanguine as to suppose that, by
appealing to experience, they are going to avoid what Mr. Stephen
describes as "endless and hopeless controversies." **Alas, this is not so!
The field of experience is no well-defined and protected region under
whose clear skies useful knowledge flourishes unchallenged, while the
mist-enshrouded territories of its metaphysical neighbours are devas-
tated by unending disputations. On the contrary, it is the very battle-
field of philosophy, the cockpit of metaphysics, strewn with
abandoned arguments, where every strategic position has been taken
and retaken, to which every school lays formal claim, which every
contending system pretends to hold in effective occupation.** Indeed, by
a singular irony, the thinkers who, at this particular moment, talk most
about experience are those metaphysicians of the Absolute in whose speculations Mr. Stephen saw no beginning of interest, except that of being
(as he supposed) at once the refuge and the ruin of traditional religion.
But these philosophers have no monopoly. All men nowadays speak well

of experience. They begin to differ only when they attempt to say what experience is, to define its character, explain its credentials, and expound its message. But, unhappily, when this stage is reached their differences are endless.

Agnosticism and Science

In order, therefore, that a man may have any rational confidence in the history of the Cosmos as revealed in the teachings of Science, he must be something more than an Agnostic. He must have very solid grounds for believing, not only that through the infinite past only one series of phenomena can be assigned capable of having produced the actual universe, but that nothing besides phenomena capable of acting on phenomena has ever existed at all— and these solid grounds of belief or disbelief must not be drawn from history; but, if derived from experience at all, must be derived from his own immediate observations.[40]

❖ Reason and Empirical Agnosticism

I am, of course, not concerned with Mr. Stephen except as a brilliant representative of a mode of thought to which I most vehemently object. I do not object to it merely because it is in my judgment insufficient and erroneous, still less because I dislike its conclusion. I object to it because it talks loudly of experience, yet never faces facts; and boasts its rationality, yet rarely reasons home. These are far graver crimes against the spirit of truth than any condemned in Locke's pretentious aphorism, and they lead to far more serious consequences.

If you ask me what I have in mind when I say that agnostic empiricism never faces facts, I reply that it never really takes account of that natural history of knowledge, of that complex of causes, rational and non-rational, which have brought our accepted stock of beliefs into being. And if you ask me what I have in mind when I say that though it reasons, it rarely reasons home, I reply that, when it is resolved not to part with a conclusion, anything will serve it for an argument; only when it is incredulous does it know how to be critical.

This is not an error into which I propose to fall. But I hope that I shall not on that account be deemed indifferent to the claims of reason, or inclined to treat lightly our beliefs either about the material world or the immaterial. On the contrary, my object, and my only object, is to bring reason and belief into the closest harmony that at present seems practicable. And if you thereupon reply that such a statement is by itself enough to prove that I am no ardent lover of reason; if you tell me that it implies, if not permanent contentment, at least temporary acquiescence in a creed imperfectly rationalised, I altogether deny the charge. So far as I am concerned, there is no acquiescence. Let him that thinks otherwise show me a better way. Let him produce a body of beliefs which shall be at once living, logical, and sufficient—not forgetting that it cannot be sufficient unless it includes within the circuit of its doctrines some account of itself regarded as a product of natural causes, nor logical unless it provides a rational explanation of the good fortune which has made causes which are not reasons, mixed, it may be, with causes which are not good reasons, issue in what is, by hypothesis, a perfectly rational system. He who is fortunate enough to achieve all this may trample as he likes upon less successful inquirers. But I doubt whether, when this discoverer appears, he will be found to have reached his goal by the beaten road of empirical agnosticism. This, though it be fashionably frequented, is but a blind alley after all.

In the meanwhile we must, I fear, suffer under a system of beliefs which is far short of rational perfection. But we need not acquiesce, and we should not be contented. Whether this state of affairs will ever be cured by the sudden flash of some great philosophic discovery is another matter. My present aim, at all events, is far more modest. But they, at least, should make no complaint who hold that common-sense beliefs, and science which is a development of common-sense beliefs, are, if not true, at least on the way to truth. For this conviction I share. I profess it; I desire to act upon it. And surely I cannot act upon it better than by endeavouring, so far as I can, to place it in the setting which shall most effectually preserve its intellectual value. This at all events, is the object to which the four lectures that immediately follow are designed to contribute.

———————————— Nature's Indifference ————————————

For it must be recollected that the same natural forces which tend to the evolution of organs which are useful tend also to the suppression of organs that are useless. Not only does Nature take no interest in our general education, not only is she quite indifferent to the growth of enlightenment, unless the enlightenment improve our chances in the struggle for existence, but she positively objects to the very existence of faculties by which these ends might, perhaps, be attained. She regards them as mere hindrances in the only race which she desires to see run; and not content with refusing directly to create any faculty except for a practical purpose, she immediately proceeds to destroy faculties already created when their practical purpose has ceased; for thus does the eye of the cave-born fish degenerate and the instinct of the domesticated animal decay.[41]

6

Perception, Common Sense and Science

On this foundation science proceeds to build up a theory of nature by which the foundation itself is shattered. It saws off the branch on which it is supported. It kicks down the ladder by which it has climbed. It dissolves the thing perceived into a remote reality which is neither perceived nor perceivable. It turns the world of common sense into an illusion, and on this illusion it calmly rests its case.

THE EXTERNAL WORLD
Mr. Balfour on the Tangle of Science
Causal and Cognitive Beliefs
(From Our Special Correspondent)
GLASGOW, JAN. 23

Speaking as usual from a few notes on the back of an envelope, Mr. Balfour to-day performed the feat of making clear to an audience of more than 1,500 people his views on the external world. He made no reference to the disputes of conflicting philosophical systems, and gave only slight indications that he was treading on the perpetual battleground of philosophers. His point of view was that of common sense and of science.

The Common-Sense View

The lecturer applied to the scientific view of the external world his distinction between the causal series involved in belief and the rational, or as he to-day preferred to call it, the cognitive series—that is, a series having relation to knowledge. What, he asked, is the common-sense view of the external world? It would be generally admitted that common sense never considers that external objects, pieces of matter, the solid globe, the heavens above, are mental states, and that it thinks of them as independent of the person who perceives them. These objects affect us when we perceive them and we do not affect them by perceiving them. Further, he thought—but of this he was not so certain—that when we look at a material object we do not think that its reality is exhausted by the aspects of it that we perceive. He summed up by saying that, according to common sense, the cognitive series which is our belief in external things is a direct and immediate perception of objects themselves, and he proceeded to make the point on which his whole argument depended.

The Foundation of Science

This simple and direct perception of external objects is the foundation upon which the whole superstructure of science is built up, because the physicist and the physiologist look on the materials of their researches "exactly as you and I look upon chairs and tables." The causal series which combines with the cognitive series to produce the belief in the external world is the business of science, and there is nothing immediate or simple or direct about it. It is a very elaborate process, not yet thoroughly understood. Here Mr. Balfour indicated the various kinds of knowledge required to give a causal explanation of our perception of the sun, astronomy, solar physics, optics, physiology, and so forth. When all these elaborate investigations were completed, one arrives at the threshold of the mind, only to be confronted with the chasm between brain and mind—a chasm not yet bridged over. One must also recollect that our perceptions of an object are profoundly modified by associations, memories, and other psychological considerations. He took the analogy of a message sent by letter post from one town to another to illustrate how many processes had to be completed before a message, starting from reality, could reach mind.

Having thus described the contrast between the causal series and the cognitive series in our belief in the external world, Mr. Balfour pointed out that the distinction which modern science draws between matter and perceiving mind is a distinction not fundamentally different from the old distinction between primary and secondary qualities of matter. That distinction has been carried further by science, which teaches that reality is hid from us behind the screen of its own effects. We cannot perceive an electron, ether, or the retinal image in our own retina. Science can never be content till it gets to the unperceivable, and the real world, as science pictures it, is more and more remote from the real world as we perceive it or are capable of perceiving it. **It is science that insists on the separation between our sensations and perceptions and the outside causes producing them. Science, then, is in a logical tangle.**

The lecturer pointed out, again, that what the scientist sees is the common-sense perception of the plain man, but what is actually there is something quite different. The position of science is something like that of Locke, who has been justly criticized for developing a theory of the external world which never gives direct access to that world but only to sensations and feelings produced by it. Here Mr. Balfour again insisted that science is entirely dependent upon the common-sense view of direct perception, and argued that it destroys its own foundation, and that it provides its own premises to be interfused with illusion. He quoted Hume's statement in the "Dialogues on Natural Theology" that we can only argue from an effect to a cause when we have seen a similar cause producing a similar effect. Nobody, he says, has ever seen electrons and ether-producing sensations. We have never seen the causes, and on Hume's principle we cannot found theories of the causes upon the effect.

External Reality

All this does not diminish the faith which everyone has in the fact of reality. Can we, he asked, imitate Hume's serene acquiescence in having one set of doctrines for the study and another for the market place, doctrines about things of everyday life? It would be arrogant to speak of solving the difficulty, but he thought that it would be mitigated if we gave up the idea that we could get our notion of an independent external reality as a conclusion from immediate perception. We must start with external reality as an inevitable belief. We know that cause is there and that is independent of the perceiver, and if we are not to make nonsense of the whole process of learning by experience we must begin with the assumption of an external material mechanism acting upon us and try to find out how it acts.

—*The Times,* Sat. Jan. 24, 1914, 5a.

❖ Common Sense and the External World

Nothing would seem easier, at first sight, than to give a general description of the ordinary beliefs of ordinary people about our familiar world of things and persons. It is the world in which we live; it is for all men a real world; it is for many men the real world, it is the world of common sense, the world where the plain man feels at home, and where the practical man seeks refuge from the vain subtleties of metaphysics. Our stock of beliefs about it may perhaps be difficult to justify, but it seems strange that they should be difficult to describe; yet difficult, I think, they are.

Some statements about it may, however, be made with confidence. It is in space and time; i.e. the material things of which it is composed, including living bodies, are extended, have mutual position, and possess at least some measure of duration.

Things are not changed by a mere change of place, but a change of place relative to an observer always changes their appearance for him. Common sense is, therefore, compelled in this, as in countless other cases, to distinguish the appearance of a thing from its reality; and to hold, as an essential article of its working creed, that appearances may alter, leaving realities unchanged.

Common sense does not, however, draw the inference that our experience of material things is other than direct and immediate. It has never held the opinion—or, if you will, the heresy—that what we perceive (at least by sight and touch) are states of our own mind, which somehow copy or represent external things. Neither has it ever held that the character or duration of external things in any way depends upon our observations of them. In perception there is no reaction by the perceiving mind on the object perceived. Things in their true reality are not affected by mere observation, still less are they constituted by it. When material objects are in question, common sense never supposes that *esse* and *percipi* are identical.

But then, what, according to common sense, are things in their true reality? What are they "in themselves," when no one is looking at them, or when only some of their aspects are under observation? We can, at all events, say, what (according to common sense) things are not. They are more than collections of aspects. If we could simultaneously perceive a "thing" at a thousand different distances, at a thousand different angles, under a thousand varieties of illumination, with its interior ideally exposed in a thousand different sections, common sense, if pressed, would, I suppose, still hold that these were no more than specimens of the endless variety of ways in which things may appear, without either changing their nature or fully revealing what that nature is. But though common sense might give this answer, it would certainly resent the question being put. It finds no difficulty in carrying on its work without starting these disturbing inquiries. It is content to say that, though a thing is doubtless always more than the sum of those aspects of it to which we happen to be attending, yet our knowledge that it is and what it is, however imperfect, is, for practical purposes, sufficiently clear and trustworthy, requiring the support neither of metaphysics nor psychology.—This, with all its difficulties, is, I believe, an account, true as far as it goes, of the world of things as common sense conceives it. This is the sort of world which science sets out to explain. Let me give an illustration. We perceive some object—let us say the sun. We perceive it directly and not symbolically. What we see is not a mental image of the sun, nor a complex of sensations caused by the sun; but the sun itself. Moreover, this material external object retains its identity while it varies in appearance. It is red in the morning; it is white at midday; it is red once more in the evening; it may be obscured by clouds or hidden in eclipse; it vanishes and reappears once in every twenty-four hours; yet, amid all these changes and vanishings, its identity is unquestioned. Though we perceive it differently at different times, and though there are times when we do not perceive it at all, we know it to be the same; nor do we for a moment believe (with Heraclitus) that when it is lost to view it has, on that account, either altered its character or ceased to exist.

In the main, therefore, experience is, according to common sense, a very simple affair. We see something, or we feel something, or, like Dr. Johnson, we kick something, and "there's an end on't." Experience is the source of all knowledge, and therefore of all explanation; but, in itself, it seems scarcely to require to be explained. Common sense is prepared to leave it where it finds it. No doubt the occurrence of optical or other illusions may disturb this mood of intellectual tranquillity. Common sense, when it has to consider the case of appearances, some of which are held, on extraneous grounds, to be real and others to be illusory, may feel that there are, after all, problems raised by perception—by the direct experience of things—which are not without their difficulties. But the case of illusions is exceptional, and rarely disturbs the even tenor of our daily round.

──────────── **Systems Only for the Few** ────────────

Systems are, and must be, for the few. The majority of mankind are content with a mood or a temper of thought, an impulse not fully reasoned out, a habit guiding them to the acceptance and assimilation of some opinions and the rejection of others, which acts almost as automatically as the processes of physical digestion.[42]

❖ Science and the External World

Now science, as it gladly acknowledges, is but an extension of common sense. It accepts, among other matters, the common-sense view of perception. Like common sense, it distinguishes the thing as it is from the thing as it appears. Like common sense, it regards the things which are experienced as being themselves unaffected by experience. But, unlike common sense, it devotes great attention to the way in which experience is produced by things. Its business is with the causal series. This, to be sure, is a subject which common sense does not wholly ignore. It would acknowledge that we perceive a lamp through the light which it sheds, and recognise a trumpet through the sound which it emits; but the nature of light or sound, and the manner in which they produce our experience of bright or sonorous objects, it hands over to science for further investigation.

And the task is cheerfully undertaken. Science also deems perception to be the source of all our knowledge of external nature. But it regards it as something more, and different. For perception is itself a part of nature, a natural process, the product of antecedent causes, the cause of subsequent effects. It requires, therefore, like other natural facts, to be observed and explained; and it is the business of science to explain it.

Thus we are brought face to face with the contrast on which so much of the argument of these lectures turns: the contrast between beliefs, considered as members of a cognitive series, and beliefs considered as members of a causal series. In the cognitive series, beliefs of perception are at the root of our whole knowledge of natural laws. In the causal series, they are the effects of natural laws in actual operation. This is so important an example of this dual state that you must permit me to consider it in some detail.

We may examine what goes on between the perceiving person and the thing he perceives from either end; but it is by no means a matter of indifference with which end we begin. If we examine the relation of the perceiver to the perceived it does not seem convenient or accurate to describe that relation as a process. It is an experience, immediate and intuitive; not indeed infallible, but direct and self-sufficient. If I look at the sun, it is the sun I see, and not an image of the sun, nor a sensation which suggests the sun, or symbolises the sun. Still less do I see ethereal vibrations, or a retinal image, or a nervous reaction, or a cerebral disturbance. For, in the act of perceiving, no intermediate entities are themselves perceived.

But now if we, as it were, turn round, and, beginning at the other end, consider the relation of the perceived to the perceiver, no similar statements can be made. We find ourselves concerned, not with an act of intuition, but with a physical process, which is complicated, which occupies time, which involves many stages. We have left behind cognition; we are plunged in causation. Experience is no longer the immediate apprehension of fact; it is the transmission of a message conveyed from the object to the percipient by relays of material messengers. As to how the transmission is effected explanations vary with the growth of science. They have been entirely altered more than once since the modern era began, and with each alteration they become more complicated. They depend, not on one branch of science only, but on many. Newtonian astronomy, solar physics, the theory of radiation, the optical properties of the atmosphere, the physiology of vision, the psychology of perception, and I daresay many other branches of research, have to be drawn upon: and all this to tell us what it is we see, and how it is we come to see it.

❖ Primary and Secondary Qualities

Now there is no one who possesses the least smattering of philosophy who does not know that the views I have just endeavoured to describe are saturated with difficulties: difficulties connected with the nature of perception; difficulties connected with the nature of the object as perceived; difficulties connected with its unperceived physical basis; difficulties connected with the relation in which these three stand to each other. For common sense the material object consists of a certain number of qualities and aspects which are perceived, an inexhaustible number which might be perceived, but are not, and (perhaps) a vaguely conceived "somewhat" lying behind both. The medieval Aristotelian, if I rightly understand him (which very likely I do not), developed this "'somewhat" into the notion of substance—an entity somewhat loosely connected with the qualities which it supported, and in no way explaining them. There was "substance" in a piece of gold, and "substance" in a piece of lead; but there was nothing unreasonable in the endeavour to associate the qualities of gold with the substance of lead, and thus for all practical purposes to turn lead into gold.

Modem science teaches a very different lesson. It has, perhaps, not wholly abandoned the notion of material substance, if this be defined as the unperceivable support of perceivable qualities; but it persistently strives to connect the characteristics of matter with its structure, and, among other characteristics, that of producing, or helping to produce, in us those immediate perceptions which we describe as our experience of matter itself.

An important stage in this endeavour was marked by the famous distinction between the primary and the secondary qualities of matter: the primary qualities being the attributes of external material things which were deemed to be independent of the observer (for example, impenetrability, density, weight, configuration); the secondary qualities being those which, apart from observers endowed with senses like our own, would either exist differently, or would not exist at all (for example, colour and taste). On this view, the primary qualities were among the causes of the secondary qualities, and the secondary qualities were transferred from the thing perceived to the person perceiving.

I am not the least concerned to defend this theory. It has been much derided, and is certainly open to attack. But something like it seems to be an inevitable stage in the development of modern views of nature. The whole effort of physical science is to discover the material or non-psychical facts which shall, among other things, account for our psychical experiences. It is true that there are men of science, as well as philosophers, who regard all such constructions as purely arbitrary—mere labour-saving devices which have nothing to do with reality. But though I shall have something to say about these theories in my next course of lectures, for the present I need only observe that they do not represent ordinary scientific opinion, either as it is, or as it has ever been. Science thinks, rightly or wrongly, that she is concerned with a real world, which persists independently of our experience: she has never assented to the doctrine that the object of her patient investigations is no more than a well-contrived invention for enabling us to foretell, and perhaps to modify, the course of our personal feelings.

But then, if science is right, we are committed to a division between the contents of immediate experience and its causes, which showed itself dimly and tentatively in the distinction between the secondary and the primary qualities of matter, but has become deeper and more impassable with every advance in physics and physiology. It was possible to maintain (though, I admit, not very easy) that, while the secondary qualities of matter are due to the action of the primary qualities on our organs of perception, the primary qualities themselves are, nevertheless, the objects of direct experience. The fact, for example, that colour is no more than a sensation need not preclude us from perceiving the material qualities which, like shape, or motion, or mass, are the external and independent causes to which the sensation is due. I do not say that this view was ever explicitly entertained—nor does it signify. For, if we accept the teaching of science, it can, I suppose, be entertained no more. The physical causes of perception are inferred, but not perceived. The real material world has been driven by the growth of knowledge further and further into the realm of the unseen, and now lies completely hidden from direct experience behind the impenetrable screen of its own effects.

❖ Perception as a Causal Series

For consider what the causal process of perception really is if we trace it from the observed to the observer—if we follow the main strands in the complex lines of communication through which the object seen reveals itself to the man who sees it.

I revert to my previous example—the sun. We need not consider those of its attributes which are notoriously arrived at by indirect methods—which are not perceived but inferred—its magnitude, for example, or its mass. Confining ourselves to what is directly perceived, its angular size, its shape (projected on a plane), its warmth, its brightness, its colour, its (relative) motion, its separation from the observer in space—how are these immediate experiences produced?

The answers have varied with the progress of science; nor, for my present purpose, does it greatly matter which answers we adopt. Let us take those which are commonly accepted at the present moment. They are not only the truest, but the fullest; and for that very reason they put the difficulty with which we are concerned in the highest relief. We begin our causal series with electrons, or, if you do not accept the electric theory of matter in any of its forms, then with atoms and molecules. We start with these, because the sun is a collection of them, and because it is their movements which set going the whole train of causes and effects by which the sun produces in us the perception of itself.

We may take, as the next stage, ethereal vibrations, of various lengths and various amplitudes, sent travelling into space by the moving particles. A fraction of these waves reaches our atmosphere, and of that fraction a fraction reaches our eyes, and of that fraction a further fraction falls within the narrow limits of length to which our eyes are sensitive. It is through these that we are able to see the sun. Still another fraction, not necessarily identical in wave-lengths, affects the nerves which produce in us the sensation of warmth. It is through these that we are able to feel the sun.

But, before we either see or feel, there is much still to be accomplished. The causal series is not nearly completed. Complicated neural

processes, as yet only imperfectly understood; complicated cerebral processes—as yet understood still less—both involving physiological changes
far more complicated than the electrical "accelerations" or electromagnetic disturbances with which we have hitherto been dealing, bring us to
the end of the material sequence of causes and effects, and lay the message from the object perceived on the threshold of the perceiving consciousness. So does a postman slip into your letter-box a message which
has been first written, then carried by hand, then by a mail-cart, then by a
train, then by hand again, till it reaches its destination, and nothing further
is required except that what has been written should be read and understood.

Thus far the material process of transmission. The psychical process
has still to come. Psychology is a science, not less than physiology or
physics; and psychology has much to say on the subject of perception. It
is true that scientific explorers whose point of departure is introspective;
who concern themselves primarily with ideas, conceptions, sensations,
and so forth, rarely succeed in fitting their conclusions without a break to
those of their colleagues who begin with the "external" causes of perception. The two tunnels, driven from opposite sides of the mountain, do not
always meet under its crest. Still, we cannot on that account ignore the
teaching of psychology on the genesis of perceptual experience regarded,
not as the ground of knowledge, but as a natural product.

I do not mean to attempt a summary of psychology from this point of
view, any more than I have attempted a summary of physics or physiology. My argument is really independent, in this case as in the other, of
particular systems. All I ask for is the admission that in perception there
are conditions antecedently supplied by the perceiving consciousness
which profoundly modify every perceptual experience—and that these
conditions (unlike Kant's forms) are natural growths, varying, like other
natural growths, from individual to individual. This admission must, I
think, be made by every empirical psychologist, to whatever school he
happens to belong.

If this statement seems obscure in its general and abstract form, consider a particular application of it. Let us assume, with many psycholo-
gists, that Will, in the form of selective attention, lies at the root of our
perceptual activities; that we may therefore be said, in a sense, voluntarily
to create the objects we perceive; that experience of the present is largely
qualified by memories of the past, and that the perceptual mould into
which our sensations are run is largely a social product—born of the
intercourse between human beings, and, in its turn, rendering that intercourse possible. Is it not clear that, on assumptions like these, conscious-

ness, so far from passively receiving the messages conveyed to it through physical and physiological channels, actively modifies their character?

❖ Perception as a Cognitive Act

But why, it may be asked, should these considerations involve any difficulty? And, if there be a difficulty, what is its exact character?

In its most general form the difficulty is this. It is claimed by science that its conclusions are based upon experience. The experience spoken of is unquestionably the familiar perception of external things and their movements as understood by common sense; and, however much our powers of perception be increased by telescopes, microscopes, balances, thermometers, electroscopes, and so forth, this common-sense view suffers no alteration. The perceptions of a man of science are, in essence, the perceptions of ordinary men in their ordinary moments, beset with the same difficulties, accepted with the same assurance. Whatever be the proper way of describing scientific results, the experimental data on which they rest are sought and obtained in the spirit of "naïf realism."

On this foundation science proceeds to build up a theory of nature by which the foundation itself is shattered. It saws off the branch on which it is supported. It kicks down the ladder by which it has climbed. It dissolves the thing perceived into a remote reality which is neither perceived nor perceivable. It turns the world of common sense into an illusion, and on this illusion it calmly rests its case.

But this is not the only logical embarrassment in which we are involved. When science has supplied us with a description of external things as they "really are," and we proceed to ask how the physical reality reveals itself to us in experience, a new difficulty arises, or, if you like, the old difficulty with a new face. For science requires us to admit that experience, from this point of view, is equivalent to perception; and that perception is a remote psychological effect of a long train of causes, physical and physiological, originally set in motion by the external thing, but in no way resembling it. Look carefully at this process from the outside, and ask yourselves why there should be any such correspondence between the first of these causes and the last of these effects, as should enable us to know or infer the one from the other? Why should the long train of unperceivable intermediaries that connect the perceived with the perceiver be trusted to speak the truth?

I just now likened these intermediaries to relays of messengers. But messengers are expected to hand on their message in the form in which they have received it. The messengers change, but not the message. The metaphor, therefore, is far too complimentary to the train of physical causes which reveal the material thing to the perceiving consciousness. The neural changes which are in immediate causal contiguity with that psychical effect which we call "the experience of an external object" have no resemblance whatever either to the thing as it is perceived or to the thing as it really is. Nor have they any resemblance to the proximate cause which sets them going, namely, the ethereal vibrations; nor have these to the accelerated electrons which constitute the incandescent object which we "experience" as the sun. Nor has the sun, as experienced, the slightest resemblance to the sun as it really is.

Hume, in his *Dialogues on Natural Religion,* urges the absurdity of arguing from an effect like the universe to a cause like God, since the argument from a particular effect to a particular cause, or from a particular cause to a particular effect, is only legitimate when we have had some previous experience of that particular class of causal sequence; and nobody, it is plain, has had the opportunity of observing Creation. Whatever be the value of this argument in the case of God and the world, it seems to me conclusive in the case of matter and man. We cannot argue from purely psychical effects, like perceptions and sensations, to external causes, like physiological processes or ethereal vibrations, unless we can experience both sets of facts in causal relation. And this, if we accept the conclusions of science, we can never do—partly because the intermediate members of the causal series are unperceivable; partly because, if they were perceivable, perception has been reduced by science to a purely psychical effect—which obviously cannot include its material cause. This last must for ever remain outside the closed circle of sensible experiences.

Here, of course, we find ourselves face to face with a familiar objection to those philosophies of perception which deny that we have any access to external reality, except through ideas which are its copy. But they are in a better case than science. They need not explicitly admit a discrepancy between their premises and their conclusions. They arrive at the subjectivity of perception by methods of introspection. They interrogate consciousness, and are convinced that every experience can be analysed into sensations and ideas, some of which, no doubt, suggest externality, but none of which are external. If, then, the worst comes to the worst, they can, and often do, lighten their philosophic ship by pitching the whole material universe overboard as a bit of superfluous cargo. But physical science cannot (at least in my opinion) do anything of the kind. Its whole business is with the material universe. Its premises are experiences of external things, not of internal sensation and ideas. And if it has associated its fortunes with a theory of perception which treats experience as a natural effect of the thing experienced; if it has thereby wandered within sight of the perilous problems which haunt the frontier where mind and matter meet, it has not done so in a spirit of reckless adventure, but in the legitimate pursuit of its own affairs.

This does not necessarily make things easier. We are not here concerned with questionings about the remoter provinces of knowledge—provinces unexplored except by specialists, negligible by ordinary men engaged on ordinary business. On the contrary, the difficulties to which I have called your attention threaten the unquestioned assumption of daily life, the presupposition of every scientific experiment, and the meaning of every scientific generalisation. They cannot be ignored.

On the other hand, threaten as they may, these difficulties can never modify our attitude either towards practical action or scientific theory. Beliefs which were inevitable before remain inevitable still. The supreme act of instinctive faith involved in the perception of external objects stands quite unshaken. Whatever we may think of Berkeley, we cannot give up Dr. Johnson."Seeing," says the proverb, "is believing"; and it speaks better than it knows.

───────────── **Science Needs Theology** ─────────────

We may, indeed, go much further and say that, unless it borrow something from Theology, a philosophy of Science is impossible. The perplexities in which we become involved if we accept the Naturalistic dogma that all beliefs ultimately trace their descent to non-rational causes, have emerged again and again in the course of the preceding argument. Such a doctrine cuts down any theory of knowledge to the root. I can end in nothing but the most impotent scepticism. Science, therefore, is at least as much as Theology, compelled to postulate a Rational Ground or Cause of the world, who made it intelligible and us in some faint degree able to understand it.[43]

❖ An Irresistible Assumption

Can we, then, adopt a middle course, and, imitating the serene acquiescence of Hume, accept the position of sceptics in the study and believers in the market-place? This seems eminently unsatisfactory; and, since believers on this subject we must perforce remain, it behoves us to consider how, and on what terms, we can best qualify our scepticism.

Observe, then, that the particular difficulty which has been occupying our attention arises in the main from the assumption that our common-sense beliefs in the reality and character of material things have no other foundation than the fact that we so perceive them. From such premises it was impossible, it seemed, to infer that they exist otherwise than as they are perceived; and still more impossible to regard the immediate intuition by which we apprehend the object, and the long-drawn sequence of causes by which the object is revealed, as being the same process looked at from different ends.

But this difficulty is greatly mitigated if we hold that our belief in an independent world of material objects, however it may be caused, is neither a conclusion drawn from this or that particular experience nor from all our experiences put together, but an irresistible assumption. Grant the existence of external things, and it becomes possible and legitimate to attempt explanations of their appearance, to regard our perceptions of them as a psychical and physiological product of material realities which do not themselves appear and cannot be perceived. Refuse, on the other hand, to grant this assumption, and no inductive legerdemain will enable us to erect our scientific theories about an enduring world of material things upon the frail foundation of successive personal perceptions.

If this does not seem clear at first sight it is, I think, because we do not consider our experiences as a whole. A limited group of experiences—say Faraday's experiments with electro-magnets—may guide us into new knowledge about the external world, including aspects of that world which are not open to sense perception. But then these experiences assume that this external world exists, they assume it to be independent of perception, they assume it to be a cause of perception. These assumptions once granted, experiment may be, and is, the source of fresh discoveries. But experiment based on these assumptions never can establish their truth; and if our theory of knowledge requires us to hold that "no proposition should be entertained with greater assurance than the proofs it is built on will warrant," our fate is sealed, and we need never hope to extricate ourselves from the entanglements in which a too credulous empiricism has involved us. This means that one at least of the inevitable beliefs enumerated in the first lecture—the belief in an external world—is a postulate which science is compelled to use but is unable to demonstrate. How, then, are we to class it? It is not a law of thought in the accepted meaning of that expression. We are not rationally required to accept it by the very structure of our thinking faculties. Many people, indeed, theoretically reject it; none, so far as I know, regard it as self-evident. On the other hand, it is not an inference from experience; neither is it an analytic judgment in which the predicate is involved in the subject. Described in technical language, it would seem to be *a priori* without being necessary, and synthetic without being empirical—qualities which, in combination, scarcely fit into any familiar philosophic classification.

According to the view which I desire to press in these lectures, this marks a philosophic omission. I regard the belief in an external world as one of a class whose importance has been ignored by philosophy, though all science depends on them. They refuse to be lost in the common herd of empirical beliefs; though they have no claim to be treated as axioms. We are inclined to accept them, but not rationally compelled. The inclination may be so strong as practically to exclude doubt; and it may diminish from this maximum to a faint feeling of probability. But, whatever be the strength of these beliefs, and whatever the nature of their claims, the importance of the part they play in the development and structure of our current creed cannot easily be exaggerated.

Before, however, I consider other specimens of this class, I must interpolate a long parenthesis upon probability. I have just described these fundamental beliefs as being "probable" in varying degrees. Gradations of probability are familiar to the mathematical theorist. Are we, then, here concerned with probability as conceived by the mathematician? It is evidently essential to settle this question before proceeding with the main argument; and I propose, therefore, to turn aside and devote the next lecture to its consideration.

─────────── **Values Refuse to be Ignored** ───────────

With the arguments of *Foundations of Belief* I do not propose to trouble the reader. But it may make clearer what I have to say about *L'Evolution créatrice* if I mention that (among other conclusions) I arrive at the conviction that in accepting science, as we all do, we are moved by "values" not by logic. That if we examine fearlessly the grounds on which judgments about the material world are founded, we shall find that they rest on postulates about which it is equally impossible to say that we can theoretically regard them as self-evident, or practically treat them as doubtful. We can neither prove them nor give them up. "Concede" (I argued) the same philosophical weight to values in departments of speculation which look beyond the material world [such as religion], and naturalism will have to be abandoned. But the philosophy of science would not lose thereby. On the contrary, an extension of view beyond phenomena diminishes rather than increases the theoretical difficulties with which bare naturalism is beset. It is not by a mere reduction in the area of our beliefs, that, in the present state of our knowledge, certainty and consistency are to be reached. Such a reduction could not be justified by philosophy. But justifiable or not, it would be quite impractical. "Values" refuse to be ignored.[44]

THEISM AND HUMANISM

7

Probability, Calculable and Intuitive

An agnostic declines to offer any opinion on the being of God because it is a matter about which he professes to know nothing. But the universe either has a spiritual cause, or it has not. If the agnostic is as ignorant as he supposes, he cannot have any reason for preferring the first alternative to the second, or the second to the first.

MR. BALFOUR ON CHANCE
Probability in Theory and Practice
The Mathematical Calculus
(From Our Special Correspondent)

GLASGOW, JAN. 26

The "January blast" did not seriously diminish the size of the audience which gathered this afternoon to hear Mr. Balfour's seventh Gifford lecture.

He began by classifying beliefs into inevitable and probable, and in the interests of this classification he offered a criticism of the mathematical theory of probability. Traditional logical theory had confined itself to this particular kind of probability, and though the mathematical statement of chances had yielded results of the first importance both for science and for practical life, it did not cover the whole ground. It had not distinguished clearly different kinds of probabilities, and in particular it had failed to give any account of that large range of beliefs which were neither inevitable nor axiomatic, but which were yet conterminous with our inevitable beliefs and were part of the necessary basis of all our knowl-edge. These beliefs Mr. Balfour called "probable," and it was in this sense that Butler had used the term in his dictum that probability was the guide of life.

Probability and Knowledge

Mr. Balfour's first task was to show precisely under what conditions the mathematical calculus was applicable. He began, to the delight of his audience, by expressing the wish that he were a great mathematician, or even a mathematician at all, for mathematics enjoyed unique advantages in method and in terminology so that no ambiguity could occur in his expression or in his reasoning. But Mr. Balfour thought that mathematicians did not set forth their premises with the same rigour as they deducted their conclusions, and they did not appreciate the abstract character of their reasoning. He indicated the limits of the mathematical treatment of probability by considering an interesting excerpt from M. Poincaré, to whose memory he paid a pious and graceful tribute. M. Poincaré had argued that chance could not be, as previous logic had taken it to be, merely the measure of our ignorance, for the statement of chances was often the basis of useful knowledge. Mr. Balfour developed this thesis by considering some typical cases in which knowledge was furnished by statement of chances.

These were, first of all, such cases as the tables of mortality or the laws of the explosiveness of radium. There we were dealing with groups of facts in a purely empirical fashion. A second set of cases was that in which the statement of chances was based on *a priori* considerations. Though experience confirmed the results of such theorizing it was possible to argue *a priori* that the chances were one in two that the tossing of a penny would result in heads and it was equally possible to say on purely *a priori* grounds that the chances were much against a visitor's leaving Monte Carlo with as much money in his pockets as he had had on entering.

Probable Beliefs

But Mr. Balfour argued that there was a definite limit to this kind of reasoning. There was the difference in feeling, if not in logic, between the argument from objective knowledge and the argument from subjective ignorance. But these arguments were usually in the same logical form, and logical theory did not distinguish them. The results of the confusion between these two became serious when the attempt was made to carry the argument from probability into more fundamental spheres.

For example, an agnostic might say that he could form no conclusion as to whether or not the world was created by an intelligent being. It might be replied to him that either it must have been so created or it must not, and he might be forced by this argument to agree that the chances of there being an intelligent Creator were even. To assert this, however, was to assert a great deal about the world—indeed as Mr. Balfour put it, it implied that the chances of the existence of an intelligent Creator were rather more favourable than the chances of winning on the black or red at Monte Carlo.

But this argument Mr. Balfour believed to be manifestly unfair. It was a case which the calculation of probability could not cover, and it plainly rested on an imperfect analysis of the conditions under which mathematical calculation was valid. Mathematical probability, he considered, had meaning only within a system already determined, and the knowledge of that system must have been arrived at by other methods. For problems such as these he believed that another kind of probability was required different from that resting on the highly abstract mathematical calculation. **But he was confirmed in his view that, in addition to inevitable beliefs, there were probable beliefs to which we were inclined but not driven. They varied in degree of coercive power, but were capable of being detected throughout the whole of scientific knowledge.** These beliefs had not received sufficient treatment from philosophers, either of the critical school or of the empirical. Kant and Mill alike had thought more of the grounds of belief than of the actual content of belief, and Mr. Balfour pleaded for as impartial an investigation into what men of science had actually believed as had been given to outworn philosophical creeds. He proposed to undertake, in his next two lectures, a survey of some of those beliefs. They would go to support his general Theistic argument, but apart from that, they were of the utmost significance for a sound philosophy of science.

—*The Times,* Tue. Jan. 27, 1914, 10a.

THEISM AND HUMANISM

❖ Mathematicians and Probability

I wish I were a mathematician. There is in the history of the mathematical sciences, as in their substance, something that strangely stirs the imagination even of the most ignorant. Its younger sister, Logic, is as abstract, and its claims are yet wider. But it has never shaken itself free from a certain pretentious futility: it always seems to be telling us, in language quite unnecessarily technical, what we understood much better before it was explained. It never helps to discover, though it may guarantee discovery; it never persuades, though it may show that persuasion has been legitimate; it never aids the work of thought, it only acts as its auditor and accountant-general. I am not referring, of course, to what I see described in recent works as "modem scientific logic." Of this I do not presume to speak. Still less am I referring to so-called Inductive Logic. Of this it is scarce worth while to speak.[45] I refer to their more famous predecessor, the formal logic of the schools.

But in what different tones must we speak of mathematics! Mill, if I remember rightly, said it was as full of mysteries as theology. But while the value of theology for knowledge is disputed, the value of mathematics for knowledge is indisputable. Its triumphs can be appreciated by the most foolish, they appeal to the most material. If they seem sometimes lost to ordinary view in the realms of abstract infinities, they do not disdain to serve us in the humbler fields of practice. They have helped mankind to all the greatest generalisations about the physical universe: and without them we should still be fumbling over simple problems of practical mechanics, entangled in a costly and ineffectual empiricism.

But while we thank the mathematician for his aid in conquering Nature, we envy him his powers of understanding her. Though he deals, it would seem, entirely with abstractions, they are abstractions which, at his persuasion, supply the key to the profoundest secrets of the physical universe. He holds the clues to mazes where the clearest intellect, unaided, would wander hopelessly astray. He belongs to a privileged caste.

I intend no serious qualification of this high praise when I add that, as regards the immediate subject of this lecture, I mean Probability, mathematicians do not seem to have given ignorant inquirers like myself all the aid which perhaps we have a right to ask. They have treated the subject as a branch of applied mathematics. They have supplied us with much excellent theory. They have exercised admirable skill in the solution of problems. But I own that, when we inquire into the rational basis of all this imposing superstructure, their explanations, from the lay point of view, leave much to be desired.

"Probability," says an often-quoted phrase of Butler, "is the guide of life." But the Bishop did not define the term; and he wrote before the theory of probability had attained to all its present dignities. Neither D'Alembert nor Laplace had discussed it. Quetelet had not applied it to sociology, nor Maxwell to physics. Jevons had not described it as the "noblest creation of the intellect." It is doubtful whether Butler meant by it exactly what the mathematicians mean by it, and certain that he did not suspect any lurking ambiguity in the expression.

Nor, indeed, would the existence of such ambiguity be commonly admitted by any school of thought. The ordinary view is that the theory of probabilities is, as Laplace described it, "common sense reduced to calculation." That there could be two kinds of probability, only one of which fitted this description, would be generally regarded as a heresy. But it is a heresy in which I myself believe; and which, with much diffidence, I now propose to defend.

--------- **Editor's Note** ---------

In this chapter, Balfour draws a distinction between two sorts of probabilities. One—which he calls *calculable*—is the kind routinely used by scientists and river-boat gamblers. It allows us to move from things we know, such as the change in temperature of a cylinder of compressed gas, to things we do not yet know, such as the pressure inside the cylinder at the new temperature. The result is statistical because to calculate the result we do not need to know about how each individual molecule responds to the temperature change. Balfour constrasts that to a different sort of probability, an *intuitive* one which deals with things that cannot be so easily measured. As an example of the latter he gives a "belief in an independent physical universe." Can we calculate the probability that the world we see around us really exists and isn't simply a dream of fevered minds? Of course not. But it is, nevertheless, something that has the "highest degree of *intuitive* probability." Behind Balfour's reasoning lies the idea that the debate between Naturalism and Theism is more a matter of *intuitive* than *calculable* probabilities. It makes no sense to say that God has "a 63 percent chance of existing." Our knowledge of God isn't that sort of knowledge. In Chapter 8, Balfour will apply that same principle to the scientific belief in the uniformity of nature and the consistency of its laws.

❖ Calculable Probability

The well-known paradox of the theory of probabilities is that, to all seeming, it can extract knowledge from ignorance and certainty from doubt. The point cannot be better put than by Poincaré in discussing the physical theory of gases, where the doctrine of probability finds an important application. Let me give you his view—partly in paraphrase, partly in translation. "For omniscience," he says in substance, "chance would not exist. It is but the measure of our ignorance. When we describe an event as accidental we mean that we do not fully comprehend the conditions by which it was brought about."

But is this the full truth of the matter? Are not the laws of chance a source of knowledge? And, stranger still, is it not sometimes easier to generalise (say) about random movements than about movements which obey even a simple law—witness the kinetic theory of gases? And if this be so, how can chance be the equivalent of ignorance? Ask a physicist to explain what goes on in a gas. He might, perhaps, express his views in some such terms as these: "You wish me to tell you about these complex phenomena. If by ill luck I happened to know the laws which govern them, I should be helpless. I should be lost in endless calculations, and could never hope to supply you with an answer to your questions. Fortunately for both of us, I am completely ignorant about the matter; I can, therefore, supply, you with an answer at once. This may seem odd. But there is something odder still, namely, that my answer will be right."

Now, what are the conditions which make it possible thus to extract a correct answer from material apparently so unpromising? They would seem to be a special combination of ignorance and knowledge, the joint effect of which is to justify us in supposing that the particular collection of facts or events with which we are concerned are happening "at random." If we could calculate the complex causes which determine the fall of a penny, or the collisions of a molecule, we might conceivably deal with pennies or molecules individually; and the calculus of probability might be dispensed with. But we cannot; ignorance, therefore, real or assumed, is thus one of the conditions required to provide us with the kind of chaos to which the doctrine of chances may most fittingly be applied. But there is another condition not less needful, namely, knowledge—the knowledge that no extraneous cause or internal tendency is infecting our chaotic group with some bias or drift whereby its required randomness would be destroyed. Our penny must be symmetrical, and Maxwell's demons[46] must not meddle with the molecules.

─────────── **Editor's Note** ───────────

James Maxwell's hypothetical demons were intelligent beings so small they could manipulate nature in ways that seemed to defy the laws of science. For example, by opening and closing a tiny door at precisely the right time they could move all the gas molecules from one chamber into another.

───────────────────

The slow disintegration of radium admirably illustrates the behaviour of a group or collection possessing all the qualities which we require. The myriad atoms of which the minutest visible fragment is composed are numerous enough to neutralise eccentricities such as those which, in the case of a game of chance, we call "runs of luck." Of these atoms we have no individual knowledge. What we know of one we know of all; and we treat them not only as a collection, but as a collection made at random. Now, physicists tell us that out of any such random collection a certain proportion will disintegrate in a given time; and always the same proportion. But whence comes their confidence in the permanence of this ratio? Why are they so assured of its fixity that these random explosions are thought to provide us with a better timekeeper than the astronomical changes which have served mankind in that capacity through immemorial ages? The reason is that we have here the necessary ignorance and the necessary knowledge in a very complete form. Nothing can well exceed our ignorance of the differences between one individual radium atom and another, though relevant differences there must be. Nothing, again, seems better assured than our knowledge that no special bias or drift will make one collection of these atoms behave differently from another. For the atomic disintegration is due to no external shock or mutual reaction which might affect not one atom only, but the whole group. A milligram of radium is not like a magazine of shells, where if one spontaneously explodes all the rest follow suit. The disruption of the atom is due to some internal principle of decay whose effects no known external agent can either hasten or retard. Although, therefore, the proportion of atoms which will disintegrate in a given time can only be discovered, like the annual death-rate among men, by observation, yet once discovered it is discovered for ever. Our human death-rate not only may change, but does change. The death-rate of radium atoms changes not. In the one case, causes are in operation which modify both the organism and the sur-roundings on which its life depends. In the other case, it would seem that the average of successive generations of atoms does not vary, and that, once brought into existence, they severally run their appointed course unaffected by each other or by the world outside.

So far we have been concerned with groups or collections or series; and about these the doctrine of chances and the theory of error may apparently supply most valuable information. But in practical affairs—nay, even in many questions of scientific speculation—we are yet more concerned about individual happenings. We have, therefore, next to ask how we can infer the probability of a particular event from our knowledge of some group or series to which it belongs.

There seems at first sight no difficulty in this, provided we have sufficient knowledge of the group or series of which the particular event is a member. If we know that a tossed penny will in the long run give heads and tails equally often, we do not hesitate to declare that the chances of a particular throw giving "heads" are even. To expect in any given case heads rather than tails, or tails rather than heads, is inconsistent with the objective knowledge of the series which by hypothesis we actually possess.

But what if our information about the group or series is much less than this? Suppose that, instead of knowing that the two possible alternatives do in fact occur equally often, we are in the less advantageous position of knowing no reason why they should not occur equally often. We ought, I suppose, still to regard the chances of a particular toss as even; although this estimate, expressed by the same fraction (1/2) and held with the same confidence, is apparently a conclusion based on ignorance, whereas the first conclusion was apparently based on knowledge.

If, for example, we know that a die is fairly made and fairly thrown, we can tell how often a particular number will turn up in a long series of throws, and we can tell what the chances are that it will turn up on the occasion of a single throw. Moreover, the two conclusions seem to be logically connected.

But if we know that the die is loaded we can no longer say how the numbers will be distributed in a series of throws, however long, though we are sure that the distribution will be very different from what it would have been had the die been a fair one. Nevertheless, we can still say (before the event) what the chances are of a particular number turning up on a single throw; and these chances are exactly the same whether the die be loaded or whether it be fair—namely, one-sixth. Our objective knowledge of the group or series has vanished, but, with the theory of probability to help us, our subjective conviction on this point apparently remains unchanged.

There is here, surely, a rather awkward transition from the "objective" to the "subjective" point of view. We were dealing, in the first case, with groups or series of events about which the doctrine of chances enabled us to say something positive, something which experience would always confirm if the groups or series were large enough. A perfect calculator, endowed with complete knowledge of all the separate group members, would have no correction to make in our conclusions. His information would be more complete than our own, but not more accurate. It is true that for him "averages" would have no interest and "chance" no meaning. Nevertheless, he would agree that in a long series of fair throws of a fair die any selected face would turn up one-sixth times as often as all the others taken together. But in the second case this is no longer so. Foresight based on complete knowledge would apparently differ from foresight based on the calculation of chances. Our calculator would be aware of the exact manner in which the die was loaded, and of the exact advantage which this gave to certain numbers. He would, therefore, know that in asserting the chance of any particular number turning up on the first throw to be one-sixth, we were wrong. In what sense, then, do we deem ourselves to have been right?

The answer, I suppose, is that we were right not about a group of throws made with this loaded die, but about a group of such groups made with dice loaded at random—a group in which "randomness" was so happily preserved among its constituent groups that its absence within each of these groups was immaterial, and no one of the six alternative numbers was favoured above another.

A similar reply might be given if we suppose our ignorance carried yet a step further. Instead of knowing that our die was loaded, and being ignorant only of the manner of its loading, we might be entirely ignorant whether it was loaded or not. The chances of a particular number turning up on the first throw would still be one-sixth. But the series to which this estimate would refer would neither be one composed of fair throws with a fair die, nor one composed of a series of throws with dice loaded at random, but one composed of a series of throws with dice chosen at random from a random collection of dice, loaded and not loaded!

It seems plain that we have no experimental knowledge of series piled on series after this fashion. Our conclusions about them are not based on observation, nor collected from statistics. They are arrived at *a priori*; and when the character of a series is arrived at *a priori,* the probability of a particular event belonging to it can be arrived at independently by the same method. No reference to the series is required. The reason we estimate the chances against any one of the six possible throws of a die as five to one under each and all of the suppositions we have been discussing is that under none of them have we any ground for thinking any one of the six more probable than another—even though we may have ground for thinking that in a series of throws made with that particular die, some number, to us unknown, will in fact turn up with exceptional frequency.

The most characteristic examples, therefore, of problems in probability depend for their solution on a bold use of the "principle of sufficient reason." We treat alternatives as equally likely when we cannot see any ground for supposing that one is more likely than another. This seems sensible enough; but how far may we carry this process of extracting knowledge from ignorance? An agnostic declines to offer any opinion on the being of God because it is a matter about which he professes to know nothing. But the universe either has a spiritual cause, or it has not. If the agnostic is as ignorant as he supposes, he cannot have any reason for preferring the first alternative to the second, or the second to the first. Must he, therefore, conclude that the chances of Theism are even? The man who knows this knows much. He knows, or may know, that God's existence is slightly more probable than his own chance of winning a coup at Monte Carlo. He knows, or may know, the exact fraction by which the two probabilities differ. How, then, can he call himself an agnostic?

Every one must, I think, feel that such reasoning involves a misuse of the theory of probability. But is that misuse without some justification? The theory, unless I misread it, permits, or rather requires, us to express by the same fraction probabilities based on what is little less than complete knowledge, and probabilities based on what is little more than complete ignorance. To arrive at a clear conclusion, it seems only necessary to apply the "law of sufficient reason" to defined alternatives; and it is apparently a matter of perfect indifference whether we apply this law in its affirmative or its negative shape; whether we say "there is every reason for believing that such and such alternatives happen equally often," or whether we say "there is no reason for thinking that one alternative happens more often than the other." I do not criticise this method; still less do I quarrel with it. On the contrary, I am lost in admiration of this instrument of investigation, the quality of whose output seems to depend so little on the sort of raw material with which it is supplied.

❖ Intuitive Probability

My object, indeed, is neither to discuss the basis on which rests the calculus of probabilities—a task for which I own myself totally unfit—nor yet to show that a certain obscurity hangs over the limits within which it may properly be employed. I desire rather to suggest that, wherever those limits are placed, there lies beyond them a kind of probability yet more fundamental, about which the mathematical methods can tell us nothing, though it possesses supreme value as a "guide of life."

Wherein lies the distinction between the two? In this: the doctrine of calculable probability (if I may so call it) has its only application, or its only assured application, within groups whose character is either postulated, or is independently arrived at by inference and observation. These groups, be they natural or conventional, provide a framework, marking out a region wherein prevails the kind of ignorance which is the subjective reflection of objective "randomness." This is the kind of ignorance which the calculus of probabilities can most successfully transmute into knowledge: and herein lies the reason why the discoverers of the calculus found their original inspiration in the hazards of the gaming-table, and why their successors still find in games of chance its happiest illustrations. For in games of chance the group framework is provided by convention; perfect "randomness" is secured by fitting devices; and he who attempts to modify it is expelled from society as a cheat.

None of these observations apply to the kind of probability on whose importance I am now insisting. If calculable probability be indeed "common sense reduced to calculation," intuitive probability lies deeper. It supports common sense, and it supplies the ultimate ground—be it secure or insecure—of all work-a-day practice and all scientific theory. It has nothing to do with "randomness"; it knows nothing of averages; it obeys no formal laws; no light is thrown on it by cards or dice; it cannot be reduced to calculation. How, then, is it to be treated? What place is it to occupy in our general scheme?

These are all important questions. But no answer to them can be given till we have pressed somewhat further the line of thought which the discussion in this present lecture has for a moment interrupted. Before I began this long parenthesis on the theory of chance, I was occupied with a most important example of a belief which possesses the highest degree of intuitive probability, but no calculable probability at all. I mean the belief in an independent physical universe. In the next lecture I shall resume the general thread of my argument, and consider another belief of the same kind which is not less—some would say even more—essential to natural science than the one with which I have already dealt. I mean a belief in the regularity of nature.

THEISM AND HUMANISM

CHAPTER

8

Uniformity and Causation

None surely, who understand the meaning of the words they use, will dare to assert that nature appears regular. What they may assert is, that the more you examine it, the more regular it appears. The reign of law is always extending. New provinces are always being added to its domains. Anomalies vanish as knowledge grows; and the absolute uniformity which we now only know by faith, we may some day know by sight.

MR. BALFOUR ON MILL
The Law of Causation Criticized
Our Hope of Progress
(From Our Special Correspondent)
GLASGOW, JAN. 28

Mr. Balfour delighted his huge audience to-day by a brilliant discussion on the law of universal causation and an entertaining criticism of the position held by John Stuart Mill. He chose our belief in the regularity of the universe as an illustration of probable believe in the sense in which he defined the word probable in his last lecture. He would not define the word regularity to-day because it is a characteristic of all fundamental probabilities that they have taken many various forms in the history of human thought, and that they vary to-day in accordance with varying degrees of knowledge.

The Idea of Regularity

The belief in the regularity of succession among events can go far behind human consciousness and human reason; for, though the lower animals cannot be said to believe anything, they form habits which produce expectations in mankind. The expectation born of habit, or the power of habit to produce expectation, is the result of natural

selection and has survival value; but mankind does more than believe that Nature is sufficiently regular to justify expectations born of habit. We carry further this notion of regularity until it embraces the whole universe. Philosophers and scientific men have embodied this idea of regularity in the law of universal causation—that every event has a cause or antecedent, and that the same antecedent always produces the same effect. The lecture was devoted to two criticisms of this dictum, and especially to Mill's use of it. Mr. Balfour said that in his published writings he had already exposed Mill's delusion that each man by a process of logical inference can infer these wide generalities from his own individual experience. Is it, he asked, so very obvious that nature is regular? He found himself tormented by its irregularities, by the occurrence of something unexpected. We often speak of the caprice of Nature. It is true that, when we recover our temper, we do not speak of Nature's capricious behaviour, but of our own faulty observation, or of the intervention of events of which we have no knowledge; we at once put Nature in the right and ourselves in the wrong. A cheer of approval gave the lecturer his opportunity of driving home his point. "Quite right," he said, "but observe that it means our belief in the regularity of Nature does not come from experience." Experience could only show that Nature is sometimes regular and sometimes irregular. He quoted the saying that if Kepler had possessed more perfect instruments he would never had made the great generalization about the elliptical character of the orbits round the sun which was at the root of Newton's immortal discovery; that if he could have observed the deviations from the elliptical form without having our modern knowledge of the cause of the deviations he would have discarded his theory. **Mr. Balfour himself thought that, so ingrained in the mind of man is the idea that there must be something like a plan,** Kepler's robust faith would have triumphed over his observations. It was, at all events, true that nothing we can discover ever upsets our faith in the regularity of Nature; but there are unexplained aberrations and it is an act of faith.

A Category of Negligibility

The second criticism is that the law of universal causation is not sufficient for scientific purposes. Scientific experiments depend upon the admission that a great deal of Nature is, for immediate and special purposes, practically negligible, and he proposed to invent a new category—the category of negligibility. He pointed out that negligibility is a probable belief, is unprovable, and cannot be established by experience, and yet it is of vital importance for any crucial experiment. The category of negligibility is apparently inconsistent with the view that the world is an inter-related tissue of causes and effects; that if anything is different, everything is altered, perhaps invisibly, but yet really. This is the view expressed in Tennyson's poem about the flower in the crannied wall. He did not quarrel with it as an intellectual ideal, but it is because it is merely an ideal that science is possible. A world in which events of one instant could not be paired off with events of the preceding instant would be a world in which history was possible, but not sciences, for unless we can break up the world into practically separate strands and threads, no inductive logic could draw any conclusion from any experiments.

A Science of Society Impossible

He went on to say that this category of negligibility has different degrees of applicability to different areas of knowledge. Philosophers have assumed that we can use it in mentality, in history, and in biography, and have attempted to construct a science of sociology in the same sense as a science of matter. As a believer in free will, he could not accept this, but apart from free will, a science of society is impossible because you cannot neglect things outside your particular experiences as you can in a physical or chemical laboratory. Science depends on repetitions, but history never repeats itself, nor does the life of an individual. In mental experiences there can never be complete identity beyond the simplest and crudest stages of mental life. Bergson had expressed this idea more eloquently, and it was one of his great contributions to contemporary thought. Mill's idea that you can transfer the methods of physical science to the complicated phenomena of society and mental life, and that the only difference lies in the larger number of complications is an illusion. You can get analogies, suggestive lessons, and interesting parallels, but you can never get an inevitable sequence in which a cause is attached to an effect and in which, by repeating the cause, you can produce the effect. Human life cannot be resolved into such sequences. The moral is that the hope of progress lies in abandoning methods which require the law of universal causation, and in trying to see how our great body of knowledge has in fact been arrived at and what inevitable or probable beliefs lie at the root of all that we think and do in the whole of our cognitive lives.

Mr. Balfour's ninth lecture will be delivered on Wednesday, February 4.

—*The Times,* Thu., Jan. 29, 1914, 10a.

❖ Habit, Expectation, Induction

In my last lecture but one I dwelt upon the interplay of causes and reasons in one special case—the case of our immediate experiences of the external world, the world in which we move, the world investigated by the physical sciences. No case can indeed be more important; for these immediate experiences are deemed by every man to be his guide through all the hours of his waking life, and by every man of science to supply the evidence on which depends all our knowledge of natural laws.

Yet this very statement suggests the existence of another series of problems not less important and not less closely connected with my general argument. For, how do we get from particular experiences to general laws—from beliefs about individual occurrences to beliefs about the ordering of the universe? These beliefs, looked at from the scientific point of view, are, as I have so often observed, a natural product. They have a history like other natural products. They are the effects of a long train of causes; and among those causes are some which claim, rightly or wrongly, to be reasons, an uncounted multitude which make no such claim, and others, again, which occupy a doubtful position between the two.

Imagine an external intelligence studying the methods by which earth-born creatures of various types adjust themselves to future circumstances. The most primitive method is, I suppose, no more than simple nervous reaction. The most developed method involves reasoned expectation. And between these two extremes our supposed observer would see a long series of intermediate forms melting into one another by insensible gradation.

From the point of view of the argument I am endeavouring to present to you, this development is of the greatest interest. The creation of a capacity for expectation, and of an inclination to expect a future similar to the past, must be deemed one of the most remarkable triumphs of selection—if to selection it indeed be due. Here we have this irrational mimic of reason, starting from the simplest forms of response to external stimulus, improving them into such excellent imitations of inductive reasoning as those which lead a chick, no more than a few hours old, to reject food which it has once found nasty;[47] and finally evolving out of these humble beginnings a mode of inference which, according to empirical philosophy, is the true and only source of all our general knowledge, whether of nature or of man.

It must be owned, indeed, that the attempt to treat instinctive expectation as a form of rational inference has been a lamentable failure. By no exercise of ingenuity can beliefs about what is not experienced be logically extracted from particular experiences, multiply them as you will. It is in vain that empirical philosophers attempt to give an air of rationality to this leap from the known to the unknown by the use of high-sounding logical titles. "Induction by simple enumeration" is doubtless an imposing name. But those who practise the thing are in no wise improving on their predecessor, the chick. Indeed they lag behind it. For the chick expects—but gives no reason; the empirical philosopher expects—and gives a bad one.

❖ Regularity, Causation

Expectation, then, if it is to be rational, can only be rationally extracted from experiences by the aid of one or more general principles. What principles are they?

One of them, at all events, must be the regularity of nature. In some form or other, and to some degree or other, this is assumed in every scientific speculation and in every purposeful action reflectively performed. It is, as you may recollect, one of the "inevitable beliefs of common sense" to which I referred in my first lecture.

But you may also recollect that in the same lecture I pointed out that inevitable beliefs, though we cannot avoid holding them in some shape, are, and have been, held in many shapes; shapes which vary with the changes in our general outlook on men and things. In what shape, then, should our belief in regularity now be held?

The shape in which it is very commonly formulated is something of this kind: "everything is caused; and the same causes are always followed by the same effects." This is the so-called "law of universal causation." It has been treated as an assured truth by philosophers of many different schools, though not always for the same reasons; and, so far as the physical universe is concerned, the modern world accepts it without demur. It is, nevertheless, open to criticism from two points of view. It asserts somewhat more about the course of nature than experience suggests, and somewhat less than science requires. Let me take the two points separately.

When I was dealing with ethics I had occasion to point out that if the primitive manifestations of loyalty and love are products of selection, they have developed by a kind of internal momentum, to a point far beyond that to which selection can possibly have carried them. Something of the same kind has happened in the case of the causal postulate. Selection, we must suppose, has produced the capacity for acquiring habitual expectations; and habitual expectation is induction without reasoning. Like induction, it would not only be useless, but harmful, if no regularity existed; if at any moment the future ceased to bear some resemblance to the past. But the regularity asserted by the law of universal causation is far in excess of this requirement. The law applies to regions which never come within the range of experience; and, as regards regions which do come within that range, experience hardly confirms it. We may, of course, attribute the apparent irregularities in nature to our ignorance or our errors; and this, in fact, is what we always do. We must (we think) have observed wrongly or insufficiently; or it may be that a clearer insight would show how apparent aberrations really illustrate some larger law, or depend on conditions at present beyond our ken. Such explanations are easy; and, what is more, they are true. **There is no complaint to be made of a verdict in favour of absolute uniformity except that it outruns the evidence. None surely, who understand the meaning of the words they use, will dare to assert that nature appears regular. What they may assert is, that the more you examine it, the more regular it appears. The reign of law is always extending. New provinces are always being added to its domains. Anomalies vanish as knowledge grows; and the absolute uniformity which we now only know by faith, we may some day know by sight.**

To this "credo" (with reservations) I readily subscribe. But it sounds a little strange in the mouths of some who preach it. Does it not imply that we interpret our experiences in the light of a preconceived scheme of things; that we force our observations into a mould which they do not naturally fit? If, in unravelling a cypher, I come across passages which are unintelligible, I attribute the check to my own ignorance or dullness. Why? Because I know independently that the cypher has a meaning, if only I could find it. But the empirical agnostic professes to know nothing about the world, except what he has observed himself or what other people have observed for him. Why, then, should he suppose perfect regularity to exist when no perfect regularity appears? Why is he not content to accept what he finds, namely, a regularity which is real but incomplete?

It is no reply to say that patient genius is constantly detecting order in apparent chaos. So it is. And when this happens, by all means rearrange your map of the universe accordingly. But do not argue that chaos is therefore non-existent. The belief in universal causation is not based on argument, nor yet on observation. It depends on what I have described as intuitive probability. And if we refuse to regard nature as liable to lapses from perfect uniformity, this is not because such a theory is unthinkable, not because it is contrary to experience, not because it is incompatible with knowledge, not because it is fatal to purposeful action; for it is none of these things. We reject it because it is out of harmony with the ideal we have formed of what the material universe ought to be and is: and so strong is this speculative prepossession that there is no experimental evidence which would convince a man of science that, when physical causes were the same, physical consequences could be different.

Irregularity of Nature

When we come to the more complex phenomena with which we have to deal, the plain lesson taught by personal observation is not the regularity, but the irregularity of Nature. . . . The most careful series of experiments carried out by the most accomplished investigators never show identical results.[48]

❖ The Principle of Negligibility

But this observation brings me to my second commentary on the formula of universal causation. If, as I have contended, it goes beyond what mere experience suggests, it also falls short of what scientific inference requires. The uniformity it postulates lacks a certain kind of "structure" which is absolutely necessary if the past is to be explained and the future foreseen. It is not enough for this purpose that the course of Nature should be determined. It must be determined after a particular pattern; its uniformity must conform to a particular type.

At first sight this statement may seem rather obscure. What (you will ask) is this "structure" or pattern whose absence would be so disastrous to knowledge? It is a structure (I reply) which makes it possible to break up the flow of events into intelligible repetitions. It is not enough that the condition of the world at any moment should be strictly determined by its condition at the preceding moment. Such a world would, I suppose, completely conform to the doctrine of uniformity, and obey both in spirit and in letter the law of universal causation. Yet, unless it also conformed to the additional canon I have just laid down, it would provide no basis either for scientific knowledge or for practical decision. The same consequent would always succeed the same antecedent, if and when it recurred. But, unless we accept the cyclic theories of the Stoics, it never would recur. The completest knowledge of the past would tell us nothing about the future; not because the succession of events was arbitrary or (as the word is commonly misused) miraculous; but because each cross-section of the stream of Time (that is to say, the sum of all contemporaneous facts and events) had to be considered as a single cause, completely determining the whole cross-section immediately in front of it; and, as a single effect, completely determined by the whole cross-section immediately behind it. Such a world might have a history, but it could never have a science.

The reason is plain. Science requires uniformities even more than uniformity; and a universe such as I have just described has uniformity but no uniformities. The very phrase "laws of nature" shows that it is these subordinate uniformities for which we look. The whole efforts of the skilled investigator are directed towards so isolating the sequences he is examining that his experiments shall become (as the phrase goes) crucial. If no such isolation could be effected, it would never be possible to point to some "phenomenon" and say of it "Here is a cause," and to some other "phenomenon" and say of it "Here is its effect." The world, in short, must have a structure which connects its successive phases in such a way that definite parts of all that exists or happens are knit with peculiar closeness to definite parts of what existed or happened before. It is on these connecting strands that we mainly fix our gaze; they are often difficult to trace, they are sometimes hopelessly entangled; but when we can bring them into clear vision, then, and not till then, we triumphantly say that we have discovered a law of nature.

We are so familiar with this "fibrous" structure of the natural world that it seems almost a matter of course. Mill, for example, assumes it, unconsciously no doubt, through all his exposition of inductive methods: and if he had not assumed it, these methods would have come tumbling about his ears in irreparable ruin. But assuredly neither he nor any other logician has a right to make such an assumption in silence. In spite of many speculative difficulties, there is no principle more vital to knowledge, practical and theoretical, than the principle of "negligibility"; the principle which asserts that sequences can be isolated and repeated, and that vast bodies of contemporaneous facts and happenings may be wholly neglected. It is much more important than the principle of causation, if by causation is meant, not a working, though possibly imperfect, regularity, but the speculative completeness implied by the phrase "universal causation" as commonly interpreted.

It may be said, and I think with truth, that these observations scarcely apply to a material world conceived in a purely mechanical fashion. In such a world negligibility is theoretically measurable. The mass of Sirius, without doubt, modifies the weight of the pen with which I am writing. But the effect is demonstrably infinitesimal, and negligibility is not assumed, but proved. Laplace's calculator, surveying the universe, would have no difficulty either in fixing his attention on particular repetitions which exemplify the "laws of nature," or in regarding them as integral parts of a single mechanical whole, whose successive phases (if the law of energy dissipation be universal) can never be repeated.

But this does not lighten the difficulty. The world may, or may not, be a single mechanical system; but, if it is, the fact can only be empirically known to us through induction: and induction assumes negligibility, and cannot, so far as I can see, move a step without it. Choose the most perfect experiment on record, idealise its conditions to your heart's content; for greater security, suppose it repeated even to weariness, how will you be advanced? There are, I suppose, millions of circumstances, for the most part utterly unknown, which have co-existed with all the experiments already tried, but will have vanished before the next experiment is under-taken. Does this disturb you? Do you ask yourself whether, among the unnumbered circumstances in which the world of to-day differs from the world of yesterday, there may not be one which is necessary to the expected effect? Not at all. You brush them aside. You say they may be neglected. And doubtless you do well. But why? Not on any grounds which observation or reasoning can supply, not on any grounds formu-lated in the logic of induction, or the calculus of chances. You trust your-self to a feeling of antecedent probability—the intuitive probability on whose importance I dwelt in the last lecture, which is not the flower of experience but its root—and your trust will sometimes be betrayed.

The principle of negligibility, or (in terms of belief) the belief that observed regularities may often be treated as if they were complete and self-contained cases of cause and effect, separable from contemporary events, is thus a necessary presupposition of concrete science; and, like other presuppositions, it is incapable of scientific proof. We often hear it said, indeed, that principles of this kind should be regarded as hypotheses verified by an ever-increasing volume of experimental proof. They are found to work; what more can be desired?

But it is not accurate to say that these and other fundamental princi-ples are, or ever have been, regarded either by common sense or science as inferences from experience or as hypotheses requiring verification. Nor is it accurate to suggest that verification differs essentially from any other kind of experimental evidence except in the date of its occurrence. If evi-dence follows conjecture, but not otherwise, it is called verification; and though, from the point of view of method, this chronological order is of immense importance, from the point of view of logic it is nothing. A doubtful conjecture (let us suppose) is "verified" by experiment. If the experiment had come earlier there would have been no conjecture, but there would have been equal evidence, indeed the same evidence. It is true that without the conjecture there might have been no experiment, and that without the experiment there might have been no proof. But, though the conjecture occasioned the proof, it certainly adds nothing to its force, and we therefore come back to the question already discussed—namely, whether principles without which no inference from experiences is possible, can be themselves inferred from experiences?—a question to which, as I conceive, only one answer is possible. Experiences may produce habit, and habit may produce expectation, and this process may masquerade as induction. But expectations thus engendered belong to the causal series, not the cognitive. Physiology and psychology may explain them. But they can neither be proved nor treated as axiomatic.

Axiomatic they certainly are not; nor do they possess the universality and precision of outline which we are accustomed to associate with axioms. It is curious, in this connection, to note that the philosophers who are most firmly resolved to root the principle of regularity (they ignore negligibility) in experience always insist on giving it that absolute character which our inferences from experience rarely possess. The notion that fundamental beliefs should be liable to exception, should be capable of degrees, and should apply unequally in different fields of observation, is as abhorrent to them as to any metaphysician out of the opposite camp. One would suppose, to hear them talk, that, unless causation be universal, experience is worthless.

—————————— **Religious and Secular Creeds** ——————————

If faith be provisionally defined as conviction apart from or in excess of proof, then it is upon faith that the maxims of daily life, not less than the loftiest creeds and most far-reaching [scientific] discoveries, must ultimately lean. The ground on which constant habit and inherited dispositions enable us to tread with a step so easy and so assured, is seen on examination to be not less hollow beneath our feet than the dim and unfamiliar regions which lie beyond.[49]

❖ Causation and Foreknowledge

The region where these uncompromising doctrines show to least advantage is human character. I do not propose to discuss causation and free will; but I may with advantage say something on a less hackneyed theme, namely, negligibility and foreknowledge. The thesis I desire to maintain is that, in dealing with a human character, full foreknowledge is theoretically impossible, even though free will be wholly absent, and the succession of psychic states be completely determined. Practically impossible we know it to be. But most determinists would hold that this impossibility is due partly to our ignorance and partly to our incapacity. We know too little either of the general laws of mind, or of individual character, or of surrounding circumstances, to make accurate forecasts; and, even if we possessed the requisite information, we could not use it, owing to the irremediable weakness of our powers of calculation. It is this contention that I wish to traverse. I hold that, had we the supernatural powers of Laplace's calculator, armed with a knowledge of the human heart which supernatural powers of observation could alone supply, we should still fail, because we are face to face with that which is inherently incalculable.

The contrary opinion is due, I think, to an imperfect comprehension of the doctrines I have touched on in this lecture. All human foreknowledge depends on detecting old sequences in a new context. The context, of course, is always new. There is never full or complete repetition. But, unless there be partial repetitions embedded in the universal flux, prescience is impossible. This is the doctrine of "negligibility."

Now consider two illustrative examples.

First, imagine yourself standing on the edge of a valley down which a landslip has just let loose the waters of some great reservoir in the hills. The catastrophe is sudden in its onset, brief in its duration, wildly irregular in its character. Even the most tumultuous cataract retains a certain steadiness of outline: and few, sights are more impressive than the stationary waves in a great rapid. But there is here no trace of order imposed on disorder, fixity on motion. The rushing wall of water, spouting into foam over every obstacle it encounters, the tossing flood that follows furiously behind, seem in their brief violence to present the very ideal of incalculable confusion. But we know it is not so. In the presence of such a spectacle our calculator would not feel a moment's embarrassment. He could forecast without difficulty the whole scene down to its minutest eddy; the motions of each drop obey laws with which he was perfectly familiar; and the total effect, catastrophic though it be, is but the sum of all these component examples of natural uniformity.

Turn now and contemplate a calmer scene. Consider the commonplace life of a commonplace man as it develops in the untroubled prosperity of a steady business and a quiet home. Such a career seems as orderly and uniform as the flood I have been describing is terrible and strange. Surely no supernatural calculator is required to cast the horoscope of its hero: for he does, and leaves undone, the same actions, he thinks and leaves unthought the same ideas, as thousands of his contemporaries; and, so far as outward appearance goes, he is an indistinguishable member of an undistinguished crowd.

Yet, in spite of this, we know him to be unique. There never has been before, nor will there ever be again, another individual exactly like him. A similar statement, it may be urged, can be made about our catastrophic flood. Though this has plenty of parallels, none of them, strictly speaking, are exact. Where, then, lies the distinction on which I am trying to insist? Let me endeavour to mark the contrast.

If the material world be conceived as a mechanical system, the flood in my illustration may be regarded as a piece arbitrarily cut out of it at the whim of the spectator. It possesses no natural unity; and, like the whole of which it is a fraction, the moving particles which compose it do each obey laws which are, (we assume) perfectly well known, and have been endlessly exemplified. Its behaviour is the sum of the behaviour of these several parts; and it is by estimating their movements that our imaginary calculator can prophesy its course with absolute exactness. He is never perplexed by the problem of negligibility; for negligibility in such a case can be accurately measured, and, our calculator possesses all the data required for its measurement. In short, the principle of regularity may here be applied in its most uncompromising form; it requires no qualification, nor can it be pressed too boldly or too far.

But the case is otherwise when we have to abandon the strictly mechanical point of view, and investigate regions where negligibility has a small and uncertain application. Such a region is individual consciousness. This possesses a natural or intrinsic unity. Its phases are never precisely repeated; nor can it be regarded as a collection of independent elements, the sequences of which may be separately examined, verified, and repeated. Not only is the whole unique, but the parts are unique also. Or, perhaps it would be more accurate to say that there are no parts possessing a fixed character of their own apart from the whole. Not only is everything qualified by everything else, but few of these qualifications are negligible. Perfect repetition is therefore impossible, and our calculator, whatever his powers, could never feel at home with his premises, or secure in his conclusions. The present would always be new, and the future would always be doubtful.

If this seems paradoxical it is, I think, mainly for two reasons. In the first place, such a doctrine seems inconsistent with the fact that, whatever Laplace's calculator could do, humbler beings like ourselves manage somehow or other to forecast the behaviour of our neighbours with some small measure of success. This, no doubt, is true. But it is in part because the alternatives of behaviour are very few and very definite compared with the infinitely graduated variations of thought, will, and feeling. Action is "canalised." It can flow only along channels engineered for it by circumstances, and among these the choice is commonly small. But the character which lies behind action is complex beyond all power of analysis, and variable beyond all powers of anticipation. The routine which is unwaveringly pursued from month to month and year to year is pursued each day in a different spirit: and often a critical hour strikes when some well-drilled creature of custom, to his own surprise and the scandal of his friends, deserts the ancient ways and wanders suddenly forth into the unknown.

Of course, these violent aberrations are the exception. The more familiar experience is that, in an orderly society, the alternatives of action which need be taken into account are few, and the "limits of deviation" narrow. Often, therefore, we can anticipate conduct without any real insight into the depths of character or the complexities of motive from which the conduct springs. And truly this is fortunate; for, if mutual comprehension were necessary to social intercourse, how could society exist?

But there is another reason why we take little note of the distinction I am endeavouring to draw between the calculable uniformities of a material world and the incalculable regularities of psychic life. The distinction is rather speculative than practical. It does not affect the routine of daily existence. For, although the course of the material world is calculable, we mortals have neither the time nor the knowledge nor the mental powers required to calculate it. We behave, therefore, towards nature as we behave towards man. We content ourselves with approximations, with analogies, with resemblances. Even if we had the power, we should not have the time to resolve the movement of all the bits of matter with which we have to deal from minute to minute into the exact sequences of which they are composed. We would not if we could. We apply rough methods; we are satisfied with imperfect results. Nor are these results always more imperfect in the psychic than in the material sphere of observation. The ways (for example) of British weather are even more mysterious than the ways of British men. Why, then, should we interest ourselves in a speculation which tells us, however truly, that perfect foreknowledge is theoretically possible in the first case, but theoretically impossible in the second? In practice it is impossible in both. And with this we must be content.

And yet the speculation is interesting. For the distinction between the two cases lies deep. It has nothing (let me say again) to do with free will. It has nothing to do with our ignorance of facts. It has nothing to do with our intellectual insufficiency. It is due to a fundamental difference between the uniformities of matter and the regularities of mind. Perfect foresight requires perfect repetition, and in the psychic sphere perfect repetition can never happen. Every self is unique; all its experiences are unique; and these unique wholes are not compounded of interchangeable elements obeying identical laws. They do not alter by mere addition, subtraction, or rearrangement of parts. They grow. And the sequence of one phase upon another faintly resembles that which would prevail in the universe of which I spoke just now, the universe where all contemporaneous events were treated as the single effect of the immediate past and the single cause of the immediate future. Of such a universe I observed that it would have a history, but could have no science. And though we cannot go so far when speaking of psychic unities, though we cannot rule out psychology or sociology, it must be admitted that no regularities which observation discloses can ever possess the precision which we theoretically attribute to material mechanism. Instructive likenesses we shall find in abundance, complete determination we may assume if we please; but "laws," in the full and strict sense of the term, we shall not find, for they are not there.[50]

——————— God and the Uniformity of Nature ———————

The uniformity of Nature, as I have before explained, cannot be proved by experience, for it is what makes proof from experience possible. We must bring it, or something like it, to the facts in order to infer anything from them at all. . . . In the same way, I do not contend that, if we start from Nature without God, we shall be logically driven to believe in Him by a mere consideration of the examples of adaptation which Nature undoubtedly contains. It is enough that when we bring this belief with us to the study of phenomena, we can say of it, what we have just said of the principle of uniformity, namely, that "broadly speaking and in the rough," the facts harmonise with it, and that it gives a unity and a coherence to our apprehension of the natural world which it would not otherwise possess.[51]

THE RETURN OF ARTHUR.

CHAPTER

9

Tendencies of Scientific Belief

Many of those who look at these problems from (what they deem to be) a strictly scientific point of view are not likely to be more favourable. Their loyalty to experience takes the form of supposing that men accumulate knowledge by peering about for "sequences" among "phenomena," as a child looks for shells upon the beach—equally ready to go north or south, east or west, as the humour of the moment moves him. . . . Science, they think, should have no partialities . . . Scientific practice, however, has been otherwise.

MR. BALFOUR ON GUIDING BELIEFS
Favouritism in Science
The Vital Impulse of Progress
(From Our Special Correspondent)
GLASGOW, FEB. 4

Mr. Balfour devoted his ninth Gifford lecture to-day to showing that, in addition to such fundamental and inevitable postulates as the belief in an external world and the belief in the regularity of the universe, there are also tendencies, inclinations to believe, probabilities in his special sense of the word, which guide the course of human speculation. He said that the full importance of these inclinations and probabilities can be discovered only when we look back upon the history of thought; but he insisted that there are such tendencies, and that they have had, and are having, a most important effect on the structure of our beliefs. The fact was generally admitted with regard to primitive beliefs and superstitions, but it was apt to be denied with regard to modern thought. It was one of his quarrels with Positivism that the Positivists argue that the fabric of scien-

tific knowledge has been arrived at by different methods from all that was done in the earlier intellectual history of mankind.

Mr. Balfour then proceeded to show that the idea that mankind has accumulated its scientific knowledge as a child picks up shells by the sea-shore, moved only by the whim of the moment and without guiding influences or inclinations, is inconsistent with the history of scientific investigation. He selected two examples of scientific doctrine to illustrate the fallacy of the notion that there is no favouritism in science, no inclination towards one kind of thing rather than another.

Atomism

The first of these illustrations was atomism—the theory which ascribes all the variety and splendour and interest of the material world to the movements and relative positions of the very small particles of which the world consists. That theory may be found in early Oriental speculations; it was the theory of Democritus; it ran through the whole of antiquity; and though it was thrown into the shade in the Middle Ages, it burst out again at the revival of learning, and was the theory of Bacon and Gassendi and Hobbes and Boyle and Newton and Leibnitz, all of whom were in their respective fashions the heirs of Democritus. Modern physical science is atomic through and through, and modern theories of matter, of electricity, and of heat are base upon atomism.

When Tyndall, at the Belfast meeting of the British Association, gave his presidential address on the history of atomism, neither the lecturer nor his critics seemed to have thought of asking how it came about that through all these centuries this theory, which had originally no experimental or mathematical or scientific basis, came to prevail and never lost its hold, and how it turns out to be true with a degree of accuracy truly astonishing. Mr. Balfour found the answer to this question in the fact that belief had run before the evidence, and that the evidence had justified the belief.

Theories of Conservation

The second illustration was the group of theories concerned with conservation, which, he said, showed a fixed resolve on the part of scientific inquirers to find conservation wherever they can. He pointed out that matter, mass, weight, motion, force, heat, and energy have all been regarded as unchangeable in quantity, conserved among all vicissitudes, unalterable in amount. He dealt with each of these in turn, and pointed out how the idea of conservation had been wrongly applied or had been applied in the wrong form, and yet scientific investigators, after the discovery of each error, pursued their search for conservation until they were rightly happy when the desire for conservation had found its legitimate exemplar.

The discussion of changes in the idea of conservation of energy led Mr. Balfour to an interesting speculation. He had, he said, often amused himself by wondering what would have happened if, in the early forties of the 19th century, the idea of conservation of energy had been a theological dogma. He said that it might easily have been so, for

James Prescott Joule, who discovered the conservation of energy in its modern form, distinctly asserted that he believed in it because he thought it the method by which God had made the world. In an amusing passage Mr. Balfour described an imaginary Positivist criticism upon this medieval theological theory, and he represented the critic as insisting upon the fact that Joule's results attained by modern methods did not bear out his *á priori* view that the grand agencies of nature are by the Creator's fiat indestructible. Joule's results in point of fact did vary enormously, and his critic would accuse him of the fallacy of assuming his conclusion and saying that the variations in his results were errors of observation. Subsequent experiments have shown that the variations were errors of observation, but Joule started with the clear belief that he was to find his rule, and this belief kept him right about the errors in his observations.

Mr. Balfour, having illustrated these scientific tendencies to believe certain things, went on to argue that such inclinations cannot be regarded as happy accidents. He could not himself describe them by the word luck; he thought the word inspiration more to the purpose. They were, he said in conclusion, very much what M. Bergson has called vital impulse in the organic world. These tendencies of scientific belief press on definitely in one direction. They are defeated in one line of advance and victorious in another, but they always move onwards, and with them develops all that is valuable in our thought, alike about the material world and, as he himself believed, about religious themes. They have been and they are rich in fruit for human progress and for human knowledge. Experiment and observation are guided by these tendencies and inclinations.

—*The Times*, Thu., Feb. 5, 1914, 6e.

Mr. Balfour will conclude his first course of Gifford Lectures in Glasgow on February 6, and will come to London for the meeting of Parliament.

—*The Times*, Sat. Jan. 30, 1914, 9a.

❖ Beliefs that We Are Inclined to Hold

In the sixth and eighth lectures of this course I dealt with two inevitable beliefs which lie at the root of all science and all practice—the beliefs that an independent, or, as it is commonly called, an "external" world exists, and the belief that the world, whether external or internal, has at least a measure of regularity. In the seventh lecture I interpolated a discussion upon probability; and showed, or attempted to show, that we must take account of a kind of probability other than that which, in the hands of mathematicians, has so greatly contributed to knowledge.

If, now, we consider these subjects in their mutual relation, we perceive that an "inevitable" belief is one which possesses the highest degree, of this intuitive probability. These are two descriptions of the same quality—one emphasising the objective, the other the subjective, aspects of a single fact.

But this at once suggests a further inquiry. Probability is evidently a matter of degree. A belief may be more probable or less probable. Inevitableness, on the other hand, seems at first sight to be insusceptible of gradation. It is, or it is not. Yet this extreme definiteness vanishes if we regard it as a limiting case—as the last term of a series whose earlier members represent varying degrees of plausibility. On this view we should regard our beliefs about the universe as moulded by formative forces, which vary from irresistible coercion to faint and doubtful inclination. Beliefs in the reality of the external world and in its regularity are important products of the first. I now propose to call attention to some beliefs which are due to the less obvious action of the second. Both kinds, whether capable of proof or not, are more or less independent of it. Both are to be regarded rather as the results of tendencies than as the conclusions of logic.

I am well aware that a doctrine like this will find few admirers among systematic thinkers. Inevitable beliefs which are fundamental without being axiomatic; which lack definiteness and precision; which do not seem equally applicable to every field of experience; which do not claim to be of the essence of our understanding, like the categories of the critical philosophy, or the so-called laws of thought, have little to recommend them to philosophers. And when inevitableness is treated as merely an extreme form of plausibility, when guidance is discovered in tendencies which are weak and of uncertain application, leading to error as well as to truth, their objections will scarcely be mitigated.

Many of those who look at these problems from (what they deem to be) a strictly scientific point of view are not likely to be more favourable.

Their loyalty to experience takes the form of supposing that men accumulate knowledge by peering about for "sequences" among "phenomena," as a child looks for shells upon the beach—equally ready to go north or south, east or west, as the humour of the moment moves him. They would regard any antecedent preference for this or that sort of explanation as a sin against the categorical imperatives of intellectual morals. Science, they think, should have no partialities: and as the honest investigator "entertains no belief with a conviction the least in excess of the evidence,"[52] so he will resist any leaning toward one kind of conclusion rather than another. Such is their view of scientific duty. Scientific practice, however, has been otherwise.

That the practice of ordinary humanity has been otherwise seems indeed sufficiently plain. The folklore, the magic, and the religions of primitive races, with all their unborrowed resemblances, are there to attest it. But these (you will say) are superstitions. The objection is not, I think, relevant; yet, for the sake of peace, let us pass to what is not regarded as a superstition, namely, morality. Here you have the singular spectacle of a close agreement among moralists as to the contents of the moral law, and a profound disagreement as to the grounds on which the moral law is to be accepted. Can the power of "tendency" be better shown? Can there be a clearer illustration of the way in which it may guide belief and anticipate proof?

─────────── **Nature Under Cross-examination** ───────────

The common notion that he who would search out the secrets of Nature must humbly wait on experience, obedient to its slightest hint, is but partly true. This may be his ordinary attitude: but now and again it happens that observation and experiment are not treated as guides to be meekly followed, but as witnesses to be broken down in cross-examination. Their plain message is disbelieved, and the investigating judge does not pause until a confession in harmony with his preconceived ideas has, if possible, been wrung from their reluctant evidence.[53]

❖ Atomism. Beliefs of Conservation

But our business to-day is neither with magic nor morality. It is with physical science. When we survey man's strivings to understand the world in which he lives, can we detect any secular leanings toward certain types of belief, any deep-lying inclination to guess by preference in one direction rather than another? We surely can. There are some answers, for example, which we refuse to take from experiment and observation. I have already referred to one such case in connection with causation. No man of science can be provoked, by any seeming irregularities, into supposing that the course of nature is subject to lapses from the rule of perfect uniformity. Consider, again, another case, where the tendency is far less strong, but where few can doubt that it is real. I refer to the deep-seated reluctance felt by most physicists to accept as final any scientific explanation which involves a belief in "action at a distance"—a reluctance which is the more remarkable since action at a distance seems a familiar fact of experience, while action by contact, when you attempt to work it out in detail, seems hard to comprehend.

But there are tendencies feebler and less general than these which give much food for reflection. Consider for example, the familiar history of atomism. At least as far back as Democritus we find the confident assertion that the world consists of atoms, and that its infinite variety is due to the motions and positions of immutable and imperceptible units, which, if they are not exactly alike, at least differ less among themselves than do the visible objects into which they are compounded. Through successive centuries this theory never died. With the revival of learning and the beginning of modem science it burst into fresh life. It was believed in firmly by Bacon, the prophet of the new era. It was treated as almost self-evident by philosophers like Gassendi and Hobbes. Boyle held it in its most uncompromising form. Newton assumed it without question. After a period of varying fortunes in the eighteenth century, a modification of it in the hands of Dalton started a new era in chemistry.[54] Taken over by the physicists, it now lies at the root of the modem theory of gases and liquids; the modern theory of matter, the modern theory of heat, and the modern theory of electricity.

This is a very strange story; and it is not really made less strange by those who emphasise the differences between the atoms of Democritus, which are the theme of its first chapter, and the electrons of Sir Joseph Thomson, which appear in its last. Different indeed they are; but, though the difference be great, the agreement is fundamental.

There are some who think that the achievement sung by Lucretius is lessened by showing that the ancients who believed in atoms had no experimental warrant for their convictions. And this is perfectly true. They had not. Nor had Bacon, nor Gassendi, nor Hobbes, nor Boyle, nor Newton. But this only brings into clearer relief the point I desire to emphasise. If experience did not establish the belief, whence came it? If it represents nothing better than an individual guess, why did it appeal so persistently to leaders of scientific thought, and by what strange hazard does it turn out to be true? It is certainly curious that Tyndall, in a once famous address to the British Association at Belfast, should have sketched the story from Democritus to Lucretius, and from Lucretius to

1874, without ever putting these questions to his audience, or, so far as I know, to himself.

But the Atomic Theory is by no means the only example of tendencies which have played an important part in the evolution of science. There are other beliefs, or kinds of beliefs, of the most far-reaching importance which have almost exactly similar characteristics. They anticipate evidence, they guide research, and in some shape or other they turn out to be true.

Consider, for example, the group of beliefs which may be described generally as beliefs in persistence, or beliefs in conservation—the kind of belief which has been applied at different periods, and by different schools of scientific thought, to matter, mass, bulk, weight, motion, force, heat, and energy. As every one knows, these ascriptions have not always been correct. But this only emphasises the strength of the tendency. Weight was at one time supposed to be invariable. We know now that the weight of a body varies with its position relatively to other bodies. It is different, for example, at the poles from what it is at the Equator. But how was the error discovered? Not by experiment. There were experiments, no doubt. But those who undertook them already believed in the law of gravitation; and the law of gravitation made it necessary to distinguish the mass of any given fragment of matter both from its weight and from the occult quality of gravity, which is one of the factors on which its weight in any given situation depends. The desire for conservation was not, however, defeated; since physicists, till within the last few years, regarded both mass and gravity as unalterable characteristics of all material bodies.

Again, consider the case of heat. This also has been regarded by powerful schools of scientific thought as a substance that was "conserved." It is so regarded no longer. But is the inclination to believe in conservation thereby defeated? Not at all. Though heat may vanish, energy remains, and heat is a form of energy.

This doctrine of the conservation of energy is indeed the crowning triumph of the tendency I am discussing, and provides the best illustrations of its strength. For natural philosophers, intent on finding conservation wherever they could, started too boldly on their quest. Descartes regarded the conservation of motion as a self-evident inference from the rationality of God. It is true that he neither had experimental evidence of his doctrine, nor could he, under any circumstances, have obtained it; for the energy of motion, as he incorrectly described it, is not conserved. Leibnitz described it correctly, and had as great a confidence as his predecessor in its conservation, and as little proof to support him. So confident indeed was he, and so independent of experimental evidence was his faith, that he dogmatically asserted that, when motion seemed to disappear, what was lost by the bodies which we see, was exactly taken up by their component elements which we do not see; so that nothing in the nature of what he called *vis viva* was either lost or created. That this transformation of energy from molar to molecular motion is constantly occurring we now have sufficient proof. But Leibnitz had no proof; and apparently thought none was required other than the Cartesian deduction from the rationality of God. He made a bold anticipation of experience, with nothing to support him but *a priori* inclination.

His anticipation, however, was not only bold; it was fortunate. Kinetic energy may really be transformed from molar to molecular motion, and suffer no variation. It is conserved. On the other hand, it may not. It may altogether cease, and what becomes of conservation then?

The scientific formula which satisfies both the facts of the case and our desire for conservation is well known.[55] Energy, we are taught, is of two kinds. Kinetic and potential energy—energy in act and energy in possibility. Each may turn into the other, and is continually so turning. Each, therefore, may vary in quantity, and does vary in quantity. It is only their sum which is indestructible. Few scientific generalisations have been more fruitful; few have been accepted on more slender evidence; none are more certain; none more clearly illustrate our natural appetite for beliefs of conservation. For, indeed, to the over-critical this sort of conservation must needs leave something to be desired. When we assert the indestructibility of matter we mean that a real entity continues through time unchanged in quantity. But the word has a less obvious meaning when it is applied to energy. The propriety of describing motion as energy seems indeed clear enough; and if all energy were energy of motion, and if energy of motion were always conserved, the conservation of energy would be on all fours with the conservation of matter. But this is not the case. In spite of Leibnitz, the amount of *vis viva* is not indestructible. What, then, happens when some of it is destroyed? In that case, says science, energy changes its form but not its quantity. Energy of motion becomes energy of position. What was kinetic becomes potential; and, as the transformation is effected without loss, the principle of conservation is saved.

When, however, energy thus becomes potential, in what sense does it still exist, and why do we still call it energy? Energy suggests "doings" and "happenings." In the case of "potential" energy there are no "doings" and no "happenings." It is "stored"; and stored it may for ever remain, hibernating (as it were) to all eternity, neither changing nor causing change.

I do not quarrel with this; but I ask myself why "energy" should be treated more leniently than "force." Though force is now known not to be "conserved," ordinary thought attributes to it a certain continuity of existence even when it does not show itself in motion. Force may be exerted though nothing moves; as, for example, by a book pressing on a table. But this view is profoundly unsatisfactory to many scientific thinkers. For them force is nothing apart from "acceleration"; it does not represent a cause, it only measures an effect. And if in our ordinary moments we think otherwise, this (they think) is simply because we illegitimately attribute to matter something which corresponds to muscular effort in man.

It is not, perhaps, so easy as these critics suppose to extrude from scientific thought (I say nothing of scientific language) this notion of latent force—force which would produce movement if it could; and is actively, though imperceptibly, striving to show itself in motion. But why should they try? They welcome potential energy—why should they anathematise latent force?

I think the answer is to be found in the fact that, whether force has, or has not, any being apart from acceleration, it is certainly not conserved; while, if energy be as real when it is potential as when it is kinetic, it certainly is conserved. A lapse into anthropomorphism, therefore, is without excuse in the first case, while a lapse into metaphysics is justified in the second. Any heresy may be forgiven, and any evidence is worth respectful attention when conservation is the thing to be proved.

I have sometimes amused myself by wondering what would have happened about the year 1842 if the conservation of energy had been a theological dogma instead of a scientific guess. Descartes, as I mentioned just now, inferred the conservation of motion from the attributes of God. Colding and Joule used the same argument in favour of the conservation of energy. Now, if a belief in the conservation of energy had been an integral part of religious orthodoxy in the early forties of the last century surely some positivist philosopher would have used Joule's first investigation on Work and Heat to upset the very dogma they were intended to establish. "Here" (he would have said) "you have a believer in these meta-physico-theological methods of discovering the laws of nature; and mark what happens. In true medieval fashion he begins with some fanciful deductions from the way in which he thinks God must have made the world. Fortunately, however, though his principles are medieval, his methods are modern. Not only is he a most brilliant experimenter, but he has the courage to put his own speculations to an experimental test. He takes the minutest precautions, he chooses the most favourable conditions, and what happens? Does he prove his case? Do his results square with his theories? Does he find a fixed relation between work and heat? Does he justify his views of God? Not at all. Between his lowest determination of the mechanical equivalent of heat, and his highest, there is an immense and lamentable gap. What does he do? He takes their mean value:—a very proper method if he knew there was a mechanical equivalent of heat; a very improper method if the reality of such an equivalent was the thing to be proved. Clearly, if he had not put his theological opinions into his scientific premises when he began his experiment, he never would have got them out again as scientific conclusions when he had reached its end."

For my own part, I think this imaginary critic would, at that date, have had something to say for himself—supposing always we are prepared to accept his presuppositions about scientific method. If sound reason and intellectual integrity require us to follow the lead of observation and experiment with no antecedent preference for one class of conclusions rather than another, then no doubt Joule and a long line of distinguished predecessors were the spoilt children of fortune. They made their discoveries in advance of their evidence, and in spite of their methods. If they turned out to be right, or, at least, on the right road, what can we do but criticise their credulity and wonder at their luck? Unless, indeed, their luck be a form of inspiration.

Before leaving beliefs of conservation, I must say one more word about the most famous of them all—the belief in the conservation of matter. This was an important article in the scientific creed of the early atomists, who had no better evidence for it than they had for the Atomic Theory itself. The material "substance" of the medieval Aristotelians was, I imagine, also conserved; though as all that could be known about it were its qualities, and as these were not necessarily conserved, the doctrine in practice did not, perhaps, amount to much. Then came the theory which, chiefly in the hands of Boyle[56] at the end of the seventeenth century, initiated modern chemistry. What was conserved, according to this view, was not a metaphysical substance with detachable qualities, but elementary kinds of matter with inseparable qualities; and out of these qualified entities was compounded the whole material universe. I may incidentally observe that a company promoter who should issue a prospectus based on no better evidence than Boyle could advance for this tremendous theory would certainly be in peril of the law. Yet Boyle was right: and, notwithstanding subsequent developments, his conjecture remains the cornerstone of modern chemical research.

Now, what is it that we intend to assert when we say that matter is conserved, or is indestructible? We certainly do not mean that its qualities never suffer change: for most of those which are obvious and striking are always liable to change. If you sufficiently vary temperature or pressure; if you effect chemical composition or decomposition, the old characteristics will vanish and new characteristics will take their place. What, then, is conserved?

In the first place, the lost qualities can (in theory) always be restored, though not always without the expenditure of energy. Water never ceases to be convertible into steam, nor steam into water. The characteristics may vanish, but in appropriate conditions they will always reappear.

Now science, as we have just seen, is tolerant of this notion of latency or potentiality, and is ready enough to use it in aid of beliefs in conservation. It was so used in connection with heat when heat was regarded as a material substance. It is still so used in connection with energy, which is sometimes described as an immaterial substance. But (as I have already noted) it has never been so used in connection with matter. The reason, I suppose, is that the conservation of matter is much more a belief of common sense than the conservation of energy. Energy is a conception which has but recently been disengaged from other conceptions, like force and momentum, and has but recently been associated with heat, with chemical reactions, with changes of physical phase, and with electromagnetic phenomena. It is, therefore, a remote and somewhat abstract product of scientific reflection; and science may do what it will with its own.

The notion of matter, on the other hand, is the common possession of mankind. Whatever difficulties it may present to reflective analysis, it presents none to our work-a-day beliefs. We are quite ready to regard it as indestructible; but we are not ready to combine this conviction with the view that it possesses no single characteristic which may not be temporarily etherealised into a "potentiality." On such terms the eternal and unchanging identity of this or that parcel of matter would seem a difficult and elusive doctrine, inappropriate to the familiar and substantial world in which we suppose ourselves to live. A belief in the conservation of matter has therefore always, or almost always, carried with it a belief in the unchanging continuity of at least some material qualities; though as to what these qualities are there has been much dispute. Descartes, though not consistent, found unchanging continuity in the attribute of size; so also did Hobbes. I presume that the older atomists, who explained the appearances of matter by the shape of its constituent atoms, would have regarded both atomic form and atomic magnitude as persistent. But it was the assumption that the same piece of ponderable matter always possessed the same gravitating power, and that the same gravitating power was always associated with the same mass, which, in the hands of Lavoisier, made so great a revolution in eighteenth-century chemistry. Matter might change its size, its shape, its colour, its phase, its power of acting and reacting; but its mass and the quality which caused its weight it could not change; these characteristics were always associated with each other, and were never in abeyance.

To Lavoisier this double principle seemed self-evident. It was not a hypothesis that required testing, but a touchstone by which other hypotheses might safely be tested. If, in the course of some chemical operation, weight increased, then no further proof was required to show that mass had increased also, and that matter had been added. If, on the other hand, weight diminished, then no further proof was required to show that mass had diminished also, and that matter had been subtracted. Whatever other qualities matter might gain or lose, mass and gravity were indestructible and unchanging.

Men of science seemed, on the whole, content silently to assume these principles of conservation without inconveniently raising the question of evidence. Philosophers have not always been so cautious. Kant supposed himself to have demonstrated them *a priori*. Schopenhauer followed suit. Spencer declared their contraries to be inconceivable. Mill said they were proved by experience. In short, all these eminent thinkers vied with each other in conferring upon this doctrine the highest honours permitted by their respective philosophies. But apparently they were hasty. Recent discoveries have changed our point of view. Mass (it seems) is no longer to be regarded as unchanging. When bodies move at speeds approaching the velocity of light their mass rapidly increases; so that this quality, which is peculiarly characteristic of matter, must be removed from the category of those which persist unchanged, and placed in the category of those which change but can always be restored. Are we so to class gravitation? Would the weight of a body moving nearly at the speed of light increase as, in like circumstances, its inertia increases? If the answer is "no," then the link is broken which has for long been thought to connect gravity and mass. If the answer is "yes," then what Kant regarded as certain *a priori* is false; what Spencer regarded as "inconceivable" is true; another carrier of "persistence" is lost, and some fresh characteristic must be found which will remain unchanged through all time, and under all conditions.

If this characteristic should turn out to be electric charge, what a curious light it will throw upon our tendency to "beliefs of conservation"! After long seeking for some indestructible attribute of matter; after taking up and rejecting size, shape, weight, mass, and (perhaps) impenetrability, we shall at last find the object of our quest in a conception which has (I suppose) been clearly realised only within the last hundred years, about which our senses tell us nothing, and of which the general run of educated mankind are still completely ignorant![57]

─────── **Truth Because of Error and Illusion** ───────

Yet an even stronger statement would seem to be justified. We must not only say that the experiences on which science is founded have been invariably misinterpreted by those who underwent them, but that, if they had not been so misinterpreted, science as we know it would never have existed. We have not merely stumbled on the truth in spite of error and illusion, which is odd, but because of error and illusion, which is odder.[58]

❖ Epilogue

It is possible, but not, I hope, probable, that some hasty reader may suppose that in this and the preceding lectures I am recommending a new method or instrument of discovery. "If you want to reach truth, follow your unreasoned inclination," may be his summary of my doctrine: brief—but also unjust.

Of the manner in which discoveries are going to be made I say nothing, for I know nothing. I am dealing with the past: and in the historic movements of scientific thought I see, or think I see, drifts and currents such as astronomers detect among the stars of heaven. And, as the law of gravitation will hardly (I suppose) explain the last, so observation, experiment, and reasoning will hardly explain the first. They belong to the causal, not to the cognitive, series; and the beliefs in which they issue are effects rather than conclusions.

Those who feel little sympathy for such a view may be inclined to regard the relatively faint inclinations dealt with in this lecture as ordinary scientific hypotheses confirmed by ordinary scientific methods. This view, as I have already observed, is not applicable to the inevitable beliefs dealt with in earlier lectures. Whatever philosophers may say after the event, the conviction that we live in an external world of things and persons, where events are more or less regularly repeated, has never been treated as a speculative conjecture about which doubt was a duty till truth was proved. Beliefs like these are not scientific hypotheses, but scientific presuppositions, and all criticism of their validity is a speculative afterthought. The same may be said, though with less emphasis and some qualification, about beliefs fostered by the intellectual tendencies considered in this chapter. These, as we have seen, are many. They are often inconsistent; they are never inevitable; and they perpetually change their form under the pressure of scientific discovery. Atomism in one shape follows atomism in another; doctrines of conservation rise, fall, and rise again; incredulity about "action at a distance" breeds explanations whose failure (in the case of gravity) leaves the hope of final success untouched.

Now, it would be an error to say that science does not, when it can, apply to these various theories its ordinary methods of verification. They are in a different position from inevitable beliefs, which can hardly be verified because the process of verification assumes them. Yet they must not be confounded with ordinary scientific hypotheses, for they are something more and something different. Like these, they are guesses, but they are guesses directed, not by the immediate suggestion of particular experiences (which indeed they sometimes contradict), but by general tendencies which are enduring though sometimes feeble. Those who make them do not attempt the interrogation of Nature wholly free from certain forms of bias. In cross-examining that most stubborn and recalcitrant of witnesses they never hesitate to ply her with leading questions; and, whether this procedure be logically defensible or not, no lover of truth need regret its results.

Readers of M. Bergson's *Creative Evolution* may remember the picture he draws of the *élan vital*—the principle of life—forcing its way along different paths of organic evolution, some without issue or promise of progress; others leading on through regions hitherto untraversed to ends remote and unforeseen. The secular movements of science, as I conceive them, somewhat resemble this process, even though it be faintly and at a distance. There is in both a striving towards some imperfectly foreshadowed end; and in both the advance is irregular, tentative, precarious, with many changes of direction, and some reversals. Yet I would not press the parallel over-far or plunge too deeply into metaphor. It is enough to say that as, according to M. Bergson, the course followed by organic evolution cannot be wholly due to Selection, so the course followed by scientific discovery, as I read its history, cannot be wholly due to reasoning and experience. In both cases we seem forced to assume something in the nature of a directing influence, and (as I should add, though perhaps M. Bergson would not) of supramundane design. And if "a Power that makes for truth" be required to justify our scientific faith, we must surely count ourselves as theists.[59]

Doubtless if empiricism be shattered, it must drag down naturalism in its fall; for, after all, naturalism is nothing more than the assertion that empirical methods are valid, and that no others are so. But because any effectual criticism of empiricism is the destruction of naturalism, is it therefore the destruction of science also? Surely not. The adherent of naturalism is an empiricist from necessity; the man of science, if he be an empiricist, is so only from choice. The latter may, if he please, have no philosophy at all, or he may have a different one. He is not obliged, any more than other men, to justify his conclusions by an appeal to first-principles, still less is he obliged to take his first principles from so poor a creed as the one we have been discussing. Science preceded the theory of science, and is independent of it. Science preceded naturalism, and will survive it.[60]

CHAPTER
10
Summary and Conclusion

My desire has been to show that all we think best in human culture, whether associated with beauty, goodness, or knowledge, requires God for its support, that Humanism without Theism loses more than half its value.

MR. BALFOUR ON THEISM
A Summary of the Lectures and an Appeal
Beliefs as Natural Products

(From Our Special Correspondent)

GLASGOW, FEB. 6

Mr. Balfour has held his great audience together to the end. In replying to some well-chosen words in which Professor Smart conveyed to him the thanks of his listeners, the Gifford Lecturer spoke gratefully of a sympathy the existence of which he had felt from the first lecture to the last, and he added that he did not believe that in any other country such an audience would have assembled on ten occasions to hear the discussion of metaphysical topics. The large gathering in Bute Hall responded as it has never failed to do, and went home happy with a good conscience and the pleasant memory of the successful efforts of a great Scotsman to tell his fellow-countrymen his thoughts on these high themes.

To-day's lecture was partly a summary and partly an appeal to the audience. Mr. Balfour began by saying that his object had been to show that the values of our beliefs are dependent upon a Theistic setting. Beliefs, he insisted, could be and must be considered as natural products, and their values as natural products must depend on their origin. We

must find in their pedigree some source higher than our poor efforts at reason, not a source lower and more contemptible. It was no answer to say that certain fundamental truths make the world, and the world is what it is because of fundamental truths, for he had shown that among the unproved and unprovable assumptions which are required to justify common sense and scientific knowledge, there are assumptions neither necessary nor universal nor inevitable, yet assumed through the whole course of knowledge. He had also shown that there are probabilities, tendencies to believe, organizing inclinations, which can be seen in the history of science.

Natural Selection and Religion

Having thus dealt with a possible objection from the point of view of critical idealism, Mr. Balfour summarized his argument that natural selection is incapable of accounting directly for any of the great values he had dealt with. He was aware of the controversies raging among biologists about natural selection; but he had chosen it because it is the only substitute that we know of for what is commonly called design. Selection does imitate design up to a certain point, but even if it could, as it certainly cannot, be proved that the higher values of aesthetics, of ethics, and of thought have a survival value, it would not help us to maintain these values. But in fact the higher a value the further it is removed from the primitive consequences for which selection is responsible.

His own argument about the necessity of a Theistic setting for our beliefs was not attached to any great metaphysical system of thought, nor to any intuitive sense of religious values. He did not under-estimate the direct argument from religious beliefs which rests religious value on religion itself. But religious values were for him the conclusion, not the premises, of his arguments, and he could only rest the value of religion upon other values which are universally acknowledged. He did not appeal to those who are satisfied with any of the great constructive metaphysical systems, but he urged the necessity for a philosophy of science and of common sense. He did so, not in the interests of science or of common sense, but in the interests of philosophy itself.

The Gifford Lecturer's Public

With this hint to philosophical experts, Mr. Balfour proceeded to ask himself to whom his argument was addressed. He thought that a Gifford lecturer should speak to the general public; but to what public?

Fortunately, he remarked, there are many to whom God is as immediate and as certain as anything of which they have immediate experience—to whom the existence of God is a daily and hourly certainty. They were above his argument and to them it would [be] superfluous. There are others immersed in the daily task, in which the toil that cannot be put off, who have no interest in speculative questions, and who are satisfied to acquiesce in the common beliefs of science and in the religious beliefs of those among whom they live. On them depends the work of the world, and he did not think it was every man's duty to acquaint himself with all the arguments on all important issues. "God," he said, "has not made the world that its ordinary business is to be carried on by dialectic."

Turning to the classes of men who are interested in such inquiries, Mr. Balfour contrasted the shallow and infinitely tiresome skeptics who base an intellectual reputation upon a few materialistic tags with the great doubters from whose ranks have come pillars of orthodoxy, leaders of heresies, framers of systems of speculation, makers of new modes of thought and of new pictures of the universe. Between these two extremes there are many educated persons greatly perplexed about the problems which science, philosophy, and criticism were forcing upon them. Such thinkers would agree with him that a world without God is a world in which aesthetic and ethical values are greatly diminished, but they might argue that their intellectual integrity required them to make the sacrifice. He hoped that his line of argument might suggest to these men some valuable forms of consolation. Their attitude was honourable, but it was mistaken, for it was based upon an entirely false contrast between intellectual and other values. Let them not be misled by the pernicious fallacy that speculative difficulties only begin when we go into super-sensible regions under the guidance of hair-splitting metaphysicians. The real speculative difficulties touch our daily life, the very nature of the things on which our daily life depends. Let them remember, too, that the Theistic setting is not required merely for the values of religion and morality; it is an essential condition of all intellectual values, including those of the belief of science.

Belief in God

The real moral of his lectures is, he concluded, that a belief in Theism is not an accidental ornament which can be added or not added to the house where you live. It cannot be superadded or not superadded to other beliefs, those other beliefs remaining unaffected and unchanged. **A Theistic belief is essential on whatever values we cast our eyes; and for the retention of these values alike in beauty, in morality, and in science there is, if we want to retain these values undiminished, but one setting. That setting is a belief in God.**

Mr. Balfour's second series of Gifford lectures will probably be delivered in January 1915.

—*The Times*, Sat. Feb. 7, 1914, 4a.

❖ Humanism and Theism

Now that we have reached our closing lecture, those who have followed the course from the beginning may, on looking back, find themselves somewhat bewildered by the variety of subjects which I have asked them to consider. Art, History, Morals, the Theory of Probability, the Logic of Perception, the presuppositions of Science, have all been touched on. Themes that might fill volumes—nay, that have filled volumes—are made the text for an hour's discourse. Introduced one after the other with breathless rapidity, each for a moment has been shown under the lime-light, and then hurried off the stage to make room for its successor. It seems hard to believe that with such diversity of materials there can be continuity of argument. But the critic who would judge the matter fairly must bear in mind the title of the course, and the purpose for which it has been delivered. **My desire has been to show that all we think best in human culture, whether associated with beauty, goodness, or knowledge, requires God for its support, that Humanism without Theism loses more than half its value.** Though, therefore, the subjects discussed are embarrassing in their variety, no diminution of their number seems possible. The argument would have broken down had I confined myself to a narrower scope—had I, for example, been content to show the importance of Theism for morality, leaving untouched its importance for science and aesthetic. Such a limitation would have shattered the whole design. No doubt there are precedents for such a procedure. Kant, for instance, kept God out of the critique which dealt with ordinary knowledge, while giving Him a place of honour in the critique which dealt with the moral law. But the procedure has always seemed to me singularly artificial, even in a philosophy which is artificial through and through. In any case, such a limitation is quite inconsistent with the scheme of these lectures. This could not be accomplished by setting up a departmental Deity—even were his department the whole province of ethics. Right conduct is much, but it is not all. We not only act, but we know, and we admire; nor could I be quite content with any form of Theism which did not sustain in every essential part the full circle of human interests.

❖ The Doctrine of Congruity

But when all explanations have been given, and all excuses made, I am well aware that in the actual presentation of my case I have introduced so much illustrative material, and of this material so much is disputable, that some of my hearers may feel themselves distracted rather than enlightened by the number of seemingly subsidiary points of which they are asked to take account. I trust such persons are in a minority; and that, on the whole, my main contention will seem enriched and strengthened, not embarrassed or confused, by the manner of its exposition. Nevertheless, it may not be amiss, before I bring the course to an end, to restate the most important points in the general case I have endeavoured to present.

The root principle which, by its constant recurrence in slightly different forms, binds together, like an operatic *leit-motif,* the most diverse material, is that if we would maintain the value of our highest beliefs and emotions, we must find for them a congruous origin. Beauty must be more than an accident. The source of morality must be moral. The source of knowledge must be rational. If this be granted, you rule out Mechanism, you rule out Naturalism, you rule out Agnosticism; and a lofty form of Theism becomes, as I think, inevitable.

It is, I imagine, the application of this method to knowledge which will be most generally resented by those who refuse to acknowledge its validity. In the case of beauty, for example, the point will seem of small importance to those for whom art means little. It may not greatly impress many of those for whom art means much. For it proclaims no new canons of taste. It belittles no aesthetic school. It asks no critic to revise his judgments. It touches the interests neither of artist nor author. It may well be ignored.

With ethics the case is somewhat different. There are, no doubt, sceptics in religion who treat scepticism as a luxury which can be safely enjoyed only by the few. Religion they think good for morals; morals they think good for society; society they think good for themselves. Such persons may well treat the opinions expressed in the lecture on ethics with benevolent disagreement. But there are more robust thinkers who will not be so lenient. They will reject as intolerable the idea that the morality they desire to preserve depends on a religion they desire to destroy; and any doctrine which, like the present, binds the two more closely together will encounter their uncompromising hostility.

Nevertheless, it is the lectures dealing with intellectual values that will rouse, as I suppose, the most serious opposition. The endeavour to treat our beliefs about the world and, our beliefs about God as interdependent will seem to many extravagant, even unnatural. It will be urged that, for all reasonable beings, reason must be the supreme judge in matters of belief. It can neither resign its office nor delegate its authority. Let it then endorse Science, as it must; and establish Theism if it can; but do not require it to commit the folly of treating truth about which opinions are agreed as dependent on conjectures about which opinions are divided.

Theism and Humanism

This may be excellent advice; but it is hardly to the point. I ask for nothing better than the supremacy of reason: not one of its prerogatives do I desire to curtail. Indeed (as I have already complained) it is the agnostic empiricists who most obstinately shrink from following it to conclusions they dislike, who mutiny, like some old-time mariners, whenever they are required to navigate unfamiliar seas.

I have no sympathy with the singular combination of intellectual arrogance and intellectual timidity so often presented by this particular school of thought. I like it no better than I like the attitude of those who declare that, since reason is bankrupt, authority should take over its liabilities, however small be the prospect of discharging them in full. My point of view is utterly different. And if I urge that the criticism of common knowledge brings us ultimately to Theism, this involves no intolerable paradox, nor indeed anything very new or strange.

Descartes, for example, thought that all knowledge was based on clear and distinct ideas, and that clear and distinct ideas could be trusted because, being due to God, they were guaranteed by His truthfulness. That there is a God possessing every perfection was independently established by an *a priori* argument into which I need not enter. But the point of interest is that, though Descartes conceived himself to have found a refuge from scepticism in the famous "I think, therefore I am," he could only get from this narrow assurance to general knowledge by the use of "clear and distinct ideas" certified by divine veracity. If, therefore, belief in one's self was the first of truths, belief in God was the second; and on this second truth all subordinate beliefs, mathematical, physical, and metaphysical, were, in his opinion, ultimately founded. In one sense, and from one point of view, this is no doubt an exact inversion of the argument developed in these lectures. **Descartes rests the belief in science on a belief in God. I rest the belief in God on a belief in science.** Nevertheless, beneath this contrast there is deep-lying agreement. Both views reject the notion that we possess in the general body of commonsense assumptions and scientific truths a creed self-sufficing and independent, to which we may add at our pleasure Theism in such doses as suit our intellectual palate. Both views, therefore, are profoundly divided, not merely from all that calls itself agnostic, but from much that calls itself religious.

I must not, however, press the parallel too far. Descartes did not, and could not, regard our beliefs as a developing system, which is not merely increasing by external accretion, like a crystal in its mother-liquid, but is growing and changing through and through like a living organism. Such conceptions were not of his age or country, nor, if they had been, could they have been easily accommodated to his peculiar genius. His was the mathematical temperament, always striving for precise definitions and rigorous proof; always tolerant of any simplification of the concrete complexities of reality, which would make them amenable to deductive treatment. Of this, as a method, we need make no complaint. Within due limits it is invaluable. But Descartes, so to speak, "objectified" it. He assumed that any judgment which could properly be described as "clear and distinct" was not only convenient in form, but true in substance. The world, alas! is not so made. The things which are clear and distinct are usually things of our own creation. Definitions, abstractions, diagrams, syllogisms, machines—such and such like are, or may be, "clear and distinct." But the great facts which we have not made—these, at our present level of knowledge, are never clear and never distinct. Life, the organism, the self, the state, the world, freedom, causality, the flow of time, the relation between mind and body, between perceiver and perceived, between consciousness and sub-consciousness, between person and person (I say nothing of beauty, of virtue, or of God)—who is there will dare to say that he either finds in these notions, or can put into them without injury, the qualities which Descartes deemed the inevitable marks of real and certain knowledge? Truth, for us, is a plant of a different and of a slower growth. How much indeed of that growth consists in discovering that what we thought was clear is in fact obscure; what we thought was simple is in fact complex; what we thought was distinct is in fact confused; and how helpful are such discoveries to the augmentation of learning!

However this may be, there is nothing in the doctrine of "congruity" which should shock those who are jealous for the supremacy of reason and the dignity of science. It is science itself which assures us that all premises, all conclusions, and all the logical links by which they are connected must be regarded as natural products. It is science itself which assures us that they belong, like all natural products, to the tissue of causes and effects whose lengthening web is continuously thrown off by the loom of time. It is science itself which requires us to harmonise these two aspects of the knowing process—the one logical and timeless; the other causal and successive.

But how are they to be harmonised if the causal series is fundamentally non-rational? Suppose yourself able to observe the development of beliefs in some alien being (say an inhabitant of Mars) as a bacteriologist observes a growing colony of microbes: suppose, further, that your observation showed how these beliefs arose from causes which had in them no tincture of reason, and that, so far as you could see, they were quite unsupported by any independent evidence which—for you—had weight or even meaning. Would you rate their value high? Surely not.

Now it is quite true that when we examine our own system of beliefs we cannot imitate this attitude of complete detachment, since in the very act of examination some of these beliefs are assumed. But we can examine the beliefs of other people, and we do, as a matter of common-sense practice, rate low the value of the beliefs whose sources we perceive to be non-rational. How, then, can we refuse to apply to ourselves a principle of judgment which we thus apply without scruple to our neighbours?

Whenever we do so apply it, we shall, I think, be forced to admit that all creeds which refuse to see an intelligent purpose behind the unthinking powers of material nature are intrinsically incoherent. In the order of causation they base reason upon unreason. In the order of logic they involve conclusions which discredit their own premises. Nor is there, as far as I can see, any mitigation of this condemnation to be looked for except by appealing to the principle of Selection. And how far will this help us out of the difficulty?

Just so far as an imitation of intelligent purpose can be a substitute for its reality, but no further. And how far is this? At first sight we might suppose that, at the worst, the cognitive series and the causal series might be harmonised on the basis of natural selection if knowledge never aspired to rise above the level which promoted race survival, if no faculties of knowing were trusted beyond the point where they ceased effectively to foster the multiplication of the species. Up to this point it would seem that, if selection be true, there is congruity between beliefs and their origin. The sequence of events which brought them into being suggests no doubt about their value. This scheme of thought, therefore, though narrowly restricted, is apparently coherent. Yet even this modest claim must be deemed excessive: for the speculation on which it rests does violence to its own principles. Manifestly we cannot indulge ourselves in reflections upon the limits of the "knowable" without using our intellect for a purpose never contemplated by selection. I do not allege that our intellect is therefore unequal to the task. I only say that, if it be indeed equal to it, we are in the presence of a very surprising coincidence. Why should faculties, "designed" only to help primitive man, or his animal progenitors, successfully to breed and feed, be fitted to solve philosophic problems so useless and so remote? Why, indeed, do such problems occur to us? Why do we long for their solution?

To such questions Naturalism can neither find an answer nor be content without one. Wearied with unavailing efforts to penetrate the unknown, many not ignoble spirits have preached the wisdom of dulling unhealthy curiosity by the aid of healthy labour. "Let us cultivate our gardens" (they say), seeking no solution of the insoluble.

But the advice is ambiguous. Will the proposed remedy, in their opinion, cure the ill, or only help us to forget it? If the latter, then, in some circumstances and with some patients, it will doubtless fulfil its promise. Oblivion may be attained by growing vegetables, as by other less reputable expedients. But if absorption in daily labour be recommended as the final stage of a rational cure, it cannot be effectual. No rational cure is, on naturalistic principles, within our reach. Could we empty ourselves of all that makes us men, could we lower our intellectual level to the point where the scope of our mental activities harmonised with their naturalistic source, we should doubtless free ourselves from the malady of vain speculation. But though the remedy, if applied, would be effectual, it would not be rational. Reflective Agnosticism cannot be combined with scientific Naturalism, because reflective Agnosticism is the product of process which Naturalism inevitably discredits. And if Naturalism be incompatible even with reasoned ignorance, how can we hope to harmonise it with the claims of reasoned knowledge?[61] The best imitation of creative purpose, therefore, which Naturalism can provide breaks down where it is most required—namely, at the highest levels of value. I have just shown this in connection with our powers of thought, and the beliefs to which they lead. But the failure is not confined to them. It is as wide as Humanism itself. Wherever we find great intrinsic worth, there we are in a region where the direct effect of selection is negligible. The noblest things in speculation, in art, in morals, possess small survival value; and, though the geniuses to whom we owe them have added greatly to the glory of their race, they have added but little to its animal successes. In the language of these lectures, they are "accidental"—due neither to purpose nor to any arrangement of causes by which purpose is successfully copied.

──────────────── **A Pitiless Creed** ────────────────

If naturalism be true, or, rather, if it be the whole truth, then is morality but a bare catalogue of utilitarian precepts; beauty but the chance occasion of a passing pleasure; reason but the dim passage from one set of unthinking habits to another. All that gives dignity to life, all that gives value to effort, shrinks, and fades under the pitiless glare of a creed like this; and even curiosity, the hardiest among the noble passions of the soul, must languish under the conviction that neither for this generation nor for any that shall come after it, neither in this life nor in another, will the tie be wholly loosened by which reason, not less than appetite, is held in hereditary bondage to the service of our material needs.[62]

THEISM AND HUMANISM

❖ Is this Systematic Philosophy?

You are now in a position to judge how far the hopes held out to you at the beginning of this course have been fulfilled, and to measure the merits and the demerits, the claims and the limitations, of the scheme I have endeavoured to expound.

I disowned, as you remember, any intention of providing you with a philosophical system—not because I despise philosophical systems or those who labour to construct them, but in part because I have none to recommend, and in part because it seems to me doubtful whether at our present stage of development a satisfactory system is possible.

But how (you may ask) does my point of view differ from a philosophical system? It may be a bad system, as it certainly is a most imperfect one. Yet, seeing that it touches on everything in heaven and earth, seeing that its very title embraces God and man, why should it repudiate a description which seemingly is not a whit in excess of its pretensions?

The question thus raised is more than a merely verbal one, and a few observations upon it may fittingly conclude the course. Note, then, in the first place, that my scheme of beliefs does not show itself unworthy to be considered systematic merely because it is incomplete. All systems are incomplete. All systems, however ambitious, admit their inability to exhaust reality. Nor is its unworthiness due to any mere accident of execution, such as inferior workmanship or defective learning. Its failures are essential and irremediable. They are inseparable from "the point of view."

Let me explain. Every system that deserves to be described as a constructive philosophy—be it dogmatic, critical, empirical, idealist, what you will—conceives itself not merely to be rooted in reason, but to be rationalised throughout. The conceptions with which it works should be sifted, clarified, defined. It should assume nothing which requires proof. It should rest nothing (in the last resort) on faith or probability. It should admit no inexplicable residues.

Philosophers seem to me entirely right if they think that this is what a system ought to be; but not entirely right if they think that this is what any system is, or has ever been. In any case, no description could be less applicable to the point of view which I am provisionally recommending. The philosopher refuses—in theory—to assume anything which requires proof. I assume (among other things) the common-sense outlook upon life, and the whole body of the sciences. The philosopher admits—in theory—no ground of knowledge but reason. I recognise that, in fact, the whole human race, including the philosopher himself, lives by faith alone. The philosopher asks what creed reason requires him to accept. I ask on what terms the creed which is in fact accepted can most reasonably be held. The philosopher conceives that within the unchanging limits of his system an appropriate niche can be found for every new discovery as it arises. My view is that the contents of a system are always reacting on its fundamental principles, so that no philosophy can flatter itself that it will not be altered out of all recognition as knowledge grows.

This last statement may look like a truism; but it is a truism which few philosophers are, in practice, disposed to accept; and the generality of mankind are perhaps even less disposed to accept it even than philosophers. That there are beliefs which can and should be held, with the same shade of meaning, by all men, in all ages, and at all stages of culture, is a view to which by nature we easily incline. But it is, to say the least, most doubtful. Language is here no true or certain guide. Even when beliefs have not outgrown the formulas by which they have been traditionally expressed, we must beware of treating this fixity of form as indicating complete identity of substance. Men do not necessarily believe exactly the same thing because they express their convictions in exactly the same phrases. And most fortunate it is, in the interests of individual liberty, social co-operation, and institutional continuity that this latitude should be secured to us, not by the policy of philosophers, statesmen, or divines, but by the inevitable limitations of language.

This is, however, by the way. The point I wish to press is that, speaking generally, we must not conceive the development of knowledge as a process of adding new truths to old truths, in the course of which old truths are supplemented but are not changed. It rather resembles the increase of some plastic body which, wherever it takes place, involves are adjustment of every part. Add brick to brick, and you may finish your house, yet never alter its foundation. Add belief to belief, and you will set up strains and stresses within your system of knowledge which will compel it to move towards some new position of equilibrium. Sometimes, no doubt, the process is more violent and catastrophic than this metaphor naturally suggests. Then occurs in the moral world the analogue of the earthquake, the lava flood, and the tidal wave, which shatter mountains and sweep cities to destruction. Men's outlook on the universe suffers sudden revolution: the obvious becomes incredible, and the incredible obvious; whole societies lose their balance, and stately systems are tumbled in the dust.

More often, however, the movements of belief are gradual. They resemble the slow rise or fall of ancient coast-lines, where, by imperceptible degrees, sea turns into land, or land into sea. So, without shock or clamour, man smoothly modifies his point of view, till, gazing over the spaces he has traversed, he greatly marvels at the change.

But we must look forward as well as backward. The spaces still to be traversed far exceed those that have been traversed already. We can set no limits to the intellectual voyage which lies before the race. Even if we arbitrarily limit the life of men to that which is possible under terrestrial conditions, we must anticipate transformations of belief comparable in magnitude with those which already divide us from primitive mankind. How, in circumstances like these, can we hope to sketch, even in outline, an enduring system of philosophy? Why should we succeed where under similar conditions the greatest of our forefathers have already failed?

If, then, we cannot attain to a scheme of belief which, whatever be its shortcomings, is good (so far as it goes) for all time, we must be content with something less. We must put up with what I have called in these lectures "a point of view." We must recognise that our beliefs must be provisional, because, till we approach complete knowledge, all beliefs are provisional. We cannot claim that they are good "so far as they go"; but only that they are as good as we are at present able to make them. And we must recognise that the two statements are profoundly different.

Now, if I were asked what categories or conceptions such a "point of view" required for its expression, I should answer Providence and Inspiration—categories for which systematic philosophy has so far found no great use. These terms, it must be owned, are now a little the worse for wear. Defaced and battered by centuries of hard usage, they have suffered the fate which the current coin of popular discussion cannot easily avoid. But they have merits negative and positive, which make them peculiarly apt for my present purpose.

In the first place, they do not suggest a philosophy of the universe. They openly evade the great problems of theological metaphysics. No one, for example, would employ them in discussing the essential nature of an Absolute God, or His relation to time, to the act of creation, to the worlds created. They belong to a different level of speculation.

In the second place, they concentrate attention on the humanistic side of Theism, on the relation of God to man, and to man's higher spiritual needs. Divine "guidance"—purposeful working of informing Spirit—is the notion on which emphasis is specially laid. The term "Providence" suggests this in a broad and general way. The term "Inspiration" suggests it in the narrower sphere of beliefs and emotions. And do not complain that no endeavour is made to explain the mode in which divine guidance works either on matter or on spirit. These are mysteries as hard of solution, as those which surround the action of mind on matter, and of mind on mind. But the difficulties are difficulties of theory, not of practice. They never disturb the ordinary man—nor the extraordinary man in his ordinary moments. Human intercourse is not embarrassed by the second, nor simple piety by the first. And perhaps the enlightened lounger, requesting a club-waiter to shut the window, brushes aside, or ignores, as many philosophic puzzles as a mother passionately praying for the safety of her child.

❖ Conclusion

To some this conclusion of a long and intricate discussion will seem curiously trivial in its unambitious simplicity. Especially will this be true of those who accept empirical Naturalism in any of its forms. "There is" (they may admit) "something grandiose about the great metaphysical systems which appeals even to those who are least able to accept them. It was no ignoble ambition which inspired their architects. It was no light labour, or trivial ingenuity, which brought them into being. On the other hand," (they will say), "if naturalistic methods are more modest, naturalistic results are more secure. They aim lower, but they reach the mark. If the long-drawn 'conflict between religion and science' has robbed us of some illusions which we abandon with regret, the knowledge it has spared us we may hold with assurance. But when we turn to the narrow Theism of these lectures, fittingly couched in the outworn language of the pulpit and the Sunday-school, can we find in it either the glory of metaphysical speculation or the security of positive knowledge? It has not the courage to explore the unknowable, nor the power to add to the known. It dare not fly; it will not walk. It is neither philosophy nor science; nor does it seek the modest security of some middle way. How, then, are we to class this strange amalgam of criticism and credulity? What purpose can it serve? To whom will it appeal? Whose beliefs will it alter even by a hair's breadth?"

These are pertinent questions. Let me try to answer them.

The customary claims of Naturalism, which I have here put into the mouth of my imaginary critic, seem to me (as you know) to be quite unreasonable. Otherwise I have no great objection to the statements contained in his indictment—however little I may agree with its spirit. In particular I admit the charge that the argument of these lectures, elaborate as it may appear, does not after all carry us far beyond the position occupied by uncritical piety and simple faith. Could it be otherwise? If we build, as I build, upon our common-sense beliefs about the natural world, our theories of the supernatural world will surely share the defects inherent in their foundation. It may—or may not—be possible to know all about the evolution of God as the Absolute Idea, while lamentably ignorant of much that pertains to the Particular. But if we begin with the Particular— and that most imperfectly apprehended—we cannot hope to grasp the full reality of the Absolute. On this line of advance the philosopher will not far outstrip the peasant.

When, therefore, my supposed critic satirically asks who it is that I hope to influence, I grant at once that it is not the plain man who already accepts without doubt or commentary a theistic view of the Universe. He is beyond my arguments—perhaps above them.

Neither do I greatly hope to influence the trained man of speculation, who has already found a theory of things which satisfies his reason, or is sure that no such theory is within his reach. Even he may, I trust, find in these lectures discussions of some philosophic interest. I ask him to con- sider whether his system provides an honourable place for the actual beliefs by which his waking life is ruled; whether all the gradations of intuitive probability, from inevitable compulsion to faint inclination, find house-room not merely in his psychology of belief, but in his theory of knowledge; whether he is satisfied with his logic of science, or can bring into one harmonious scheme his creed regarded as a body of rational con- clusions and his creed regarded as a bundle of natural effects. If he replies in the affirmative, his state is the more gracious. But he is not likely to be interested in my arguments; and assuredly they will not convert him to my views.

I need say nothing about his pretentious imitator, who, under many names, has long been a familiar figure in certain societies. With no deep desire for truth, and poorly equipped for pursuing it, his main ambition is to indicate discreetly that he holds what the fashion of the moment regards as "advanced" views in their most advanced form. Wherein the quality of "advancement" consists, it might be hard to determine; nor is it (in this connection) a subject worthy of investigation. It is enough to say that "advanced" views must have an air of novelty, must be making some stir in the world, must be sufficiently unorthodox to shock the old-fashioned, and either sufficiently plausible to deceive the simple or sufficiently imposing to overawe them. I do not think that I shall find many converts among members of this class; nor is it to them that I desire to speak.

But there are many persons, both earnest and sincere, to whom the conclusions which modern Naturalism extracts from modem science are a source of deep perplexity and intellectual unrest. Their mood, if I rightly read it, is something of this kind. They would agree that a world where God is either denied or ignored is a world where some higher values are greatly impoverished. They would read the lectures I have devoted to Beauty and Morals with sympathy, if not with agreement. Life, they would admit, is but a poor thing if it does no more than fill with vain desires the brief interval between two material "accidents"—the "accident" which brought it into being, and the "accident" which will extinguish it for ever. But this (they will say) is no argument. A wise man faces facts, a good man prefers the hardest truth to the most alluring illusion. If there be no ground for assuming a living purpose behind the indifferent mask of nature, let us not fill the vacancy with a phantasm of our own creation. Let us at least sink back into the nothingness from which we rose with our intellectual integrity undamaged. Let all other values perish, so long as rational values remain undimmed.

Here, according to my view, lies the great illusion. Those who in all sincerity, and often with deep emotion, plead after a fashion like this, profoundly misunderstand the situation. They are indeed worthy of respect. They must not be confounded with those unstable souls who ignore God when they are happy, deny Him when they are wretched, tolerate Him on Sundays, but truly call on Him only when life, or fortune, hangs doubtfully in the balance. They are of a different and more virile temper. But are they less mistaken? They search for proofs of God, as men search for evidence about ghosts or witches. Show us, they say, the marks of His presence. Tell us what problems His existence would solve. And when these tasks have been happily accomplished, then will we willingly place Him among the hypothetical causes by which science endeavours to explain the only world we directly know, the familiar world of daily experience.

But God must not thus be treated as an entity, which we may add to, or subtract from, the sum of things scientifically known as the canons of induction may suggest. He is Himself the condition of scientific knowledge. If He be excluded from the causal series which produces beliefs, the cognitive series which justifies them is corrupted at the root. And as it is only in a theistic setting that beauty can retain its deepest meaning, and love its brightest lustre, so these great truths of aesthetics and ethics are but half-truths, isolated and imperfect, unless we add to them yet a third. We must hold that reason and the works of reason have their source in God; that from Him they draw their inspiration; and that if they repudiate their origin, by this very act they proclaim their own insufficiency.

11

A Distinctively Christian Setting

Now it can, I think, be shown that the central doctrine of Christianity, the doctrine which essentially differentiates it from every other religion, has an ethical import of great and even of an increasing value.

-------------------- **Editor's Note** --------------------

Constrained by the conditions of the Gifford endowment, in his speeches Balfour could argue for no more than the existence of the God of Theism. In his other writings, however, Balfour made it clear that he felt an equally strong case can be made for the God of Christianity. He laid special stress on something that distinguishes Christianity from all other religions, a belief in the Incarnation, that in Jesus Christ God uniquely became man and entered our world. John's gospel expressed that belief in its first chapter when it said that the Word which was God, "became flesh and lived for a time among us." In this supplemental chapter, which was not part of the original *Theism and Humanism*, I have included remarks Balfour made elsewhere on this topic.

❖ An Epilogue on the Incarnation

So far the argument has gone to show that the great body of our beliefs, scientific, ethical, aesthetic and theological, form a more coherent and satisfactory whole in a Theistic than in a Naturalistic setting. Can the argument be pressed further? Can we say that those departments of knowledge, or any of them, are more coherent and satisfactory in a distinctively Christian setting than in a merely Theistic one? If so, the *a priori* presuppositions which have induced certain learned schools of criticism to deal with the Gospel narratives as if these were concerned with events intrinsically incredible will need modification, and there may even on consideration appear to be an *a priori* presupposition in favour of their general veracity.

Now it can, I think, be shown that the central doctrine of Christianity, the doctrine which essentially differentiates it from every other religion, has an ethical import of great and even of an increasing value. The Incarnation as dogma is not a theme within the scope of this work; but it may not be amiss, by way of Epilogue, to enumerate three aspects of it in which it especially ministers, as nothing else could conceivably minister, to some of the most deep-seated of our moral necessities.

(a) The whole tendency of modern discovery is necessarily to magnify material magnitudes to the detriment of spiritual ones. The insignificant part played by moral forces in the cosmic drama, the vastness of the physical forces by which we are closed in and overwhelmed, the infinities of space, time, and energy thrown open by Science to our curious investigations, increase (on the Theistic hypothesis) our sense of the power of God, but relatively impoverish our sense of His moral interest in His creatures. It is surely impossible to imagine a more effective cure for this distorted yet most natural estimate than a belief in the Incarnation.

(b) Again, the absolute dependence of mind on body, taught, and rightly taught, by empirical science, confirmed by each man's own humiliating experience, is of all beliefs the one which, if fully realised, is most destructive of high endeavour. Speculation may provide an answer to physiological materialism, but for the mass of mankind it can provide no antidote; nor yet can an antidote be found in the bare theistic conception of a God ineffably remote from all human conditions, divided from man by a gulf so vast that nothing short of the Incarnation can adequately bridge it.

(c) A like thought is suggested by the "problem of evil," that immemorial difficulty in the way of a completely consistent theory of the world on a religious basis. Of this difficulty, indeed, the Incarnation affords no speculative solution, but it does assuredly afford a practical palliation. For whereas a merely metaphysical Theism leaves us face to face with a Deity who shows power but not mercy, who has contrived a world in which, so far as direct observation goes, the whole creation travails together in misery, **Christianity brings home to us, as nothing else could do, that God is no indifferent spectator of our sorrows, and in so doing affords the surest practical alleviation to a pessimism which seems fostered alike by the virtues and the vices of our modern civilisation.**[63]

❖ Our Significance in the Cosmic Drama

Critics have made merry over the naive self-importance which represented man as the centre and final cause of the universe, and conceived the stupendous mechanism of nature as primarily designed to satisfy his wants and minister to his entertainment. But there is another, and an opposite, danger into which it is possible to fall. The material world, howsoever it may have gained in sublimity, has, under the touch of science, lost (so to speak) in domestic charm. Except where it affects the immediate needs of organic life, it may seem so remote from the concerns of men that in the majority it will rouse no curiosity, while of those who are fascinated by its marvels, not a few will be chilled by its impersonal and indifferent immensity.[64]

Among the needs ministered to by Christianity are some which increase rather than diminish with the growth of knowledge and the progress of science; and this Religion is therefore no mere reform, appropriate only to a vanished epoch in the history of culture and civilisation, but a development of theism now more necessary to us than ever.

I am aware, of course, that this may seem in strange discord with opinions very commonly held. There are many persons who suppose that, in addition to any metaphysical or scientific objections to Christian doctrines, there has arisen a legitimate feeling of intellectual repulsion to them, directly due to our more extended perception of the magnitude and complexity of the material world. The discovery of Copernicus, it has been said, is the death-blow to Christianity: in other words, the recognition by the human race of the insignificant part which they and their planet play in the cosmic drama renders the Incarnation, as it were, intrinsically incredible. This is not a question of logic, or science, or history. No criticism of documents, no haggling over "natural" or "supernatural," either creates the difficulty or is able to solve it. For it arises out of what I may almost call an aesthetic sense of disproportion. "What is man, that Thou art mindful of him; and the son of man, that Thou visitest him?" is a question charged by science with a weight of meaning far beyond what it could have borne for the poet whose lips first uttered it. And those whose studies bring perpetually to their remembrance the immensity of this material world, who know how brief and how utterly imperceptible is the impress made by organic life in general, and by human life in particular, upon the mighty forces which surround them, find it hard to believe that on so small an occasion this petty satellite of no very important sun has been chosen as the theatre of an event so solitary and so stupendous.

Reflection, indeed, shows that those who thus argue have manifestly permitted their thoughts about God to be controlled by a singular theory of His relations to man and to the world, based on an unbalanced consideration of the vastness of Nature. They have conceived Him as moved by the mass of His own works; as lost in spaces of His own creation. Consciously or unconsciously, they have fallen into the absurdity of supposing that He considers His creatures, as it were, with the eyes of a contractor or a politician; that He measures their value according to their physical or intellectual importance; and that He sets store by the number of square miles they inhabit or the foot-pounds of energy they are capable of developing. In truth, the inference they should have drawn is of precisely the opposite kind. The very sense of the place occupied in the material universe by man the intelligent animal, creates in man the moral being a new need for Christianity, which, before science measured out the heavens for us, can hardly be said to have existed. Metaphysically speaking, our opinions on the magnitude and complexity of the natural world should, indeed, have no bearing on our conception of God's relation, either to us or to it. Though we supposed the sun to have been created some six thousand years ago, and to be "about the size of the Peloponnesus," yet the fundamental problems concerning time and space, matter and spirit, God and man, would not on that account have to be formally restated. But then, we are not creatures of pure reason; and those who desire the assurance of an intimate and effectual relation with the Divine life, and who look to this for strength and consolation, find that the progress of scientific knowledge makes it more and more difficult to obtain it by the aid of any merely speculative theism. The feeling of trusting dependence which was easy for the primitive tribes, who regarded themselves as their God's peculiar charge, and supposed Him in some special sense to dwell among them, is not easy for us; nor does it tend to become easier. We can no longer share their naive anthropomorphism. We search out God with eyes grown old in studying Nature, with minds fatigued by centuries of metaphysic, and imaginations glutted with material infinities. It is in vain that we describe Him as immanent in creation, and refuse to reduce Him to an abstraction, be it deistic or be it pantheistic. The overwhelming force and regularity of the great natural movements dull the sharp impression of an ever-present Personality deeply concerned in our spiritual well-being. He is hidden, not revealed, in the multitude of phenomena, and as our knowledge of phenomena increases, He retreats out of all realised connection with us farther and yet farther into the illimitable unknown.

Then it is that, through the aid of Christian doctrine, we are saved from the distorting influences of our own discoveries. **The Incarnation throws the whole scheme of things, as we are too easily apt to represent it to ourselves, into a different and far truer proportion.** It abruptly changes the whole scale on which we might be disposed to measure the magnitudes of the universe. What we should otherwise think great, we now perceive to be relatively small. What we should otherwise think trifling, we now know to be immeasurably important. And the change is not only morally needed, but is philosophically justified. Speculation by itself should be sufficient to convince us that, in the sight of a righteous God, material grandeur and moral excellences are incommensurable quantities; and that an infinite accumulation of the one cannot compensate for the smallest diminution of the other. Yet I know not whether, as a theistic speculation, this truth could effectually maintain itself against the brute pressure of external Nature. In the world looked at by the light of simple theism, the evidences of God's material power lie about us on every side, daily added to by science, universal, overwhelming. The evidences of His moral interest have to be anxiously extracted, grain by grain, through the speculative analysis of our moral nature. Mankind, however, are not given to speculative analysis; and if it be desirable that they should be enabled to obtain an imaginative grasp of this great truth; if they need to have brought home to them that, in the sight of God, the stability of the heavens is of less importance than the moral growth of a human spirit, I know not how this end could be more completely attained than by the Christian doctrine of the Incarnation.[65]

❖ Our Ethical Needs

If the reality of scientific and of ethical knowledge forces us to assume the existence of a rational and moral Deity, by whose preferential assistance they have gradually come into existence, must we not suppose that the Power which has thus produced in man the knowledge of right and wrong, and has added to it the faculty of creating ethical ideals, must have provided some satisfaction for the ethical needs which the historical development of the spiritual life has gradually called into existence?

Manifestly the argument in this shape is one which must be used with caution. To reason purely *a priori* from our general notions concerning the working of Divine Providence to the reality of particular historic events in time, or to the prevalence of particular conditions of existence through eternity, would imply a knowledge of Divine matters which we certainly do not possess, and which, our faculties remaining what they are, a revelation from Heaven could not, I suppose, communicate to us. My contention, at all events, is of a much humbler kind. I confine myself to asking whether, in a universe which, by hypothesis, is under moral governance, there is not a presumption in favour of facts or events which minister, if true, to our highest moral demands? and whether such a presumption, if it exists, is not sufficient, and more than sufficient, to neutralise the counter-presumption which has uncritically governed so much of the criticism directed in recent times against the historic claims of Christianity? For my own part, I cannot doubt that both these questions should be answered in the affirmative; and if the reader will consider the variety of ways by which Christianity is, in fact, fitted effectually to minister to our ethical needs, I find it hard to believe that he will arrive at any different conclusion.[66]

❖ Our Material Bodies

Of all creeds, materialism is the one which, looked at from the inside—from the point of view of knowledge and the knowing Self—is least capable of being philosophically defended, or even coherently stated. Nevertheless, the burden of the body is not, in practice, to be disposed of by any mere process of critical analysis. From birth to death, without pause or respite, it encumbers us on our path. We can never disentangle ourselves from its meshes, nor divide with it the responsibility for our joint performances. Conscience may tell us that we ought to control it, and that we can. But science, hinting that, after all, we are but its product and its plaything, receives ominous support from our experiences of mankind. Philosophy may assure us that the account of body and mind given by materialism is neither consistent nor intelligible. Yet body remains the most fundamental and all-pervading fact with which mind has got to deal, the one from which it can least easily shake itself free, the one that most complacently lends itself to every theory destructive of high endeavour.[67]

What we need, then, is something that shall appeal to men of flesh and blood, struggling with the temptations and discouragements which flesh and blood is heir to; confused and baffled by theories of heredity; sure that the physiological view represents at least one aspect of the truth; not sure how any larger and more consoling truth can be welded on to it; yet swayed towards the materialist side less, it may be, by materialist reasoning than by the inner confirmation which a humiliating experience gives them of their own subjection to the body.

What support does the belief in a Deity ineffably remote from all human conditions bring to men thus hesitating whether they are to count themselves as beasts that perish, or among the sons of God? What bridge can be found to span the immeasurable gulf which separates Infinite Spirit from creatures who seem little more than physiological accidents? What faith is there, other than the Incarnation, which will enable us to realise that, however far apart, they are not hopelessly divided? The intellectual perplexities which haunt us in that dim region where mind and matter meet may not be thus allayed. But they who think with me that, though it is a hard thing for us to believe that we are made in the likeness of God, it is yet a very necessary thing, will not be anxious to deny that an effectual trust in this great truth, a full satisfaction of this ethical need, are among the natural fruits of a Christian theory of the world.[68]

❖ Our Difficulties with Evil

I have already said something about what is known as the "problem of evil," and the immemorial difficulty which it throws in the way of a completely coherent theory of the world on a religious or moral basis. I do not suggest now that the Doctrine of the Incarnation supplies any philosophic solution of this difficulty. I content myself with pointing out that the difficulty is much less oppressive under the Christian than under any simpler form of Theism; and that though it may retain undiminished whatever speculative force it possesses, its moral grip is loosened, and it no longer parches up the springs of spiritual hope or crushes moral aspiration.

For where precisely does the difficulty lie? It lies in the supposition that an all-powerful Deity has chosen out of an infinite, or at least an unknown, number of possibilities to create a world in which pain is a prominent, and apparently an ineradicable, element. His action on this view is, so to speak, gratuitous. He might have done otherwise; He has done thus. He might have created sentient beings capable of nothing but happiness; He has in fact created them prone to misery, and subject by their very constitution and circumstances to extreme possibilities of physical pain and mental affliction. How can One of Whom this can be said excite our love? How can He claim our obedience? How can He be a fitting object of praise, reverence, and worship? So runs the familiar argument, accepted by some as a permanent element in their melancholy philosophy; wrung from others as a cry of anguish under the sudden stroke of bitter experience.

This reasoning is in essence an explication of what is supposed to be involved in the attribute of Omnipotence; and the sting of its conclusion lies in the inferred indifference of God to the sufferings of His creatures. There are, therefore, two points at which it may be assailed. We may argue, in the first place, that in dealing with subjects so far above our reach it is in general the height of philosophic temerity to squeeze out of every predicate the last significant drop it can apparently be forced to yield; or drive all the arguments it suggests to their extreme logical conclusions. And, in particular, it may be urged that it is erroneous, perhaps even unmeaning, to say that the universality of Omnipotence includes the power to do that which is irrational; and that, without knowing the Whole, we cannot say of any part whether it is rational or not.

These are metaphysical considerations which, so long as they are used critically, and not dogmatically, negatively, not positively, seem to me to have force. But there is a second line of attack, on which it is more my business to insist. I have already pointed out that ethics cannot permanently flourish side by side with a creed which represents God as indifferent to pain and sin; so that, if our provisional philosophy is to include morality within its circuit (and what harmony of knowledge would that be which did not?), the conclusions which apparently follow from the co-existence of Omnipotence and of Evil are not to be accepted. Yet this speculative reply is, after all, but a fair-weather argument; too abstract easily to move mankind at large, too frail for the support, even of a philosopher, in moments of extremity. Of what use is it to those who, under the stress of sorrow, are permitting themselves to doubt the goodness of God, that such doubts must inevitably tend to wither virtue at the root? No such conclusion will frighten them. They have already almost reached it. Of what worth, they cry, is virtue in a world where sufferings like theirs fall alike on the just and on the unjust? For themselves, they know only that they are solitary and abandoned; victims of a Power too strong for them to control, too callous for them to soften, too far for them to reach, deaf to supplication, blind to pain. Tell them, with certain theologians, that their misfortunes are explained and justified by an hereditary taint; tell them, with certain philosophers, that, could they understand the world in its completeness, their agony would show itself an element necessary to the harmony of the Whole, and they will think you are mocking them. Whatever be the worth of speculations like these, it is not in the moments when they are most required that they come effectually to our rescue. What is needed is such a living faith in God's relation to Man as shall leave no place for that helpless resentment against the appointed Order so apt to rise within us at the sight of undeserved pain. And this faith is possessed by those who vividly realise the Christian form of Theism. **For they worship One Who is no remote contriver of a universe to whose ills He is indifferent. If they suffer, did He not on their account suffer also? If suffering falls not always on the most guilty, was He not innocent? Shall they cry aloud that the world is ill-designed for their convenience, when He for their sakes subjected Himself to its conditions?** It is true that beliefs like these do not in any narrow sense resolve our doubts nor provide us with explanations. But they give us something better than many explanations. For they minister, or rather the Reality behind them ministers, to one of our deepest ethical needs; to a need which, far from showing signs of diminution, seems to grow with the growth of civilisation, and to touch us ever more keenly as the hardness of an earlier time dissolves away.[69]

A

A Catechism for Naturalism

I am not aware that any one has as yet endeavoured to construct the catechism of the future, purged of every element drawn from any other source than the naturalistic creed. It is greatly to be desired that this task should be undertaken in an impartial spirit; and, as a small contribution to such an object, I offer the following pairs of contrasted propositions, the first member of each pair representing current teaching, the second representing the teaching which ought to be substituted for it if the naturalistic theory be accepted.

Reason

Traditional: The universe is the creation of Reason, and all things work together towards a reasonable end.

Naturalism: So far as we can tell, reason is to be found neither in the beginning of things nor in their end; and though everything is predetermined, nothing is fore-ordained.

Love

Traditional: Creative reason is interfused with infinite love.

Naturalism: As reason is absent, so also is love. The universal flux is ordered by blind causation alone.

Moral Law

Traditional: There is a moral law, immutable, eternal; in its governance all spirits find their true freedom and their most perfect realisation. Though it be adequate to infinite goodness and infinite intelligence, it may be understood, even by man, sufficiently for his guidance.

Naturalism: Among the causes by which the course of organic and social development has been blindly determined are pains, pleasures, instincts, appetites, disgusts, religions, moralities, superstitions; the sentiment of what is noble and intrinsically worthy; the sentiment of what is ignoble and intrinsically worthless. From a purely scientific point of view these all stand on an equality; all are action-producing causes developed, not to improve, but simply to perpetuate, the species.

Beauty

Traditional: In the possession of reason and in the enjoyment of beauty, we in some remote way share the nature of that infinite Personality in Whom we live and move and have our being.

Naturalism: Reason is but the psychological expression of certain physiological processes in the cerebral hemispheres; it is no more than an expedient among many expedients by which the individual and the race are preserved; just as Beauty is no more than the name for such varying and accidental attributes of the material or moral worlds as may happen for the moment to stir our aesthetic feelings.

Individual Worth

Traditional: Every human soul is of infinite value, eternal, free; no human being, therefore, is so placed as not to have within his reach, in himself and others, objects adequate to infinite endeavour.

Naturalism: The individual perishes; the race itself does not endure. Few can flatter themselves that their conduct has any appreciable effect upon its remoter destinies; and of those few none can say with reasonable assurance that the effect which they are destined to produce is the one which they desire. Even if we were free, therefore, our ignorance would make us helpless; and it may be almost a consolation to reflect that our conduct was determined for us by unthinking forces in a remote past, and that if we are impotent to foresee its consequences, we were not less impotent to arrange its causes.

The doctrines embodied in the second member of each of these alternatives may be true, or may at least represent the nearest approach to truth of which we are at present capable. Into this question I do not yet inquire. But if they are to constitute the dogmatic scaffolding by which our educational system is to be supported; if it is to be in harmony with principles like these that the child is to be taught at its mother's knee, and the young man is to build up the ideals of his life, then, unless I greatly mistake, it will be found that the inner discord which exists, and which must gradually declare itself, between the emotions proper to naturalism and those which have actually grown up under the shadow of traditional convictions, will at no distant date most unpleasantly translate itself into practice.[70]

APPENDIX
B

The Evolution of Belief

Ever since there has been speculation on the subject of varieties of opinion, this fact must have been obvious, that a man's beliefs are very much the results of antecedents and surroundings with which they have no proper logical connection.[71] That the sons of Christians are much more often Christians, and the sons of Mahommedans much more often Mahommedans, that a man more commonly holds the opinions of those with whom he lives, and more commonly trusts the policy of the party with whom he acts, than on the theory of probability could happen supposing that conviction was in all cases the result of an impartial comparison of evidence, must always have been plain to the most careless observer. It other words, it must always have been known that there were causes of belief which were not reasons.[72]

The progress of knowledge has not led us to increase, but rather to diminish, our estimate of the part which reasons as opposed to other causes have played in the formation of creeds; for it has shown that these reasons are themselves the result of non-rational antecedents, so that even when a man tempts to form opinions only according to evidence *what he shall regard as evidence* is settled for him by causes over which he has no more control than he has over the natural forces by which a particular flora is produced at any particular place and time.

The scientific evidence for this truth is various and overwhelming. It is justified *a posteriori* with regard to individuals by common observation, with regard to races by every improvement in our historic method and every addition to our historic knowledge. Physiology shows it *a priori* by demonstrating the dependence of thought on the organism and of the organism on inheritance and environment while finally evolution binds up these detached lines of proof into an imposing and organic whole.

But though in the face of such evidence, nobody doubts the fact, few people, I should think, contemplate it habitually without now and then suffering under a sort of sceptical uneasiness (if I may so express myself), when they consider its bearing on their own opinions. The multitude of beliefs which in obedience to a mechanic and inevitable law, sway for a time the minds and actions of men, and are then for ever swept away to the forgotten past, giving place to others, as firmly trusted in, as false, and as transitory as themselves, form a spectacle which is not only somewhat melancholy in itself, but which is apt to suggest uncomfortable reflections as to the permanent character of the convictions we ourselves happen to be attached to. If, indeed, the law obeyed by this intellectual dissolving view applied only to savages, or to the people with whose opinions we disagreed, we might perhaps contemplate its action with a merely speculative interest. Unfortunately, however, this is not so. We are all involved in its operations, from the most ignorant barbarian to the most advanced thinker. The existence of Comtism is explained by it not less than that of fetichism, it accounts for theories of Evolution not less than for Hindo cosmogonies, and the man of science is as certainly under its control as was the Indian whose superstitions he is making the subject of analysis and classification.

But if these things be so, wherein lies our defence against universal scepticism? It is true that we hear on all sides of the progress of knowledge, that we imagine science to be as it were a fabric of which each generation lays a tier, resting upon that which was laid by its predecessors, and serving for a foundation for that which will be laid by its successors. But after all, this metaphor only represents an opinion—like other opinions. It is the belief of an optimistic age, which may seem to future generations no more than a transitory fashion. The last ground of faith seems cut away from beneath our feet, if no belief is left which can be trusted sufficiently for us to use it as at criterion of immutable truth; and if our creed be the mere product of irrational law where is such a belief to be found?

A train of thought not unlike this must, I should imagine, have been sometimes started in the mind of the reader when he reflects on the evolution of opinion. I propose in this chapter to put in a clear form what I conceive to be the really solid element in such sceptical, if somewhat vague, speculations.

The case may be stated thus—Since all beliefs are caused, it follows that those fundamental beliefs must be caused which lie at the root of all other beliefs, and which are, as I explained in the first chapter, the rational ground on which we hold them. Now these fundamental beliefs, being the ultimate premises of all knowledge, are themselves, of course incapable of proof. So that while they resemble other beliefs in being caused, they differ from them in this, that the causes by which they are produced are of necessity, and from the very nature of the case, always non-rational. In ordinary life, when we perceive a non-rational cause for any opinion, as for instance party feeling, or self-interest, or special education, it makes us examine such reasons as there may be for it with more jealous minuteness. In contrast to this, it is curious and interesting to note that the only beliefs of which, according to received scientific theories, we may say with certainty that they *can* have no reason, but *must* have non-rational causes, are those on which the certitude of all other beliefs finally rests. The upholders, however, of the current theory of Evolution are so far from finding any difficulty here, that they even refer triumphantly to this theory of non-rational causation, as supplying a basis of philosophical certitude to these fundamental beliefs. They hold that though all opinion is the product of natural forces, the general tendency of those forces is gradually to make opinion approximate to truth; that in particular the opinions which are commonly regarded as 'self-evident' and 'known by intuition' are really the result of reiterated and uncontradicted experience acting on successive generations; and that this theory of their origin supplies a philosophic justification for believing them to be true.

This line of reasoning, however, involves a manifest argument in a circle. It cannot be that this interaction between organism and environment is a reason for believing any proposition to be true which is required to prove that interaction. Or (to put it more generally) no argument in favour of a system of beliefs can be drawn from the fact that, according to that system, its fundamental beliefs would be true.

From Evolution, then, no argument can be drawn in favour of any scientific axiom. It remains to be seen whether that theory has any less negative bearing on the philosophy of belief.

Now the theory asserts this—All phenomena whatever are evolved by regular laws and groups of laws from the phenomena next preceding them in time. Among other phenomena, beliefs; among other beliefs, fundamental beliefs. All beliefs whatever being caused, the question arises, Is there anything in the nature of the laws according to which they are caused which should make them true? To which an evolutionist would probably reply that there is, and would mention those causes to which allusion has already been made, whose tendency is gradually to make belief correspond with fact. Then (we may further ask) are these causes of such a nature as to make *all* beliefs true?

This question must undoubtedly be answered in the negative. If any result of 'observation and experiment' is certain, this one is so—that many erroneous beliefs have existed, and do exist in the world; so that whatever causes there may be in operation by which true beliefs are promoted, they must be either limited in their operation, or be counteracted by other causes of an opposite tendency. Have we then any reason to suppose that fundamental beliefs are specially subject to these truth-producing influences, or specially exempt from causes of error? This question, I apprehend, must be answered in the negative. At first sight, indeed, it would seem as if those beliefs were specially protected from error which are the results of legitimate reasoning. But legitimate reasoning is only a protection against error if it proceeds from true premises, and it is clear that this particular protection the premises of all reasoning never can possess. Have they, then, any other? Except the 'tendency' above mentioned, I must confess myself unable to see that they have; so that our position (as evolutionists) is this—From certain ultimate beliefs we infer that an order of things exists by which all beliefs, and therefore all ultimate beliefs, are produced, but according to which any particular belief, and therefore any particular ultimate belief, must be doubtful. Now this is a position which is self-destructive. No system of beliefs, giving an account of the origin of fundamental beliefs, can be consistent unless those fundamental beliefs are as certain when regarded as the result of antecedent causes, as they are when regarded as the ground of our belief in the existence and operation of those causes. It does not follow (as I pointed out by implication above) that if, according to the account of their origin given by the system, those fundamental beliefs are true, *that therefore they are true;* for the truth of the system is an inference from these beliefs, and cannot therefore prove them. What *does* follow is, that the system has one of the negative conditions of truth, and is (so far at least as this matter is concerned) consistent with itself.

To this criticism it may perhaps be replied, that there is no contradiction involved in considering a proposition from two points of view—from one of which it seems certain, and from the other doubtful. It happens every day in dealing with statements which are established by pieces of evidence of very different degrees of cogency. For example, the fact that the three angles of a triangle are invariably equal to two right angles would be doubtful if we had no better means of demonstrating it than the employment of a pair of compasses. Geometrical proof, on the other hand, makes it absolutely certain. Will it be maintained that such an inconsistency, if it can be called so, suggests any sceptical conclusion?

Assuredly not. But there is no parallelism between the two cases. Ultimate premises are not shown to be merely probable by one set of proofs, and shown to be certain by another. They are not shown to be certain at all. They are assumed to be so: and the first stage of the difficulty arises from the fact that while they are assumed without evidence to be certain, the evidence we possess as to their origin shows that they are *not* certain.

If this were all, however, the difficulty would be a slight one. We should merely have to modify our original position, and concede to the sceptic that the assurance we possessed respecting the validity of our ultimate premises was not quite so strong as we had supposed. It is at the next stage that the real difficulty arises, when we consider the fact that our whole ground for thinking these ultimate premises doubtful is founded in the last resort upon their certainty. This is a manifest flaw or defect, which must be fatal to the validity of any system from which it cannot be removed.

The difficulty only arises, it may be observed, when we are considering *our own* beliefs. If I am considering the beliefs of some other person—say of some mediaeval divine—there is no reason why I should regard them as anything but the results of his time and circumstances. I observe that he lived in such a country, fell under the influence of such and such teachers, came across such and such incidents, and then I infer, with much self-contentment, that his beliefs could not have been other than they were. I may even pay them the compliment of pointing out that they form a necessary stage in the general evolution of humanity. But when I come to consider *my own* beliefs as a stage in the general evolution of humanity, then there emerges the contradiction mentioned above. If they represent such a stage, all of them *may* be, and many of them *must* be, false. Why not the particular belief in Evolution? Because it is scientifically demonstrated? This only removes the difficulty a stage further back. It must be demonstrated ultimately from something which is not demonstrated: and these undemonstrated beliefs are necessarily rendered doubtful by the reflection that they form part of the stage in the evolution of humanity.

"But if this is all," the advocates of Evolution may be inclined to reply, "you have proved nothing more than we are quite prepared to grant. We concede, without difficulty, that our theory is not at present rigorously certain; and even that it can never become so. You have shown that doubt must always attach to our original data; we will go further, and admit that error may always creep into our most careful deductions. But this only shows—what nobody ever disputed—that we must content ourselves in science, as in everything else, with something short of rigorous demonstration. Unless you can show us that our system has some other defect, not necessarily incident to the work of fallible man, your arguments will be wasted on people who in the main agree with you." I reply that I *can* show that it has some other defect; and the defect is this: If we suppose Evolution to become what every evolutionist must wish it to be—though he may admit that it is not—namely, a solid piece of demonstration resting on axiomatic premises, from that moment it becomes self-contradictory. It is impossible as soon as it is certain; because, by the very fact of its becoming certain, we obtain demonstrative proof that the premises of the system, and therefore the system itself, is uncertain. A system of which this can be said is not merely doubtful, it is incoherent.

The precise nature of this objection will perhaps be more clear if, instead of being put in this its most abstract and general form, a concrete example of it is taken.

We may suppose, then, a conversation between an Evolutionist and an Enquirer, in which, when the former has explained in the usual ways how human beliefs, after passing through infinite gradations of diminishing error, have at length reached the highest development they are now capable of in the opinion he himself professes, the Enquirer continues the dialogue by asking—

Enquirer: Do you suppose that this development of beliefs has now reached its limits, or do you anticipate as great a change in the future as has occurred in the past?

Evolutionist: However great the superiority of my views may be over those of my remote ancestors, or indeed over those of my contemporaries who are still under the influence of tradition, there is every reason to suppose that the causes which have produced this superiority are still in operation, and that we may look forward to a time when the opinion of mankind will bear the same relation to ours as ours bear to those of primitive man.

Enquirer: A glorious hope! One, nevertheless, which would seem to imply that many of our present views are either entirely wrong, or will require profound modification.

Evolutionist: Doubtless.

Enquirer: It would be interesting to know which of our opinions, or which class of them, is likely to be improved in this way off the face of the earth. For example, is the opinion you have just expressed, that beliefs are developed according to law—is that opinion likely to be destroyed by development?

Evolutionist: To answer your question in the affirmative would appear to involve a contradiction. If (as we assume) development is truthwards, it is impossible that development should produce a disbelief in development.

Enquirer: I understand you to hold then that a belief in development is true, and therefore indestructible and that in this it differs from many of our other beliefs, of which we cannot, unfortunately, say the same. It would be important to know the grounds of this distinction, in order that we might see how far it was capable of general application.

Evolutionist: Evolution is a theory arrived at by received scientific methods. Doubtless, all results of which the same may be said are equally true, and will be equally permanent.

Enquirer: You talk of scientific methods—but a method must proceed on a principle or principles. How do you get at these?

Evolutionist: The principles you speak of are, I suppose, the assumptions which every one must start from, who expects to make any progress in knowledge.

Enquirer: These assumptions, as I understand you, are what render a scientific method possible They cannot, therefore, be arrived at by a scientific method, nor can they belong to that class of beliefs which, as you just pointed out, the progress of evolution will leave uninjured.

Evolutionist: Still you must assume something.

Enquirer: But the difficulty here, as it seems to me, is, that if you start from your idea of evolution, these assumptions, like all other beliefs not arrived at by 'received scientific methods,' are, or may be, mere transient phases in the development of opinion, like the doctrines involved in ancestor worship or theism. Nevertheless, it is only by starting from these assumptions that you ever get to your theory of evolution at all. In other words, if Evolution is certain, these assumptions must be certain, when regarded as premises, and uncertain when regarded as products. This is not easy to believe.

Evolutionist: Still, you know, you must assume something.

Enquirer: Nevertheless, it is a pity you cannot so order your assumptions as to make your system more self-consistent. At present you seem somewhat to resemble an astronomer who should base his whole theory of the real motion of the heavenly bodies on the supposition that his own planet was at rest; but should unfortunately discover that one of the necessary conclusions from his theory was that his planet, in common with all the others, was in motion. Of such a one we should probably say, that if his deductions were correct his premises must have been wrong, while if his premises were correct his deductions must have been wrong.

So far I have only considered this difficulty as it applies to Evolution, because it seemed to me that he issue to which I wished to call attention could be thus most conveniently raised. It is a mistake, however, to suppose that the difficulty necessarily attaches to Evolution alone. Every theory is obnoxious to it according to which all beliefs are supposed to be caused, while fundamental beliefs are caused in such a manner as to make them uncertain. Now it is to be noted that this description is rather a wide one: and must undoubtedly be held to include the world of Science as ordinarily conceived.

For it is plain that current scientific methods can lead to no other result than that belief is a product. If experience can prove anything, it can prove that. There is here none of that doubt which has been thrown on the existence or non-existence of free will by the real or supposed discrepancy between the deliverances of introspective consciousness and the verdict of ordinary historical experience. In this case, whether we consult statistics, whether we interrogate consciousness, whether we judge of the matter on grounds furnished by physiology, or ethnology, or history, or natural selection—whatever scientific doctrine or scientific method be brought to bear on the question, but one result is obtained: beliefs, all beliefs, are the result of the operation of natural causes, and of these alone. And since it is no less certain, **I apprehend, that these causes are of a kind to throw doubts on the beliefs they produce, it follows according to our canon, that ordinary scientific methods land us in contradiction. It must, however, be observed that there is a justification, beyond mere convenience of exposition, for making Evolution especially the subject of their criticism, because it is Evolution alone which *necessarily* claims to regulate the whole world of phenomena.** The special sciences—physics, chemistry, and so forth—might very well go on, even if their methods were not universally applied, though it must be admitted that it is not easy to find a principle of limitation. But if Evolution is not universal, it is nothing. If certain phenomena are to be left outside it, if it cannot without contradiction and confusion explain, potentially at least, how the whole world as it is follows necessarily from the world as it was, it certainly appears to me that it ought to modify either its methods or its pretensions.

Note: In the preceding chapter [of *A Defence of Philosophic Doubt*] the argument has turned in part on the manner in which the nature of the causes of belief in general (and therefore of ultimate beliefs) may affect their validity. At first sight there may seem to be some contradiction between this portion of the argument and the general principles laid down in the first chapter. For it was there pointed out that no enquiry into the origin of ultimate beliefs can be of any philosophic value, and the reader may be tempted to interpret this canon into an assertion that the origin of ultimate beliefs is a matter of absolute philosophic indifference—an interpretation for which my own language offers, perhaps, some excuse. Thus interpreted however, the doctrine is incorrect. It is true that the origin of ultimate beliefs never can supply any ground for believing them, simply because the fact of their having any particular origin can only be shown by inference founded ultimately on these beliefs themselves. But it is quite possible that the converse of this proposition may be true, and that inference from ultimate beliefs as to their origin may furnish logical grounds for doubting or disbelieving them. The preceding chapter contains an example of this drawn from actual science, and an imaginary instance may perhaps serve to put the matter in a still more forcible light. We might imagine it to be a conclusion demonstrable from our ultimate beliefs, that those beliefs were implanted in us by a being who had the power and invariably had the wish, to deceive and mislead us. Now I say that under such circumstances we should be compelled either to think that our creed was essentially incoherent, or that we had committed some blunder in our inference; and this is the dilemma which, though in a less obvious shape, I maintain we are brought face to face with by the doctrine of Evolution when applied, as it must be applied, to our ultimate beliefs.

―――――――――― **Educated above our Natural Station** ――――――――――

Our capacity for standing outside ourselves and taking stock of the position which we occupy in the universe of things has been enormously, and, it would seem, unfortunately, increased by recent scientific discovery. We have learned too much. We are educated above that station in life in which it has pleased Nature to place us. We can no longer accept it without criticism and without examination. We insist on interrogating that material system which, according to naturalism, is the true author of our being, as to whence we come and whither we go, what are the causes which have made us what we are, and what are the purposes which our existence subserves. And it must be confessed that the answers given to this question by our oracle are extremely unsatisfactory. We have learned to measure space, and we perceive that our dwelling-place is but a mere point, wandering with its companions, apparently at random, through the wilderness of stars. We have learned to measure time, and we perceive that the life not merely of the individual or of the nation, but of the whole race, is brief, and apparently unimportant. We have learned to unravel causes, and we perceive that emotions and aspirations whose very being seems to hand on the existence of realities of which naturalism takes no account, are in their origin contemptible and in their suggestion mendacious.[73]

APPENDIX
C

The Discrepancy Between Religion and Science

In the preceding chapter [of *A Defence of Philosophical Doubt*] there was a good deal of reference to the discrepancy which exists, or is supposed to exist, between Religion and Science. To determine the actual amount of such discrepancy, or even to decide whether it has any reality or not, was in no way necessary to my main argument; but it may be convenient to indicate in a note the general view which I should be disposed to take of a question which, though its importance has been greatly exaggerated, is not without interest.[74]

The discord between Science and Religion has reference chiefly, if not entirely, to the interference by the supernatural with the natural, which Religion requires us to believe in; and the amount of this discord may be measured by the importance of the scientific doctrines which such a belief would require us to give up, if we were determined at all hazards to make the two systems consistent with each other. In discussing this subject, I shall assume, for the sake of argument, that this interference is not, as has been often suggested, produced immediately by the operation of some *unknown* though *natural* law; but that the common opinion is correct which attributes it to the direct action of a Supernatural Power. The question therefore we have to ask, is this: What scientific beliefs do we contradict if we assert that a Supernatural Power has on various occasions interfered with the operation of natural laws? "We contradict," it will be replied, "the belief in the uniformity of Nature." Is the belief which is thus contradicted particularly important then to Science? "So important," many people would answer, "that it lies at the foundation of all our scientific reasoning, as well as all of our practical judgments." This I understand to be the opinion of the two most recent assailants of Theology who, so far as I know, have touched on the subject—namely, the author of *Supernatural Religion* and Mr. Leslie Stephen. The former of these, whose treatment of the whole question suggests a suspicion that he is hardly equal to dealing with the profounder problems which he has undertaken to solve, I need not further allude to. Mr. Stephen, however, may be quoted with advantage. "If it is not contrary," he says, "to the laws of Nature that the dead shall be raised, or one loaf feed a thousand men, the occurrence of the fact does not prove that an Almighty Being has suspended the laws of Nature. If such a phenomenon is contrary to the laws of Nature, then a proof that the events had occurred would establish the inference. But, on the other hand, it must always be simpler to believe that the evidence is mistaken; *for such a belief is obviously consistent with a belief in the uniformity of Nature, which is the sole guarantee (whatever its origin) of our reasoning.* Really to evade Hume's reasoning is thus impossible," &c.[75]

From the sentence in this extract which I have put in italics, it would appear that Mr. Stephen holds, and thinks that Hume implicitly held, the doctrine that a belief in occasional Divine interference is inconsistent with that belief in the uniformity of Nature which is "the sole guarantee of our reasoning." I doubt whether this was Hume's opinion; in any case it is incorrect.

The scientific belief which, with least impropriety, may be termed the "sole guarantee" of our reasoning, is *that* belief in the uniformity of Nature which is equivalent to a belief in the law of universal causation; which again is equivalent to a belief that similar antecedents are always followed by similar consequents. But this belief, as the least reflection will convince the reader, is in no way inconsistent with a belief in supernatural interference.

A belief in the uniformity of Nature, which is equivalent to a belief that natural effects are uniformly preceded by natural causes, no doubt *is* inconsistent with supernatural interference; but of what pieces of reasoning it is our sole guarantee, except those directed to show that in any given case the hypothesis of supernatural interference must be rejected, I am not able to say.

It is clear, then, that the most important discrepancy which has been, or could be, alleged to exist between Science and Religion has no real existence. The only great general principle on which scientific philosophers have as yet been able to rest their scientific creed is untouched. Let us therefore now turn our attention to the more special and derivative doctrines of Science, and consider how far they are affected by a belief in supernatural interference.

In this enquiry it will be convenient to keep in mind a distinction drawn in the fourth chapter of this essay, between what were there called the *abstract* and the *concrete* parts of Science. By the abstract parts of Science were meant the general laws by which phenomena are connected;

by the concrete parts were meant (what may be sufficiently described as) particular matters of fact.

Does, then, Theology require us to modify in any way our beliefs concerning the abstract part of Science?

I apprehend that it does not. Such beliefs are in themselves as true and as fully proved if supernatural interference be possible as they are if such interference be impossible. A law does not do more than state that under certain circumstances (positive and negative) certain phenomena will occur. If on some occasions these circumstances, owing to supernatural interference, do not occur the fact that the phenomena do not follow proves nothing as to the truth or falsehood of the law. If we believe that oxygen and hydrogen will combine under given conditions to produce water, we believe so none the less because we happen also to believe that some Supernatural Power may interpose, or has on certain occasions interposed, to prevent that result. I need not further insist on this point, which is obvious enough in itself, and on which I believe I am in agreement with Mr. Mill and others who are not commonly suspected of a theological bias.

There remains then the concrete part of Science: the matters of fact which compose history in its widest sense, or which belongs to that fraction of the future which Science can pretend to foresee. Now with regard to the former of these the question is complicated by a consideration which does not affect us when we are dealing with other portions of the scientific system—by the consideration, namely, that it is a matter of controversy *what*, in certain very pertinent particulars, the scientific version of history really is. For the Theologians usually maintain that the kind of scientific inference which I call Historical, compels a belief in the intervention on certain occasions of supernatural causes: a great part of what are commonly called Christian evidences being indeed nothing more than a detailed attempt to prove this thesis, just as most of the direct attacks on Christianity are attempts to prove the precise opposite. Now, if the Theologians are right in their opinions on this point, there can be no discrepancy whatever between Religion and Science as regards matters of fact, because it is Science itself which compels us to accept the account of miracles in which Religion teaches us to believe. Before, therefore, discussing the nature and magnitude of the discrepancy which is supposed to exist between them, it would seem necessary to enter fully into all the disputes respecting the authenticity of documents, the credibility of witnesses, the interpretation of texts, the growth of myths, the natural history of religions, the abstract question as to the possibility of inferring supernatural facts from natural data, and, in short, all the topics which supply theological and anti-theological writers with so much material for discussion. Such a task is of course impossible. But it may be worth while to note the conclusions that would have to be faced if on all these disputed questions the Theologians are wrong and the Anti-theologians are right; if known natural causes are able in all cases, without straining, to account for the historical facts which both sides allow to have occurred, and if, either for this, or for some more abstract reason, only natural causes can rationally be admitted to have been in operation. On such a hypothesis theological beliefs would, without doubt, modify opinions framed out of purely scientific materials, though the modification may easily be exaggerated. Regarded in their relation to us as men, the facts which Theology asserts to have happened are unquestionably of transcendent importance. Regarded in their relation to Science, this can hardly be maintained. As *phenomena*, the few events which are said to have occurred in Palestine and elsewhere of a supernatural character are scarcely worth noting. Being supernatural, they furnish no grounds either for believing in any new law of Nature or for disbelieving any which we had before supposed to be established; and being few, they are lost in the mass of facts which have succeeded each other since the earth came into being. "Is the supernatural creation of the world, then, nothing?" the reader may be tempted to exclaim. I have always understood[76] that this is a subject on which men of science professed to be altogether out of their sphere. "What, then, do you say about a belief in Providence, and in the possible interference of Supernatural Power in answer to prayer?" These, again, are not convictions which require us to modify our adherence to known laws. They may cast, indeed, an additional shade of doubt over our expectation of the events which are to occur in the future, as well as over the explanation of the events which have occurred in the past; and if our actual scientific inferences were (as I have shown in the fourth chapter that they are not) of a satisfactory character on these points, this might prove a matter of some, though not, I think, of very great importance. As it is, however, the Supernatural Power is only one of an indefinite number of known and unknown natural powers, which we never have seen, and perhaps can never hope to see, reduced to law, and which even if we leave miraculous interference out of account would suffice to make demonstrative prophecy or retrospection an absolute impossibility.

It would appear then that the discrepancy between Religion and Science which vanishes altogether if we take the hypothesis most favourable to the Theologians is comparatively insignificant in its amount even on the hypothesis most favourable to the Freethinkers: and if many writers who certainly know a great deal about Science, and may be supposed to know something about Theology, are of an altogether different opinion, this may, I apprehend, be attributed to the fact that they approach the question with their minds completely saturated with a theory of the logical relation which ought to subsist between Religion and Science, according to which the grounds, if any, for believing the first, are to be found, if anywhere, among the doctrines of the second. It is not hard to see that on any presupposition of this sort (combined as it is with the assumption that Science is philosophically established), the smallest want of harmony between the two systems may, or rather must, lead to the most important consequences: since the mere discovery that they are not rationally connected would remove all ground for accepting the dependent creed; while the least appearance of contradiction would supply a positive ground for rejecting it. As, however, I have in the preceding chapter sufficiently expressed my dissent from this view, it is not necessary that I should here any further allude to it. I merely desired to point out the principal reason which I believe exists for the great exaggeration which is occasionally to be observed in the estimate of the importance of the contradiction between current Religion and current Science put forward by thinkers of reputation.

────────── **Naturalism's Scientific Pretence** ──────────

Who would pay the slightest attention to naturalism if it did not force itself into the retinue of science, assume her livery, and claim, as a kind of poor relation, in some sort to represent her authority and to speak with her voice?[77]

APPENDIX

D

Changes from the 1915 Text

Every effort has been made to follow the original text, retaining British punctuation and spellings. In a few cases, however, changes were made.

- Page 30 of the original (Chap. 3, Sec. 3 of this edition) "their reigns" was replaced with "there reigns."

- Page 179 (Chap. 7, Sec. 2) corrected the quotation marks in the sentence beginning with "For omniscience."

- Page 222 (Chap. 9, Sec. 2) the spelling of "Tyndal" is corrected to "Tyndall."

- Page 230 (Chap. 9, Sec. 2) capitalized "unless."

- Page 240f. (now an endnote at the conclusion of Chap. 9), ellipses were added to Lodge's letter to indicate gaps that Balfour placed in his quotations from Sir Oliver Lodge.

- Page 264 (Chap. 10, Sec. 3), "is" was added to "This, however, by the way."

- Page 268 (Chap. 10, Sec. 4), fixed the quotation marks around "There is."

- In three places a note in the text was transferred to an endnote.

  - Page 215, the note at the end of Chap. 8.

  - Page 236–37, the note at the end of Chap. 9, Sec. 2.

  - Sir Oliver Lodge's letter at the end of Chap. 9.

   In addition, other minor textual changes were made to bring the book into accord with modern typesetting practices. For instance, many of the book titles that were placed quotation marks in the original were put into italics, and awkward looking;— and:— were replaced with a simpler — to improve the appearance. Also, for consistency with modern practices, I have added Balfour's name to the end of the preface.

   In Appendix, A, "A Catechism for Naturalism," "A" and "B" were changed to "Traditional" and "Naturalism." In Appendix B, "The Evolution of Belief," "Enq." and "Evl." were changed to "Enquirer" and "Evolutionist."

The book's division into four 'parts' was removed and minor changes made to headings of chapters and sections to make what Balfour was saying clearer to modern readers unaccustomed to complex book divisions. In addition, I have made bold the text when Balfour makes a particularly interesting remark. Finally, numerous quotes from Balfour's other writings, the articles from *The Times,* all of Chapter 11, several appendices, a glossary and an index were added and footnotes changed to endnotes.

A P P E N D I X
E
Letters from C. S. Lewis to Sheldon Vanauken

——————— **Editor's Note** ———————

During 1950 and 1951 the Oxford writer, C. S. Lewis, wrote three letters to Sheldon Vanauken (later the author of *A Severe Mercy*). In them Lewis answered some questions that Vanauken was having about spiritual matters. Subsequently, Lewis gave Vanauken permission to publish the letters, which Vanauken then released into the public domain. They are included here because they tackle issues similar to those that Arthur Balfour dealt with in this book. This does not necessarily imply that Lewis got his ideas from Balfour, merely that both were attempting to deal in an intelligent way with questions many people raise about the truths of Christianity.

In his first letter, Lewis dealt with those who attempt to explain away Christianity rather than refute it, a topic Balfour mentions in Chapter 2. The desire of some to be "their own masters" is not all that different from Naturalists who dogmatically exclude God from the universe. Lewis rejected their viewpoint—which he calls "the materialistic world picture"—in the second paragraph. He also rejected "primitive religions" because they fail to provide an adequate moral foundation—exactly what Balfour said about Naturalism in Chapter 4.

In his second letter, Lewis dealt with faith in much the same common-sense manner that Balfour used in his lectures. Both argue that the way we live our everyday lives is a better model for how we should deal with questions about God than the endless speculations of philosophy. And Balfour would have agreed with Lewis' remark that there is no "demonstrative proof" of Christianity of the sort found in Euclid's geometry. Instead, our faith in God is like the trust we expect from our friends. In addition, both writers point to our desires as evidence that their fulfillment exists. Lewis used our need for food. Balfour pointed to our love of beauty, our moral yearnings, and our search for the truth.

Finally, in the third letter Lewis stressed that what we need most in life aren't irrefutable answers to life's biggest questions, but a fleeting glimpse of a small portion of the dark and dangerous mountain road of life in front of us. This fits well with Balfour's belief that no world view—least of all Naturalism—can provide rationally perfect answers to all life's important questions.

To make reading easier, I have taken the liberty of filling out abbreviations Lewis used in his original letters and formatting the text for publication.

December 14, 1950

Dear Mr. Vanauken,

My own position at the threshold of Christianity was exactly the opposite of yours. You wish it were true; I strongly hoped it was *not*. At least, that was my conscious wish: you may suspect that I had unconscious wishes of quite a different sort and that it was these which finally shoved me in. True: but then I may equally suspect that under your conscious wish that it were true, there lurks a strong unconscious wish that it were not. What this works out to is that all the modern thinking, however useful it may be for explaining the origin of an error which you already know to be an error, is perfectly useless in deciding which of two beliefs is the error and which is the truth. For (a.) One never knows all one's wishes, and (b.) In very big questions, such as this, even one's conscious wishes are nearly always engaged on both sides. What I think one can say with certainty is this: the notion that everyone would like Christianity to be true, and that therefore all atheists are brave men who have accepted the defeat of all their deepest desires, is simply impudent nonsense. Do you think people like Stalin, Hitler, Haldane, Stapledon (a corking good writer, by the way) would be pleased on waking up one morning to find that they were not their own masters, that they had a Master and a Judge, that there was nothing even in the deepest recesses of their thoughts about which they could say to Him "Keep out! Private. This is *my* business"? Do you? *Rats!* Their first reaction would be (as mine was) rage and terror. And I have much doubt whether even you would find it *simply* pleasant. Isn't the truth this: that it would gratify some of our desires (ones we feel in fact pretty seldom) and outrage a good many others? So let's wash out all the wish business. It never helped anyone to solve any problem yet.

I don't agree with your picture of the history of religion. Christ, Buddha, Mohammed and others elaborating on an original simplicity. I believe Buddhism to be a simplification of Hinduism and Islam to be a simplification of Christianity. Clear, lucid, transparent, simple religion (Tao *plus* a shadowy, ethical god in the background) is a late development, usually arising among highly educated people in great cities. What you really start with is ritual, myth, and mystery, the death and return of Balder or Osiris, the dances, the initiations, the sacrifices, the divine kings. Over against that are the Philosophers, Aristotle or Confucius, hardly religion at all. The only two systems in which the mysteries and the philosophies come together are Hinduism and Christianity: there you get both the Metaphysics and Cult (continuous with primeval cults). That is why my first step was to be sure that one or the other of these had the answer. For the reality can't be one that appeals either only to savages *or* only to high brows. Real things aren't like that (e.g. *matter* is the first most obvious thing you meet: milk, chocolates, apples, and also the object of quantum physics). There is no question of just a crowd of disconnected religions. The choice is between (a.) The materialist world picture: which I can't believe. (b.) The real archaic primitive religions; which are not moral enough. (c.) The (claimed) fulfilment of these in Hinduism. (d.) The claimed fulfilment of these in Christianity. But the weakness of Hinduism is that it doesn't really merge the two strands. Unredeemable savage religion goes on in the village; the Hermit philosophizes in the forest: and neither really interfaces with the other. It is only Christianity which compels a high brow like me to partake of a ritual blood feast, and also compels a central African convert to attempt an elightened code of ethics.

Have you ever tried Chesterton's *The Everlasting Man*? The best popular apologetic I know.

Meanwhile, the attempt to practice Tao is certainly the right line. Have you read the *Analects* of Confucius? He ends up by saying, "This is the Tao. I do not know if anyone has ever kept it." That's significant: one can really go direct from there to the Epistle of the Romans.

I don't know if any of this is the least use. Be sure to write again, or call, if you think I can be of any help.

Yours sincerely,

C.S. Lewis

December 23, 1950

Dear Mr. Vanauken,

The contradiction "we must have faith to believe and must believe to have faith" belongs to the same class as those by which the Eleatic philosophers proved that all motion is impossible. And there are many others. You can't swim unless you can support yourself in water and you can't support yourself in water unless you can swim. Or again, in an act of volition (e.g. getting up in the morning) is the very beginning of the act itself voluntary or involuntary? If voluntary then you must have willed it, . . you were willing it already, . . it was not really the beginning. If involuntary, then the continuation of the act (being determined by the first movement) is involuntary too. But in spite of this we *do* swim, and we *do* get out of bed.

I do not think there is a *demonstrative* proof (like Euclid) of Christianity, nor of the existence of matter, nor of the good will and honesty of my best and oldest friends. I think all three (except perhaps the second) far more probable than the alternatives. The case for Christianity in general is well given by Chesterton; and I tried to do something in my *Broadcast Talks*. As to *why* God doesn't make it demonstrably clear; are we sure that He is even interested in the kind of Theism which would be a compelled logical assent to a conclusive argument? Are *we* interested in it in personal matters? I demand from my friend a trust in my good faith which is *certain* without demonstrative proof. It wouldn't be confidence at all if he waited for rigorous proof. Hang it all, the very fairy tales embody the truth. Othello believed in Desdemona's innocence when it was proved: but that was too late. "His praise is lost who stays till all commend." The magnanimity, the generosity which will trust on a reasonable probability, is required of us. But supposing one believed and was wrong after all? Why, then you would have paid the universe a compliment it doesn't deserve. Your error would even so be more interesting and important than the reality. And yet how could that be? How could an idiotic universe have produced creatures whose mere dreams are so much stronger, better, subtler than itself?

Note that life after death, which still seems to you the essential thing, was itself a *late* revelation. God trained the Hebrews for centuries to believe in Him without promising them an afterlife, and, blessings on Him, he trained me in the same way for about a year. It is like the disguised prince in a fairy tale who wins the heroine's love *before* she knows he is anything more than a woodcutter. What would be a bribe if it came first had better come last.

It is quite clear from what you say that you have *conscious* wishes on both sides. And now, another point about *wishes*. A wish may lead to false beliefs, granted. But what does the existence of the wish suggest? At one time I was much impressed by Arnold's line, "Nor does the being hungry prove that we have bread." But surely though it doesn't prove that one particular man will *get* food, it *does* prove that there is such a thing as food! i.e. if we were a species that didn't normally eat, weren't designed to eat, would we feel hungry? You say the materialist universe is "ugly." I wonder how you discovered that! If you are really a product of a materialistic universe, how is it you don't feel at home there? Do fish complain of the sea for being wet? Or if they did, would that fact itself not strongly suggest that they had not always, or would not always be, purely aquatic creatures? Notice how we are perpetually *surprised* at Time. ("How time flies! Fancy John being grown-up and married! I can hardly believe it!") In heaven's name, why? Unless, indeed, there is something about us that is *not* temporal.

Total humility is not in the Tao because the Tao (as such) says nothing about the Object to which it would be the right response: just as there is no law about railways in the acts of Queen Elizabeth. But from the degree of respect which the Tao demands for ancestors, parents, elders, and teachers, it is quite clear what the Tao *would* prescribe towards an object such as God.

But I think you are already in the meshes of the net! The Holy Spirit is after you. I doubt if you'll get away!

Yours,

C.S. Lewis

April 17, 1951

Dear Vanauken,

My prayers are answered. No: a glimpse is not a vision. But to a man on a mountain road by night, a glimpse of the next three feet of road may matter more than a vision of the horizon. And there must perhaps be always just enough lack of demonstrative certainty to make free choice possible: for what could we do but accept if the faith were like the multiplication table?

There will be a counter attack on you, you know, so don't be too alarmed when it comes.

The enemy will not see you vanish into God's company without an effort to reclaim you.

Be busy learning to pray and (if you have made up your mind on the denominational question) get confirmed.

Blessings on you and a hundred thousand welcomes. Make use of me in any way you please: and let us pray for each other always.

Yours,

C.S. Lewis

Tao Defined

[Lit."way"] 1. The creative principle that orders the universe as conceived by Taoists. 2. The path of virtuous conduct as conceived by Confucians.
—*Webster's Ninth New Collegiate Dictionary*

Notes

1 Editor: From "Rationalist Ortho-doxy" in *Foundations of Belief.* (Henceforth *Foundations.*) Quoted in Wilfrid M. Short, *The Mind of Arthur James Balfour* (New York: George H. Doran, 1918), 255. (Henceforth, *Mind.*)

2 Editor: From the Henry Sidgwick Memorial Lecture delivered at Newnham College, Cambridge, January 25, 1908. Quoted in *Mind,* 96.

3 Written before the war.

4 Editor: From *Foundations.* Quoted in *Mind,* 249–50.

5 Editor: From *Foundations.* Quoted in *Mind,* 337.

6 Editor: From *Foundations.* Quoted in *Mind,* 254.

7 Editor: From *Foundations.* Quoted in *Mind,* 252.

8 Editor: The humor linking a pledge with a drink of water probably came from abstinence campaigns in that era which encouraged people to pledge not to drink anything alcoholic.

9 Editor: In the early nineteenth century many believed that the argument from design described in books such as William Paley's *Natural Theology* proved that God was the creator of our complex, biological world. By Balfour's day, however, that idea had been displaced by an equally widespread belief that Darwinian selection could mimic intelligent design, depending on nothing but chance variations in living creatures.

10 Editor: In the "Prologue" to his second (1922–23) Gifford lecture series, Balfour noted: "As this reference may be obscure to my younger readers, it may be worth saying by way of explanation that about ninety years ago eight treatises by various authors, selected by the President of the Royal Society, were published on "the Power, Wisdom, and Goodness of God, as manifested in the Creation." This originated in a benefaction by the last Earl of Bridgewater, who died in 1829." Arthur J. Balfour, *Theism and Thought* (London: Hodder and Stoughton, *circa* 1923), 23.

11 Editor: Balfour speech to the Pan-Anglican Congress, London, June 22, 1908 as published in the (London) *Times.* Quoted in *Mind,* 369–70.

12 Editor: From Part IV of *Foundations.* Quoted in *Mind,* 344.

13 Editor: In modern terms, Pierre Simon Laplace's hypothetical calculator would be a computer so powerful that, given the present position and velocity of every object in the universe, it could calculate precisely what the universe would be like at any point in the past or future. Of course, Laplace's calculator assumes that there is no such thing as free will, and that all events in the universe are completely determined by previously existing conditions.

14 Editor: From a speech at the celebration of the Darwin Centenary, June 23, 1909. In *Report of Proceedings by Darwin Centenary Committee.* Quoted in *Mind,* 85.

15 As I shall often have to mention "selection" in the course of these lectures, I must observe that it is no part of my business to weigh the comparative merits of competing evolutionary theories. It may be that the hypothesis of small random variations accumulated or eliminated according as they help or hinder survival, is, in

the light of recent research, insufficient and unsatisfactory. From my point of view this is immaterial. I use the word "selection" as a convenient name for any non-rational process, acting through heredity, which successfully imitates contrivance. Darwin's theory, be it true or false, still provides, I suppose, the only suggestion as to how this feat may be accomplished, and his terminology may be used without danger of misunderstanding.

16 Editor: From Arthur J. Balfour, "Introduction" in *Science Religion and Reality* ed. Joseph Needham (New York: Macmillan, 1925), 17.

17 Editor: From Balfour's Presidential Address to the British Association for the Advancement of Science, August 17, 1904 as reprinted in his *Essays and Addresses*. Quoted in *Mind*, 208.

18 Editor: From the chapter on "Naturalism and Aesthetics" in *Foundations*. Quoted in *Mind*, 213–14.

19 I greatly regret having to stretch the ordinary meaning of the word "aesthetic" to the extent required by the argument of this chapter. I got into trouble in a previous work by the extension I gave to the word "Authority." And as, in that case, no explanation seemed sufficient to avoid misconception, so I am afraid it will be in the present case.

But what better course is open to me? I require a word to express a concept which is vital to the doctrines I am preaching. Where am I to get it? If there is no such word in ordinary use, I must either invent a new word, or I must modify the familiar meaning of an old word. There are objections to both courses; yet one of them must be taken. I have chosen the second; and

can do no more than ask for the indulgence of those readers who think I should have chosen the first.

20 Editor: From the chapter on "Naturalism and Aesthetics" in *Foundation*. Quoted in *Mind*, 213.

21 Editor: From "Naturalism and Aesthetics" in *Foundation*. Quoted in *Mind*, 238.

22 Editor: From "Beauty, and the Criticism of Beauty" given as the Romanes Lecture at Oxford University, November 24, 1909. Quoted in *Mind*, 215.

23 Editor: From the summary to Part I of *Foundations*. Quoted in *Mind*, 241. Balfour isn't saying that an artist's message is "never important." He is claiming that if naturalism is true, then art has no real meaning.

24 Cf. Plato in the "Pheedrus."

25 Editor: From "Philosophy and Rationalism" in *Foundations*. Quoted in *Mind*, 253–54.

26 It is perhaps to this tendency we may (in part) attribute the eagerness with which poetry and fine art have used and abused the personifications of natural objects provided for them by primitive superstition. If not, it is curious that these tedious mythologies should have been cherished by poets long after they were abandoned by everybody else; and that we still use every expedient for endowing material nature with fictitious sympathies and powers. But it is, I think, an error to see nothing in such metaphors but a trick of style. They represent the same deep-rooted tendency which finds significance in such phrases as "Mother Earth," which has suggested certain poetic forms of Pantheism; or which gathers a vague, semi-spiritual consolation from the thought that, when we die, our bodies, resolved into their elements, may still share in the new manifestations of life which Nature (half personified) pours out in exhaustless profusion.

27 Editor: From "Naturalism and Ethics" in *Foundations*. Quoted in *Mind*, 233–34.

28 Written in 1913. Editor: That is, before World War I and the strong nationalism the war generated.

29 Doubtless under such circumstances ideal virtue might also have survival value in the biological sense.

30 Editor: From "Naturalism and Ethics" in *Foundations*. Quoted in *Mind*, 233.

31 Editor: Balfour is referring to Huxley's controversial 1893 Romanes Lecture, "Evolution and Ethics," that, with the addition of a "Prolegomena," was published the next year as a book with the same name. The loose quotation that follows was taken from pages 139–40 of the 1894 edition.

32 Editor: From the summary to Part I of *Foundations*. Quoted in *Mind*, 242.

33 Editor: The quotation is from the apostle Paul in Romans 7:19

34 Indirectly, no doubt, sanctions may perform a most important educational work in stimulating and guiding the higher loyalties. The approval or disapproval of our fellows, the "terrors of the law," the belief in future rewards and punishments, though their immediate appeal is only to self-interest, may powerfully aid in the creation of moral judgments sufficiently free from any "empirical elements of desire" to have satisfied Kant himself.

35 Editor: From "Naturalism and Ethics" in *Foundations*. Quoted in *Mind*, 233.

36 Editor: From "Naturalism and Ethics" in *Foundations*. Quoted in *Mind*, 237.

37 Editor: From Part IV of *Foundations*. Quoted in *Mind*, 345–46.

38 Editor: From the summary of *Foundations*. Quoted in *Mind*, 141.

39 Editor: From the summary of *A Defence of Philosophic Doubt*. Quoted in *Mind*, 102.

40 Editor: From the summary of *A Defence of Philosophic Doubt*. Quoted in *Mind*, 100.

41 Editor: From "Naturalism and Reason" in *Foundations*. Quoted in *Mind*, 239.

42 Editor: From "Philosophy and Rationalism" in *Foundations*. Quoted in *Mind*, 251.

43 Editor: From the summary of *A Defence of Philosophic Doubt*. Quoted in *Mind*, 145.

44 Editor: From "Creative Evolution and Philosophic Doubt," *Hibbert Journal*, (October, 1911). Quoted in *Mind*, 50.

45 Although, as a matter of fact, I do speak of it in the next lecture.

46 Maxwell, as all who interest themselves in physics are aware, arrived at very interesting conclusions by considering what would happen if little demons interfered with the random motions of the molecules constituting a gas.

47 Extract from Morgan's *Habit and Instinct*, page 40. "A young chick two days old, for example, had learnt to pick out pieces of yolk from others of white of egg. I cut little bits of orange-peel of about the same size as the pieces of yolk, and one of these was soon seized, but at once relinquished, the chick shaking his head. Seizing another, he held it for a moment in the bill, but then dropped it and scratched at the base of his beak. That was enough; he could not again be induced to seize a piece of orange-

peel. The obnoxious material was now removed, and pieces of yolk of egg substituted, but they were left untouched, being probably taken for orange-peel. Subsequently, he looked at the yolk with hesitation, but presently pecked doubtfully, not seizing, but merely touching. Then he pecked again, seized, and swallowed."

48 Editor: From "The Philosophical Basis of Naturalism" in *Foundations.* Quoted in *Mind,* 247.

49 Editor: From "Philosophy and Rationalism" in *Foundations.* Quoted in *Mind,* 251.

50 Note: The shortcomings of mechanism have been discussed by M. Bergson in a manner which no other thinker is likely to rival. He has, however, usually dealt with the subject in connection with freedom; whereas in this section I have only dealt with it in connection with foreknowledge, repetition, and what I have termed the doctrine of "negligibility." He approaches it from the side of reality. I approach it from the side of inductive inference and the law of universal causation.

51 Editor: From Part IV of *Foundations.* Quoted in: *Mind,* 344.

52 See Lecture [Chapter] 6.

53 Editor: From Balfour's Presidential Address, British Association for the Advancement of Science (August 17, 1904). Reprinted in *Essays and Addresses.* Quoted in *Mind,* 206.

54 Editor: This may refer to John Dalton's *A New System of Chemical Philosophy, circa* 1810.

55 See note at the end of the lecture. Editor: this note is now endnote 59 and referenced at the end of this chapter.

56 I got this view of Boyle's relation to modern chemistry from Ostwald's work.

57 In this chapter, especially in that part of it which deals with beliefs of conservation, I am greatly indebted to Meyerson's *Identité et Réalité.* This acute and learned work is not written from the same point of view as that which I have adopted; but this in no way diminishes the amount of my obligation to its author.

58 Editor: From "The Philosophical Basis of Naturalism," *Foundations.* Quoted in *Mind,* 245.

59 Extracts from a letter from Sir Oliver Lodge on certain passages in this lecture relating to Energy and its transformation.

You say, on page 226 [published as 225, Chap. 9, Sec. 2 in this edition], "Energy, we are taught, is of two kinds, kinetic and potential energy— energy in act and energy in possibility."

So long as emphasis is laid upon the words "we are taught," I have no objection. People have taught that, though I strongly object to such teaching, because I object to the idea "Energy in possibility" or "possible Energy" of any kind. I teach the identity of Energy in much the same terms as the identity of Matter; not merely the conservation, with the idea that one quantity can disappear and another quantity reappear. It is not another quantity, but the same; though it may have been locked up for any length of time. But then it has not been usually taught so, and I think you are dealing with what is usual. . . .

Again, you say on page 228 [published as 227, chap. 9, sec. 2], "Energy suggests 'doings' and 'happenings.'" No, say I, activity suggests doings and happenings, and activity is Energy in transformation. Energy alone is something stored, like Capital. The earth's rotational energy, for instance, is stored just as really as, and for a longer time than, the vegetation of the carboniferous epoch.

Lower down you observe that "Force may be exerted though nothing moves." Certainly it may, when resisted by an equal opposite force. But I fully admit that a lot of nonsense has been talked about the acceleration measure of force, as if it were the only measure, and that some criticism on this procedure is useful. But I should not speak of "latent" force; it is real force you have in mind, or at least real stresses—i.e. two equal and opposite forces. It is latent Activity which becomes active when the other factor, *viz.* Motion, is supplied or allowed—e.g. by the release of a bent bow, or a woundup spring, or a raised weight.

So it is also with the Energy of a flywheel. That, too, is latent Activity until the other factor, *viz.* Force, is supplied, i.e. when it is employed to overcome resistance, and therefore do work. Otherwise its Motion will be stored to all eternity.

In short, activity, or doing of work, has two factors, Force and Motion. When both are present, work is done; when either is present alone, Energy is stored. Static Energy is the Force factor, with the possibility of a certain range of effectiveness understood; like a head of water, for instance, a certain height above the sea. Kinetic Energy is the Motion factor, with a certain inertia or possibility of Force understood; not Motion alone, but a mass in motion, so that it may be able to overcome resistance.

There is no real reason why one form of Energy should be considered more "actual" or real than another; our eyes appreciate the one form, our muscles could appreciate the other.

In considering cases of Potential Energy, it is wise to realise that our knowledge about Gravitation is altogether too vague to make the case of a raised weight useful. And our knowledge of solid elasticity, though not so insignificant, is small enough to make the case of a bent bow or wound spring not very easy for fundamental contemplation. A case of chemical Energy, like gun-cotton, is in much the same predicament.

But a typical and satisfactory example of Potential Energy is the case of a vessel of compressed air. Here is Energy stagnant enough, and violent enough when released, and one that can be locked up apparently to all eternity, and yet released by the pulling of a trigger. It represents, however, a case of which we know something concerning the internal mechanism; and we have learnt that in this case the force statically exerted on the walls of a vessel is really a kinetic bombardment of the molecules. In other words, we recognise in this case that Potential Energy is ultimately resolvable into Kinetic. It may be so in the other cases. And on Kelvin's Kinetic Theory of Elasticity, which he showed a tendency in later life to abandon, all strain or stress in Ether may be ultimately due to its ultramicroscopic vortex circulation.

But none of this is yet proven. . . .

The general argument of your lecture deals with the ease with which certain general propositions are accepted as it were intuitively, without real conclusive evidence. I am entirely with you. And the way we feel secure about general laws, when adequate evidence for them is really impossible, has often struck me as remarkable. Even when facts appear to go against them, we question the facts, and find after all that in so doing we have been right.

60 Editor: From "The Philosophical Basis of Naturalism" in *Foundations*. Quoted in *Mind*, 248.

61 Let me here parenthetically remind you that again (as I observed in an earlier lecture) the Naturalism of which I speak is Naturalism in what, from our present point of view, must be regarded as its most plausible shape. Those who have followed, even at a distance, the trend of biological thought are aware that many naturalists of the highest authority are shaken in their allegiance to natural selection. They do not, indeed, exclude it from the evolutionary drama, but they reduce its role to insignificance. Why then, you may ask, do these lectures so constantly refer to selection, but say never a word about other theories of organic evolution?

The answer is that selection, and only selection, really imitates contrivance. Other theories may deal, and do deal, with variation and heredity. But selection alone can explain adjustment; whence it follows that selection alone can imitate design.

62 Editor: From the summary of Part I of *Foundations*. Quoted in *Mind*, 241.

63 Editor: From the summary of *Foundations*. Quoted in *Mind*, 147–48.

64 Editor: From the Henry Sidgwick Memorial Lecture, delivered at Newnham College, Cambridge, January 25, 1908. Quoted in *Mind*. 96–97.

65 Editor: From Part IV of *Foundations*. Quoted in *Mind*, 363–65.

66 Editor: From Part IV of *Foundations*. Quoted in *Mind*, 362–63.

67 Editor: From Part IV of *Founda-tions*. Quoted in *Mind*, 365–66.

68 Editor: From Part IV of *Foundations*. Quoted in *Mind*, 366.

69 Editor: From Part IV of *Foundations*. Quoted in *Mind*, 366–68.

70 Editor: From the summary to Part I in *Foundations*. Quoted in *Mind*, 242–44

71 The substance of this chapter appeared originally in the *Fortnightly Review* of 1877, p. 698. I have attempted to cure the obscurity which some of my friends professed to find in it, at the cost of a little amplification, and I fear a certain amount of repetition.

72 Editor: This appendix is taken from: Arthur J. Balfour, *A Defence of Philosophic Doubt* (London: Macmillan, 1879), 260–76.

73 Editor: From the summary to Part I of *Foundations*. Quoted in *Mind*, 242

74 Editor: This appendix is taken from: Arthur J. Balfour, *A Defence of Philosophic Doubt* (London: Macmillan, 1879), 328–34.

75 *English Thought in the Eighteenth Century,* p. 341

76 If the literal interpretation of the Mosaic account of the creation is to be accepted as an essential part of religion, no doubt the discrepancy between Religion and Science will be greater than that stated in the text. I have, however, assumed (in accordance with what I understand to be the opinion of theological experts) that this is not the case.

77 Editor: From "The Philosophical Basis of Naturalism" in *Foundations*. Quoted in *Mind*, 248.

Glossary

Adams, Walter S. (1876–1956) An American astronomer best known for his spectroscopic studies at Mt. Wilson observatory in California.

Agnosticism Derived from the Greek word *agnostos* (unknowable), the term refers to the belief that we cannot know anything beyond our own experiences. In popular use, however, it is used of the belief that we cannot know whether God exists or not and contrasts with atheism, which asserts that we can know that God does not exist. Though the idea behind agnosticism is not new, the term was first used publicly in 1869 by Thomas H. Huxley.

Aristotle (384–322 B.C.) A Greek philosopher whose influence on the development of Western thought was enormous, particularly during the Middle Ages.

Augustine, Saint (354–430 A.D.) A North African bishop and theologian who was one of the most brilliant thinkers Christianity has ever produced.

Babbage, Charles (1791–1871) A prominent English mathematician who pioneered the development of practical programmable mechanical calculators known as "analytical engines." Many of his ideas were adapted to electronic computers.

Bacon, Francis (1561–1626) A talented writer and statesman who claimed to understand every field of knowledge. He argued that science was intuitive and that it should be used for the benefit of mankind.

Beethoven, Ludwig van (1770–1827) A brilliant German composer who dominated music during the transition between the classical and romantic styles. His music was particularly effective at conveying philosophical ideas.

Bergson, Henri Louis (1859–1941) A French philosopher best known for his 1889 *Essai sur les données immédiates de conscience* (Trans. 1910, *Time and Free Will*). Before World War I, Bergson had a large popular following, and in 1928 he won the Noble Prize for Literature.

Berkeley, George (1685–1753) An English philosopher and Anglican bishop whose radical ideas about perception are given in his 1709 *An Essay Towards a New Theory of Vision* and can be summarized as "to be is to be perceived." Some of his criticisms of Newtonian physics in *De Motu* anticipated Einstein's theories.

Boyle, Robert (1627–1691) A natural philosopher and chemist who helped replace the Aristotelian view of nature as forms and qualities with a scientific one based on matter and motion. He is best known for his work on gases, but he also explored the relationship between science and religion in writings such as *The Christian Virtuoso*. His will endowed a Boyle lectureship to defend Christianity against unbelief.

Bridgwater, Earl of (Alternate spelling: Bridgewater) From a reference in Balfour's 1923 *Theism and Thought*, this was apparently a cousin of Francis Egerton Bridgewater (founder of British inland navigation) who acquired the latter's title and gave a benefaction that funded the publication of eight treatises on "the Power, Wisdom. and Goodness of God, as manifested in the Creation" that were published by the Royal Society during the 1830s. According to Balfour, this particular Earl of Bridgwater was the last of his line and died in 1829.

Butler, Bishop Joseph (1692–1752) Anglican bishop and moral philosopher who defended Christianity as a biblical revelation against the challenges of rationalists and deists. He is best known for his 1726 "Sermons on Human Nature" and his 1736 *The Analogy of Religion, Natural and Revealed, to the Constitution and Course of Nature.* Some consider him to be Britain's greatest moral philosopher.

Colding, Ludvig August (1815–1888) A Danish scientist who studied the conservation of energy.

Copernicus, Nicolaus (1473–1543) A Polish astronomer best known for proposing that the earth revolves around the sun.

Creative Evolution A theory of evolution described by Henri Bergson in his 1907 *L'Évolution créatice* (English trans. 1911, *Creative Evolution*). He believed evolution was driven by an *élan vital* (vital impulse or life force) that had creative powers.

D'Alembert, Jean Le Rond (1717–1783) A French mathematician and philosopher who developed an alternative way of expressing Newton's second law of mechanics.

Dalton, John (1776–1844) A British chemist and the author of *A New System of Chemical Philosophy.*

Darwin, Charles (1809–1882) An English biologist who achieved worldwide renown in 1859 when he published his theory of organic evolution in *On the Origin of Species by Means of Natural Section.*

Democritus (*circa* 460–370 B.C.) A Greek philosopher best known for his theory that the universe is made up of small indivisible *atomon* whose existence is unchanging and eternal. He claimed that the difference between substances was not based on differences in the material of which atoms were made, but only on how that basic substance was arranged. Water, for instance, was a fluid because its atoms were round, smooth and thus able to move past one other easily.

Descartes, Rene (1596–1650) A French philosopher and mathematician who was one of the first to challenge the dominance of Aristotelian thought. His philosophy was based on intuition and used reason to build on ideas that were considered innate to the mind. His science was mechanical and based on data derived from the senses. As Balfour notes, the respect he earned in each field was independent of that earned in the other.

Euclid (*circa* 300 B.C.) The best known mathematician of the Greco-Roman era. His *Elements* explained geometry logically.

Faraday, Michael (1792–1867) A British scientist who began his career as a chemist, but made his most lasting impact in physics with fundamental discoveries about electricity and magnetism. He invented the electric motor and generator.

Galileo (1564–1642) Noted Italian scientist best known for his use of the telescope to confirm the Copernican theory.

Gassendi, Pierre (1592–1665) A French scientist, philosopher and priest. In his writing he tried to reconcile a mechanistic atomism with Christian beliefs.

Grandison, Sir Charles A fictional character created by Samuel Richardson (1689–1761) in a seven-volume novel entitled *The History of Sir Charles Grandison*. In that novel Richardson attempted to portray the character of a good man.

Hegel, Georg W. (1770–1831) A German philosopher who built a system in which history is described as the conflict between one idea, a thesis and its opposing idea or antithesis. The result of their conflict is a new idea called a synthesis. He believed that beauty could be understood by studying the work of artists.

Heraclitus (*circa* 540–480 B.C.) Alternate spelling: Heraclitus. A Greek philosopher who believed fire was the basic substance of all matter.

Hobbes, Thomas (1588–1679) An English political thinker who tried to extend Galileo's explanation of planetary behavior based mechanical laws of motion to everything that happens including the behavior of people. In his most famous work, *Leviathan,* he saw society as composed of self-centered individuals who are bent on doing as they wanted and who need the restraint of a powerful ruler much as the sun's

gravitation restrains and guides the paths of planets.

Hume, David (1711–1776) A Scottish philosopher and historian who concluded that we cannot know anything beyond what we experience. He believed it was natural to believe in cause/effect relationships even though we can never know with certainty that our beliefs are true.

Huxley, Thomas H. (1825–1895) An English biologist and bold advocate of Darwinian evolution. Near the end of his life, however, he became skeptical that evolution provided a good model for human society and his 1893 Romanes lecture on "Evolution and Ethics" created a stir in Victorian society. In that Oxford lecture he claimed that. "the practice of that which is ethically best" is in all respects "opposed to that which leads to success in the cosmic struggle for existence." Evolution and ethics, he argued, are unalterably opposed to one another.

Jevons, William Stanley (1835–1882) An English logician and political economist who wrote on marginal utility value (that the value of owning something varies in inverse proportion to how many are owned).

Johnson, Samuel (1709–1784) Often know simply as "Dr. Johnson," this essayist and biography remained for later generations one of the best known figures of late eighteenth century England and one of the most quoted of all writers.

Joule, James P. (1818–1889) An English physicist who established the principles of the law of conservation of energy.

Kant, Immanuel (1724–1804) A German philosopher whose writings have been enormously influential despite (or perhaps because of) the difficulty of understanding what he was saying.

Kelvin, Lord (1824–1907) A Scottish engineer who became one of the most influential physicists of the latter half of the nineteenth century. He believed that all forces were the result of matter in motion. (Also known as William Thomson.)

Kepler, Johannes (1571–1630) A Bavarian astronomer who discovered that the planets travel around the sun in elliptical orbits.

Laplace, Pierre-Simon (1749–1827) A brilliant French mathematician who solved a problem that had baffled Isaac Newton—why the solar system was stable despite the influence of the gravitational fields of planets on one another. His famous nebular hypothesis said that the solar system was formed from cooling and contracting gases.

Lavoisier, Antoine-Laurent (1743–1794) A French scientist who was one of the founders of modern chemistry. He established the principal that matter is always conserved in chemical reactions.

Leibnitz, Gottfried W. (1646–1716) A German thinker whose philosophy championed the value of the individual and whose mathematical accomplishments included establishing the foundation for both integral and differential calculus.

Le Verrier, Urbain–Jean–Joseph (1811–1877) A French astronomer whose study of irregularities in the orbit of Uranus led to the discovery of Neptune.

Lister, Joseph (1827–1912) A British surgeon whose techniques for preventing infections revolutionized surgery.

Locke, John (1632–1704) A British philosopher who brought the Enlightenment to England, inspired the U. S. Constitution, and described his ideas about human knowledge in his *An Essay Concerning Human Understanding*. Locke distrusted reason used alone and stressed the need to base knowledge on experience.

Lodge, Sir Oliver J. (1851–1940) A British physicist who invented devices used in early radio systems. His inventions include a detector of radio waves (called the coherer) and the use of capacitors and inductors to change the frequency of radio receivers and transmitters.

Lucretius (1st century B.C.) A Latin poet known only for a single poem *De rerum natura* (*On the Nature of Things*). It gives Epicurus' theory that the universe is made up of an infinite number of atoms differing only in shape, size and weight.

Mach, Ernst (1838–1916) An Austrian physicist and philosopher who believed that all knowledge comes from the way we organize data derived from sensory experience. Those views are explained in his 1887 *Contributions to the Analysis of the Sensations*.

Maxwell, James C. (1831–1879) A Scottish physicist whose field equations explain electromagnetic (radio) waves.

Mill, John Stuart (1806–1873) A highly influential English philosopher and economist best known for championing utilitarianism and empiricism.

Morgan, Conwy Lloyd (1852–1936) A British zoologist who studied animal psychology objectively rather than in terms of its effect on human evolution. His book, *Habit and Instinct,* was derived from lectures he gave in Boston, New York and Chicago. In later life he turned to metaphysics.

Myerson, Émile (1859–1933) A German-educated Polish Jew who immigrated to France in 1882. There he wrote books that explored scientific philosophy by studying the history of science. Balfour was influenced by his *Identité et réalité* (English trans. *Identity and Reality,* 1908).

Natural religion The belief that some theological ideas (such as the existence of a Creator God) can be derived from a study of the world around us, particularly the world of living creatures.

Naturalism The philosophical theory that all of reality is natural rather than supernatural and that everything can be studied scientifically. In general Naturalism can be said to be opposed to Theism, although there are some who claim to be theistic naturalists.

Newton, Sir Isaac (1642–1727) One of the most influential figures in the history of physics. His 1687 *Mathematical Principles of Natural Philosophy* is one of the most important books in scientific history.

Nietzsche, Friedrich W. (1844–1900) A German philosopher and cultural critic who believed the final result of the Enlightenment would be the destruction of all values that provide a foundation for traditional morality. In its place would come a "will to power" that loathed Christianity's concern for protecting the weak.

Ostwald, Wilhelm (1883–1932) A German chemist and a founder of physical chemistry. In 1909 he won the Nobel prize for chemistry.

Paley, William (1743–1805) An Anglican priest who wrote popular books giving teleological arguments for God's existence. His 1802 *Natural Theology* compares the biological world to a watch and God to a watchmaker.

Pantheism A belief that either the universe taken as a whole is God or that God exists as nothing more than the matter and forces which make up the universe.

Paul, Saint (*circa* 10—67 A.D.) A persecutor of early Christianity who became one of its most influential converts. His missionary activity helped spread Christianity around the Mediterranean.

Philo Judaeus (10/15 B.C.–45/50 A.D.) A Greek-speaking Jewish philosopher who attempted to reconcile Judaism with Greek philosophy.

Plato (428/427—378/377 B.C.) A Greek philosopher who, together with Socrates and Aristotle, provided the philosophical roots of Western civilization.

Poincaré, Henri (1854–1912) A brilliant French mathematician and talented writer who, in the first decade of the twentieth century, wrote a series of books popularizing scientific ideas.

Positivism The belief that all knowledge should be based on emperically verified natural events.

Quetelet, Adolphe (1796–1874) A Belgian mathematician who helped pioneer the use of statistics in the study of human society.

Schopenhauer, Arthur (1788–1860) A German philosopher known for his pessimism and stress on the importance of the human will.

Shakespeare, William (1564–1616) A British poet and playwright who is considered one of the greatest dramatists in history.

Shelley, Percy Bysshe (1792–1822) An English Romantic who championed romantic love and rebelled against the wealthy society in which he was reared.

Solomon, King of Israel (10th century B.C.) The son of the biblical David and a king who was known for his wisdom and political successes, including the building of the temple in Jerusalem.

Spencer, Herbert (1820–1903) An English philosopher whose greatest work, his 1896 *The Synthetic Philosophy*, attempted to provide a system that explained everything from biology to ethics.

Stephen, Sir Leslie (1832–1904) A talented English critic and writer best known as the first editor of the *Dictionary of National Biography*. He claimed that Darwin's *Origin of the Species* helped him to reject Christianity. In his 1882 *Science of Ethics* he tried to build an ethical system based on evolution.

Stoicism A Greco-Roman philosophy that stressed the importance of doing one's duty, living rationally, and accepting one's fate in life calmly.

Tennyson, Alfred Lord (1809–1892) The poet laureate of England and the best known Victorian poet. Some of his poetry dealt with the implications of scientific discoveries.

Thomson, Sir Joseph John (1856–1940) An English physicist who discovered the electron in 1897 and received the Nobel Prize in 1906.

Thucydides (*circa* 460–404 B.C.) The greatest ancient Greek historian, best known for his *History of the Peloponnesian War*.

Tyndall, John (1820–1893) A talented British physicist whose discoveries ranged from explaining why the sky is blue to disproving spontaneous generation.

Vitalism A belief that there is more to life processes than mere chemistry and physics.

Wordsworth, William (1770–1850) The greatest poet of English Romanticism and someone who described himself as a "worshipper of Nature."

Index

M

Macbeth 57
Mach, Ernst 196
Man and Superman (George Bernard Shaw) 60
Marriage 49
Mass, changes in 137
Materialism 25, 50, 160, 183
Mathematics 103, 105
Maxwell's demons 107, 189
Maxwell, James C. 106, 107, 189, 196
Metaphysics 15, 21, 86
Meyerson, Emile 190
Mill, John Stuart 83, 84, 104, 105, 113, 114, 119, 137, 176, 196
Moral Law 163
Morgan, Conwy Lloyd 189, 197
Mother earth 188
Mountain road, glimpse of 185
"Mr. Balfour's Attack on Agnosticism" (Thomas Huxley) 5
Müller, Max 11
Myerson, Émile 197

N

Nationalism 70
Natural beauty 51
Natural religion 13, 197
Natural selection 59, 68, 80, 141
Natural theology 20
Naturalism 6, 147, 183, 192, 197
   C. S. Lewis' views 181
   Catechism for 6, 163
   creative purpose 148
   empirical 152
   science 153
Negligibility, law of 120, 122, 190
Newton, Sir Isaac 114, 128, 131, 197
Nietzsche, Friedrich W. 60, 61, 72, 73, 197
Nineteenth Century, The 5

O

Omniscience 106
Optimism 29
Ostwald, Wilhelm 190, 197
Othello 42, 184

P

Paley, William 27, 187, 197
Pantheism 50, 188, 197
Patriotism 70
Paul, Saint 22, 75, 76, 189, 197
Pessimists 50
Phenomena 52, 130
Philo Judaeus 22, 197
Plain man 12, 18
Platitude 85
Plato 22, 197
Plausibility 70
Poincaré, Henri 103, 106, 197
Positivism 127, 128, 198
Posterity 70
Potential energy 133, 191
Principle of negligibility 120
Probability 103, 105
   matter of degree 129
   theory of gases 106
Providence 151, 177

Q

Quetelet, Adolphe 106, 198

R

Radioactive decay 107
Radium 107
Randomness 111
Reason 163
Religion
   and science 174
   natural 13, 20
   of Greeks 57
   primitive 55, 183
Romans, Epistle to 183

S

Scepticism, defense against 166
Schopenhauer, Arthur 50, 137, 198
Science
    and religion 174
    naturalism 153
    theism 144
Sermon on the Mount 72
Severe Mercy, A (Sheldon Vanauken)
    181
Shakespeare, William 42, 57, 72, 198
Shaw, George Bernard 60
Shelley, Percy Bysshe 198
Sidwick, Mrs. (Arthur's sister) 10
Solomon, King of Israel 52, 198
Soul 17, 76
Specialists and knowledge 14
Spectator 5
Spencer, Herbert 25, 28, 39, 42, 137, 198
Stalin, Joseph 182
Stapledon, Olaf 182
Stephen, Sir Leslie 80, 84, 174, 198
Stoicism 118, 198
Sufficient reason, law of 110
Supernatural power 174
Survival of the fittest 40, 68
Synthetic Philosophy (Herbert Spenser)
    28

T

Tao 183, 184
Tennyson, Alfred Lord 114, 198
Text
    Changes from 1915 edition 179
Theism 35
    humanism 143
    opponents 22
    science 144
Theosophy 50
Thermo-dynamics 57
Thomson, Sir Joseph John 131, 198
Thucydides 55, 198
Time 184
Tossing a coin 109

*Treatise on Comparative Embryology,
    A* (Francis Balfour) 6
Tyndall, John 128, 131, 198

U

Uniformity
    doctrine of 118
    material world 124
    none in aesthetics 45
    of nature 175
Universal causation, law of 116, 118

V

Vanauken, Sheldon 181
Vitalism 198

W

Weight thought invariable 132
Wordsworth, William 40, 198

Printed in the United States
50131LVS00003BA/55

9 781587 420054